T0305101

Energy in a Competitive Market

Energy in a Competitive Market

Essays in Honour of Colin Robinson

Edited by

Lester C. Hunt

Professor of Energy Economics, Surrey Energy Economics Centre (SEEC), Department of Economics, University of Surrey, UK

Edward Elgar

Cheltenham, UK • Northampton, MA, USA

Published by
Edward Elgar Publishing Limited
Glensanda House
Montpellier Parade
Cheltenham
Glos GL50 1UA
UK

Edward Elgar Publishing, Inc.
136 West Street
Suite 202
Northampton
Massachusetts 01060
USA

A catalogue record for this book
is available from the British Library

Library of Congress Cataloguing in Publication Data
Energy in a competitive market : essays in honour of Colin Robinson / edited by Lester C. Hunt.
       p. cm.
    Includes index.
    1. Energy industries. 2. Energy industries—Case studies. 3. Competition.
    I. Hunt, Lester C. II. Robinson, Colin, 1932–

    HD9502.A2 E54394 2003
    333.79—dc21

ISBN 1 84064 798 1   2002037931

Printed and bound in Great Britain by MPG Books Ltd, Bodmin, Cornwall

Contents

Figures

Tables

Contributors

Massimo Filippini   Centre for Energy Policy and Economics (CEPE), Swiss Federal Institute of Technology, Switzerland and Economics Department, Universita della Svizzera Italiana, Lugano, Switzerland.

Roger Fouquet   Imperial College Centre for Energy Policy and Technology, Imperial College of Science, Technology & Medicine, London, UK.

David Hawdon   Surrey Energy Economics Centre (SEEC), Department of Economics, University of Surrey, Guildford, UK.

Lester C. Hunt   Surrey Energy Economics Centre (SEEC), Department of Economics, University of Surrey, Guildford, UK.

Guy Judge   Department of Economics, University of Portsmouth, UK.

Alexander G. Kemp   Department of Economics, University of Aberdeen, UK.

Eileen Marshall   Office of Gas and Electricity Markets (Ofgem), London, UK.

Yasushi Ninomiya   Institute for Global Environmental Strategies (IGES), Kanagawa, Japan.

Mike J. Parker   Science and Technology Policy Research Unit (SPRU), University of Sussex, Brighton, UK.

Peter J.G. Pearson   Imperial College Centre for Energy Policy and Technology, Imperial College of Science, Technology & Medicine, London, UK.

Bridget Rosewell   The Environment Business Ltd, London, UK.

Laurence Smith   The Environment Business Ltd, London, UK.

Linda Stephen   Department of Economics, University of Aberdeen, UK.

Paul Stevens   Centre for Energy, Petroleum and Mineral Law and Policy, University of Dundee, Scotland.

Catherine Waddams Price   Centre for Competition and Regulation, University of East Anglia, Norwich, UK.

Thomas Weyman-Jones   Department of Economics, Loughborough University, UK.

Jörg Wild   Centre for Energy Policy and Economics (CEPE), Swiss Federal Institute of Technology, Switzerland.

Acknowledgements

Colin Robinson has been at the forefront of energy economics thinking for over 30 years and it is a pleasure and a privilege to edit this festschrift in his honour. Colin has made an outstanding contribution across the whole spectrum of energy economics; he is an inspiration to energy economists everywhere, not least me. At a time when academic economics moves ever further from its application to important policy issues, it is appropriate that this volume honours Colin; a man who has influenced the thinking of academics, researchers and policy makers alike. I sincerely thank him personally and also on behalf of the Surrey Energy Economics Centre (SEEC) at the University of Surrey.

The collection of papers in this volume originates from a SEEC conference held in the summer of 2000 to honour Colin. I am very grateful to Charlie Lye who originally set up the conference and to Katie Lowe who coordinated the event. They both undertook their tasks in a friendly and efficient way and I am for ever in their debt for the assistance they gave me. I am also indebted to Sally Rumsey for helping me to chase up a number of references at very short notice and to Diana Corbin for her invaluable assistance in putting this volume together.

I would also like to thank my wife Sue and our daughters Sam, Charlotte and Harriet for their support; they are the backbone of my existence. Their love maintains my sanity while I am working in the increasingly stressful and pressurized environment of a British university.

Lester C. Hunt

Introduction

Lester C. Hunt

Colin Robinson is an inspiration to energy economists the world over. His contribution to the study and understanding of energy markets and policy is outstanding. Colin worked as a business economist for eleven years, initially for Procter & Gamble and then as Head of the Economics Division of Corporate Planning for the Esso Petroleum Company. This was followed by his appointment as Professor of Economics at the University of Surrey in 1968. At Surrey he developed and led the Department of Economics for many years and in particular cultivated the study of energy economics, with the Surrey Energy Economics Centre (SEEC) being established in the early 1980s. SEEC became the focus of research into energy economics and policy with a specialized MSc in energy economics that still runs today, with many past students and scholars benefiting from Colin's teaching, supervision and general inspiration. Since formally retiring from his Chair in the late 1990s, Colin has remained as active as ever. He is Emeritus Professor at the University of Surrey and continues to contribute to the teaching of energy economics and the research of SEEC. In addition he is editorial director of the Institute of Economics in London.

Colin continues to write on energy economics and is sole or joint author of many exceptional publications, including over 20 books and monographs and over 150 learned articles. This is a remarkable achievement. However, it is even more remarkable than the quantity of his excellent writings for two main reasons. The first is that his publications have spanned the complete spectrum of energy economics. He has written on energy modelling and forecasting; North Sea oil and gas; the British coal industry; nuclear power; gas; electricity; utility privatization; utility regulation; the international oil, coal and gas markets; and a number of papers on business and managerial economics. His ability to write and talk with authority across all of these, often wide and varied, areas is renowned.

The second reason is that Colin has the gift to be able to influence not only the thinking of academic energy economists, but policy makers alike. He is a past member of the Monopolies and Mergers Commission (Electricity Panel); he has appeared as an expert witness in public inquiries and arbitration proceedings in Britain, abroad and in cases in the US and

Australian courts; he has given evidence on many occasions to committees of the Houses of Parliament; and is a frequent broadcaster on television and radio. His influence permeates throughout energy policy the world over.

Not surprisingly, Colin's contribution has been honoured by significant energy economics organizations. In 1992, he was named as Energy Economist of the Year by the British Institute of Energy Economics (BIEE) and in 1998 he received the Outstanding Contribution to the Profession award from the International Association for Energy Economics (IAEE).

Energy in a Competitive Market reflects Colin's belief that markets are key to an efficient allocation of resources, applying equally to energy as with any other commodity. He has put forward his belief over a considerable number of years that, wherever possible, competitive energy markets should be encouraged and developed – even before it became fashionable with academics and policy makers. This is wonderfully summarized in the published version of Colin's address at the 1998 IAEE conference when receiving his Outstanding Contribution to the Profession award (Robinson, 2000). In particular, he recalls giving a paper at the 1969 annual conference of the UK Association of University Teachers of Economics where he suggested that a market regime for energy might be an improvement on the nationalized structures in place at that time. These suggestions were seen as 'extreme, if not mildly eccentric' and 'a number of colleagues chided [him for his] paper along the lines that no sensible person could seriously believe that competitive energy markets are feasible – and anyway, even if feasible, they would not be desirable' (pp. 3–4). How wrong these 'colleagues' were. It is a testimony to Colin that he resisted the temptation to 'run with the pack' and continued to pursue the ideas that have now become the 'conventional wisdom'; ideas that in various forms now underpin energy policy across the globe.

The contributions in this book also reflect Colin's involvement with the whole spectrum of energy economics as outlined earlier. Marshall (Chapter 1) reviews the development of competition and regulation in the British gas and electricity industries. She concludes that the natural monopoly elements of gas transportation and electricity transmission and distribution are likely to require regulation in the near future. However, the unbundling that has taken place in these industries means that many services within these industries are now working within ever-increasing competitive markets. Marshall argues that it is effective competition that will eventually achieve the separation of policy, regulation and the commercial management of utility businesses, so that gas and electricity supply can be treated like any other product or service.

Waddams Price (Chapter 2) surveys various attempts of regulators to use comparative efficiency analysis in energy and water utilities. She concludes that there is little direct use of comparative performance (or yardstick competition) in regulation despite its potential and argues that these techniques are a useful addition to the regulatory process. Weyman-Jones (Chapter 3) also surveys developments in benchmarking and yardstick competition in electricity distribution; in particular the theory of yardstick competition and the implementation using data envelopment analysis (DEA). He concludes that the process has attractive incentive properties, but is sensitive to the choice of variables, measurement techniques and size of sample.

The implementation of yardstick competition within the Swiss electricity market is considered by Filippini and Wild (Chapter 4). Using results from an estimated cost function, they present an empirical application of the yardstick competition concept to the Swiss electricity distribution sector and conclude that the concept could be a powerful tool in the implementation of the proposed Swiss electricity market law. Hawdon (Chapter 5) further considers the measurement of efficiency and performance using gas industry data from over 30 countries. DEA is employed and, although there is some ambiguity with some results (such as the lack of clearly defined economies of scale), he shows that the reforms introduced in Britain and planned across the European Union are associated with high levels of technical efficiency.

The effects of competitive markets on the UK coal industry are examined by Parker (Chapter 6), who concludes that with coal it is not possible to separate the influence of politics and economics from the impact of market liberalization and privatization. However, the political agenda and market forces both contributed to the significant contraction of the industry. Stevens (Chapter 7) considers the way economists can help understand the working of the international oil industry, in particular the issue of vertical integration. Kemp and Stephen (Chapter 8) consider the economics of cluster developments in the UK continental shelf (UKCS). They conclude that cluster developments can contribute to developing the UKCS with the substantial benefits available from infrastructure cost sharing and project risk sharing.

The measurement of the underlying energy demand trend (UEDT) when estimating energy demand functions is investigated by Hunt, Judge and Ninomiya (Chapter 9). Using data from the UK, they argue that a flexible approach is required to allow for a potentially non-linear UEDT to avoid biases in the estimated income and price elasticities. Pearson and Fouquet (Chapter 10) conduct a long-run analysis of the relationship between economic development and energy-related environmental quality (carbon dioxide emissions) for a group of post-industrialized countries and a group of developing countries. They find many common elements in the relationship between emissions, income and time but also some variations in the pathways. They conclude that a country's trajectory can be influenced by a range of exogenous and endogenous factors and these factors change over time and may respond to policy intervention. Finally, Rosewell and Smith (Chapter 11) model incentive mechanisms required to reduce UK emissions, concluding that a 'performance credit' is the recommended instrument.

REFERENCE

Robinson, C. (2000), 'Energy economists and economic liberalism', *Energy Journal*, **21** (2), 1–22.

1. Electricity and gas regulation in Great Britain: the end of an era

Eileen Marshall

INTRODUCTION

Gas and electricity regulation in Great Britain is poised to change in fundamental ways which can be seen as the end of one era and the beginning of another. It is not possible to cover all aspects of the regulatory regime – instead this chapter focuses on three significant changes.

First, competition in the retail supply of gas and electricity to all customers, large and small, is becoming well established. It can be envisaged in the foreseeable future that sector-specific price regulation of these activities will be removed, with reliance being placed instead on general competition legislation to deal with any remaining concerns.

Second, the electricity wholesale trading arrangements are due to undergo radical reform with the existing spot market – 'the Pool' – being replaced by more market-based arrangements, which have become known as the new electricity trading arrangements (NETA).

Third, the Utilities Act 2000 will amend the pre-privatization regulatory regimes for the gas and electricity industries, as set out in the Gas Act 1986 and the Electricity Act 1989.

RETAIL SUPPLY COMPETITION

Gas

From an unpromising start retail supply competition in gas has come a long way. The Gas Act 1986 allowed competitors to contract to supply gas to very large industrial customers (consuming over 25,000 therms per year) using British Gas pipelines, and gave the Director General of Gas Supply (DGGS) the power to settle terms for use of the British Gas network if the parties involved failed to agree. The act did not further restructure the gas industry and British Gas continued to operate as an integrated utility.

Competition in the contract market failed to develop post-privatization. This is because significant economic barriers to entry remained. For example, open and equal access to the British Gas pipeline network had not been established, competing suppliers did not have access to wholesale gas which was all contracted to British Gas, and British Gas' authorization under the Gas Act 1986 did not guard against predatory pricing by British Gas.

However, the DGGS had a general duty to act in a way 'best calculated' to enable persons to compete effectively in the contract market, which was a late amendment to the act. Also at privatization the potentially competitive contract market for supply to very large industrial loads became subject to regulation by the Director General of Fair Trading (DGFT) under general competition legislation.

And so began the long journey towards effective competition. A process that involved eliminating the economic barriers to entry by new suppliers and removing British Gas' statutory monopoly over the supply of gas to smaller industrial and commercial customers and to households.

Within a year of privatization, after complaints from large consumers that British Gas was abusing its dominant position, the company was referred to the Monopolies and Mergers Commission (MMC) by the DGFT under the Fair Trading Act 1973.

The MMC (1988) found that British Gas' actions in the contract market involved systematic and extensive discrimination in the pricing of firm gas. In addition, there was discrimination in the willingness to supply interruptible gas. The report was a key early milestone for developing effective gas-on-gas competition. It recommended several measures to promote competition. These included requiring British Gas to price against published schedules to prevent price discrimination and requiring British Gas to contract for no more than 90 per cent of the gas from new North Sea gas fields to ensure that competitors had access to wholesale gas. The MMC also recommended that British Gas should publish more information about terms of access to its network and set up 'Chinese walls' between British Gas staff involved in access negotiation and those involved in purchasing and supplying gas, better to facilitate non-discriminatory third party access by competing suppliers.

In May 1989, following a referral of disputed terms to the DGGS, the Office of Gas Supply (Ofgas) published guidelines for third party access agreements and the first agreements were put in place in 1990, based upon an allowable rate of return on current cost assets of 4.5 per cent.

But still competition was slow to develop. In October 1991 the Office of Fair Trading (OFT) published a review of the industrial market for gas, in which it found that the remedies applied following the 1988 MMC report had not been particularly effective in encouraging competition (OFT, 1991). In 1988, British Gas continued to supply all large industrial loads. By the time of the OFT report in 1991 British Gas' share was still 95 per cent.

The OFT made several recommendations to help promote competition. Its main proposals were that some of British Gas' contracted gas supplies should be sold to competitors, that British Gas reduce its share of the contract market (other than power generation and chemical feedstock use) to 40 per cent by 1995, and that it establish a separate pipeline and storage subsidiary with transparent and non-discriminatory pricing. British Gas gave undertakings to the DGFT on this basis in March 1992. The OFT had also suggested that the government should ease the prohibition on supply by competitors to consumers of less than 25,000 therms per year, with a new threshold of 2,500 therms per year and possibly no limits at all after 1996. The government subsequently reduced the competitive market threshold to 2,500 therms in 1992.

Ofgas and British Gas were in discussion concerning a new price control over this period. They disagreed on the rate of return on new transportation investment and on the appropriate rate of return for existing assets. Ofgas was also dissatisfied with the rate of progress on the separation of British Gas' transportation activities from trading as recommended by the OFT. British Gas was concerned with the form of regulation to which it was subject, citing inconsistency in the way in which the OFT and Ofgas were regulating it. In July 1992, British Gas requested that the secretary of state refer its business to the MMC under the Fair Trading Act 1973 and there were parallel references by Ofgas under the Gas Act 1986. Thus, aside from the specific issues put to it by Ofgas on rates of return and separation, the MMC had to consider British Gas' position in the gas market more widely.

The MMC reported in August 1993. It recommended that X be relaxed from 5 to 4 in the franchise market price control formula,[1] to take account of the reduction in the competitive threshold to 2,500 therms that had occurred after the price control had been set (MMC, 1993). However, the MMC found that British Gas' operation of its gas supply business as an integrated structure could be expected to operate against the public interest by inhibiting competition. It recommended that British Gas' trading business should be separated from its transportation and storage businesses in 1994 and the subsequent divestment of its trading business by 1997. The MMC also suggested that competition should be extended to customers consuming over 1,500 therms per year from 1997 and that British Gas' statutory supply monopoly be removed entirely three to five years later.

The government did not accept the MMC's divestment proposals, relying instead on Ofgas to impose rigorous regulatory separation. But the government accelerated the pace of opening the whole supply market to competition, compared with the MMC proposals. Ofgas imposed new licence conditions on British Gas in early 1995 to ensure full, financial, physical and information separation between its trading business and its other activities, which included the appointment of a compliance officer approved by the DGGS. British Gas voluntarily divested its trading arm (Centrica) in February 1997.

With the economic conditions for effective competition in place, the 1995 Gas Act provided for the final hurdle, that is, opening the domestic market to competition. This was completed in May 1998, an event which had not even been contemplated a decade or so previously, when British Gas was privatized.

A review of the competitive industrial and commercial gas market by Ofgas in March 1995 showed good progress with the development of competition and resulted in the suspension of the requirement for British Gas to price against published price schedules for 12 months from June 1995. The pricing schedules requirement was not reimposed. Ofgem's competitive market review published in August 2000 showed British Gas' share of the total industrial and commercial market (excluding power stations and feedstocks) down to about 12 per cent.

In the domestic market competition also developed well with 28 suppliers competing for custom and nearly 30 per cent of British Gas Trading's customers having switched to an alternative supplier by 2000. The National Audit Office (NAO) reported in May 1999 that domestic gas competition had benefited consumers to the tune of about £1 billion per year (NAO, 1999).

British Gas Trading's supply price control was of one year's duration up to 31 March 2001. Direct debit domestic customers were removed from the scope of the price control at the last review, since competition in that part of the market had developed well. All other domestic customers (on BGT's PromptPay and the Standard/PrePayment tariff) are covered by the price control. When putting this price control in place the Office of Gas and Electricity Markets (Ofgem) said that, subject to satisfactory progress, it was Ofgem's firm intention to remove the remaining price controls from 1 April 2001 (Ofgem, 2000).[2]

Electricity

The Electricity Act 1989 established the regulatory regime for the electricity industry before it passed into the private sector. Fortunately, as arrangements for electricity privatization were being discussed, it was possible to learn from the lessons of gas privatization.

The electricity regulator was given a primary duty to promote competition in generation and supply, and significantly the electricity industry was restructured from the beginning to help facilitate competition. The old Central Electricity Generating Board (CEGB) was broken up and electricity generation was separated from transmission. The National Grid Company (NGC) was given responsibility for the high voltage transmission system and given a statutory duty to facilitate competition. There were also limits placed on the licences of the major generators from acting as major suppliers and limits on the Regional Electricity Companies' (RECs) licences restricting their equity interest in generation plant. But the activities of the RECs were not fully separated at privatization between distribution and supply. (The Utilities Act 2000 now requires this separation to be put in place.)

However, most importantly, the kinds of economic barriers which prevented effective competition being established for so long in gas, were addressed by the electricity legislation.

First, the licences of both NGC and the RECs required them to publish tariffs for use of their transmission and distribution systems and to provide open and equal access to all users, which meant that the RECs had to treat competitors on the same basis as their own supply businesses. Second, there were non-discrimination provisions placed on the licences of both the RECs and the large generators to help prevent the kind of anti-competitive practices which occurred early on in the development of gas competition. Also, the Director General of Electricity Supply (DGES) was given concurrent jurisdiction with the DGFT in applying competition legislation in the electricity industry.

Finally, the problem encountered in the gas industry whereby competitors could not get hold of gas to sell because it was all contracted to British Gas was also addressed in electricity. An electricity spot market was created – the Pool. Virtually all the power generated had to be sold into the Pool every day by generators and purchased by suppliers, with prices set every 30 minutes. Since electricity generation was privatized at the same time as the rest of the industry, it was also possible to match the length of power purchase contracts to the phased introduction of competition in electricity supply. As a result, there has not been the major mismatch between long-term wholesale purchase contracts and retail market shares which caused a problem in the gas market when full supply competition was introduced. Thus, as the industry was privatized and in contrast to gas, the electricity industry structure and the regime more generally were much more conducive to the development of competition in supply.

Moreover, a timetable was set out from the beginning in the licences of the RECs to provide for the phased opening of the supply market.

Customers with maximum demand above 1 MW were able to choose their supplier immediately. The 5,000 or so eligible customers accounted for about a third of total electricity demand.

Customers with maximum demand of between 100 kW and 1 MW were allowed to choose their supplier from April 1994. The 50,000 or so customers who were able to choose their supplier from that date accounted for about 17 per cent of total electricity demand. The remaining 50 per cent of total demand represents consumption by about 26 million domestic and small business customers. The licences provided for this sector of the market to be opened to competition from April 1998. This timetable was not quite met. A great deal of effort was needed to get the necessary information technology (IT) systems in place to record the switching of customers between suppliers. Also, to help ensure a smooth transfer process, the below 100 kW market was opened in tranches – from September 1998 to May 1999.

With the structure of the industry sorted out and a conducive regulatory regime, competition for the largest electricity consumers was fierce from the start. About 40 per cent of 1 MW customers switched suppliers as the market was opened and a very high percentage of these customers is now being served by a supplier other than the local REC. About 25 per cent of the smaller (100 kW–1 MW) customers switched supplier as the market was opened to competition in 1994, a figure again that has since risen considerably. The opening of the domestic market too got off to a good start. A survey carried out by Ofgem showed that by the beginning of July 1999 on average 9 per cent of customers had switched supplier.

By summer 2000, 15 per cent of electricity customers had switched away from the local REC. There were 24 licensed electricity suppliers, including 14 who also supplied gas. Almost half of electricity and gas customers who switched to an alternative supplier were subsequently supplied on 'dual fuel' contracts.

The supply price control in electricity covered a two-year period up to 31 March 2002. Small business and domestic direct debit customers were removed from the scope of price controls in April 2000 since competition had become well established for such customers, but all other domestic customers are covered by the price controls.

In electricity as in gas, Ofgem anticipated that competition would have become sufficiently effective to enable the removal of the remaining electricity price controls from April 2002.[3]

The fact that every consumer in Great Britain can now choose his or her gas and electricity supplier is already beginning to be taken for granted. But it is a major achievement, a world first. The enormous effort on the part of so many people to get competition under way should not be consigned to the history books without due recognition.

THE NEW ELECTRICITY TRADING ARRANGEMENTS

Competition in Generation

Where the electricity industry restructuring was less effective was in the limited competition created in electricity generation. In the gas industry, competition in gas production was established well before the privatization of British Gas. The development of offshore oil and gas reserves from the 1960s onwards was undertaken largely by privately owned companies. More than 50 different companies produced gas, including British Gas' own exploration and production arm.

But unlike gas production, electricity generation was not a competitive activity before privatization. Apart from a few power stations located at large industrial sites, all the power stations were owned by the government and operated as part of the CEGB which also operated the high voltage national transmission system. The publicly owned regional electricity boards then distributed the power through their low voltage systems and supplied end-use customers. But fairly late in the day the nuclear power stations were withdrawn from the generation share flotation, due to uncertainties about decommissioning costs, and were retained in the public sector. (Some of the power stations were privatized later.) These stations represented about 17 per cent of the power produced at privatization. The remaining coal- and oil-fired generation plants were divided between only two companies, National Power and Powergen, with National Power being about double the size of Powergen. This duopoly structure was initially chosen when National Power was going to own the nuclear power stations, but was not revised when they were withdrawn from the share sale. However, around the time of privatization, gas was allowed for the first time to be used for power generation.

New gas-fired plant, commissioned largely by the RECs, diluted the market power of National Power and Powergen somewhat. But these gas-fired power stations, being efficient and having low running costs, were used as baseload stations. Nuclear power also operates as baseload. National Power and Powergen had virtually all the plant that ran to meet daily and seasonal peaks in demand. These companies therefore dominated price setting in the electricity spot market – the Pool. The concentration of market power, especially the amount of control National Power and Powergen had been able to exercise over the electricity spot market prices, ensured close and repeated scrutiny by the regulator. The first Pool Price Inquiry was undertaken in 1991. By February 1994 successive inquiries had been undertaken and various measures taken, including changing the Pool rules, and changing the licences of the generators.

In February 1994, after a detailed investigation by the Office of Electricity Regulation (Offer), National Power and Powergen agreed between them to divest within two years 6 GW of plant (6,000 megawatts) – equivalent to six sizeable power stations – to reduce their significant positions in the market. Also, while the disposals were proceeding, the prices National Power and Powergen could bid into the Pool were capped for two years. The National Power and Powergen disposals were completed in 1996 with both companies selling coal-fired plants to the Eastern Group, which in 1996/97 accounted for nearly 10 per cent of the total market.

Subsequent divestments of 8 GW of plant by National Power and Powergen also occurred as a condition for acquisitions of RECs. The existing power stations, especially the nuclear stations, were run more efficiently after privatization and there was increasing power coming across the electricity interconnectors with France and Scotland. The upshot is that a combination of new entrants (25 per cent), increased efficiency and divestments have created a marked restructuring of the electricity generation market, and National Power and Powergen's combined market share was below 25 per cent.

Nevertheless, despite these encouraging developments, prices in the electricity Pool did not follow reductions in input costs and increases in efficiency, as one might have expected in a more competitive market. It was estimated by Ofgem (1999) that the total cost of pooled electricity was about £7.5 billion. If Pool prices had been set at new entrant levels (combined cycle gas turbine at 60 per cent load factor), revenues would have been £1.5 billion less. And this is assuming generators did not earn any additional revenues from selling hedging contracts or providing the national grid with ancillary services. In the year 1999/2000 Pool prices remained around £24–£25 MWh – still well above new entry costs. It seemed clear that suppliers and customers were not reaping the benefits that should be coming through from a more competitive generation market.

Prima facie, it might be expected that such a major change in the structure of the generation market would have had a major impact on margins and prices in generation. However, there is no direct, simple link between aggregate measures of market concentration and the strength of competition, as is borne out by the history of Pool prices in the 1990s. There had been no great intensification of competition in pricing among generators in the years since privatization. What is required for real competition to develop is genuine rivalry among competitors; numbers alone are not enough.

It was to unleash the competitive potential in generation that in 1998 Ofgem and the DTI proposed to introduce new electricity trading arrangements. NETA has an important role in creating effective competition by introducing more market-based trading, in which competing generators actually seek suppliers to which they can sell their power. This, in turn, should help enable effective supply competition to develop as suppliers seek to differentiate themselves by keen purchasing.

The Pool

When the CEGB was split up at privatization with generation being divided from transmission, it was necessary to establish a system for physically balancing the electricity grid in the face of competition. What was established was a regime which gave NGC responsibility for dispatching electricity generation to meet its forecast of national demand and the England and Wales electricity spot market (the Pool) was created alongside the physical dispatch arrangements.

One day ahead of real time NGC ranks generators' bids in a merit order, for every 30 minutes; prices are set for all at the highest accepted bid, which sets the marginal price. NGC then makes adjustments constraining some generators onto the system and others off, to overcome transmission constraints and to take account of unexpected changes to supply and demand on the day.

This is essentially the same centrally planned arrangement that the CEGB used before privatization, except then the CEGB ranked the generation that it owned against a cost-based merit order, instead of a merit order based on generators' bids.

The Pool was innovative at the time – the split between generation and transmission was very contentious and there was a need for a demonstrably robust way of ensuring security of supply. The Pool also facilitated competition, in generation by providing new entrants a place to sell their electricity, and in supply by providing a market from which suppliers could purchase electricity to meet their customers' requirements.

But, as mentioned earlier, there were problems with the Pool. The Pool system led to the manipulation of price setting; relatively soft price competition since all generators tend to benefit from the high prices, and to lack of liquidity in financial instruments to hedge the Pool price risk. In addition, since all suppliers purchased electricity from the Pool at the same price, the arrangements tended to have a blunting effect on supply competition – bearing in mind that for domestic customers, generation costs represent nearly 50 per cent of the final price (and more than that for industrial and commercial customers).

New Electricity Trading Arrangements

NETA introduces new arrangements for the pricing of electricity and new arrangements for ensuring that NGC can physically balance the system in real time, to maintain quality and security of supply.

The basic outline of the trading arrangements remains unchanged from that described in Offer's (1998) proposals document. The proposals were based on bilateral trading between generators, suppliers, traders and customers, and they also provided a balancing mechanism in which NGC, as system operator, can buy and sell electricity close to real time to balance the system.

NETA thus includes:

- forward and futures markets, which evolve in response to the requirements of participants, allowing contracts for electricity to be struck up to several years ahead;
- short-term power exchanges, also evolving in response to the requirements of participants, to give them the opportunity to 'fine tune' their contract positions in a simple and accessible way;
- a balancing mechanism in which NGC, as system operator, accepts offers of and bids for electricity to enable it to balance the system; and
- a settlement process for charging participants whose contracted positions do not match their metered volumes of electricity, for the settlement of accepted balancing mechanism offers and bids, and for recovering the system operator's costs of balancing the system.

The forward, futures and short-term markets were expected to become the main wholesale markets, where the vast majority of electricity will be traded and priced. By the time the balancing mechanism opens for a trading period[4] – $3^{1}/_{2}$ hours before real time – it is expected that generators' and suppliers' contract positions will closely match their anticipated metered output and metered demand. But there will be unanticipated changes within the day on the generation and demand sides, which will require intervention by NGC, as system operator.

With the introduction of NETA the Pooling and Settlement Agreement was to be replaced by the Balancing and Settlement Code (BSC) incorporating the rules of the balancing mechanism and settlement process. NGC as system operator would be obliged to maintain the code. Licensees would be obliged to conform to it. The code includes flexible and effective governance arrangements to allow for modifications to the rules. One of the major criticisms of the Pool was its slow pace of reform. Ofgem have given careful consideration to the new rules of the balancing mechanism and settlement process under NETA, in order to minimize their complexity and to speed up the rules modification process once the new arrangements are introduced.

Market Power

NETA will not solve all the problems of the electricity market. In particular, very close to real time market power in electricity systems can be intractable, deriving from steep demand and supply curves that often exist when the system operator has to balance an unbalanced supply and demand position very quickly (against unexpected changes in demand and supply).

An important innovation of NETA is the full incorporation of the demand side. For example, large customers and suppliers can bid in the balancing mechanism to reduce their demand to assist the system operator to balance the system. Contracting ahead by the system operator rather than relying only on purchases in the balancing mechanism is another way in which close to real time market power can be ameliorated. But it is still expected, especially before full demand-side participation develops, that close to real time market power could remain a problem under NETA. It is for that reason that Ofgem firmly believes that the inclusion of a market-abuse licence condition will remain necessary under NETA, similar to the licence condition we proposed to be included in the licences of some generators with substantial market power, to prevent further abuse in the Pool before the introduction of the new trading arrangements.

Together with other pro-competitive changes in the electricity market, it is believed by Ofgem that the new market-based trading arrangements offer the prospect of a truly competitive electricity market in the future. The Utilities Act 2000 provides for the implementation of NETA under powers exercisable by the Secretary of State.[5]

THE REGULATORY REGIME

The incoming Conservative government in 1979 was committed to transferring publicly owned enterprises into private ownership. Mixed motives have been ascribed to the British privatization programme. These include politically orientated motives such as providing private finance to fund growing demands for infrastructure investment thereby relieving pressure on increasingly scarce tax revenues, raising revenues to fund spending or tax cuts, and widening share ownership. They also include economically orientated motives designed to increase the efficiency of the industries in question by bringing the disciplines of the stock market to bear on their productive efficiency and reducing political interference in their management.

Most of the early privatizations involved industries which operated in competitive markets. But after the Conservative Party's further election victory in 1983 a new wave of privatizations occurred involving utility industries which did not face competition in their core activities.

This meant that a new regulatory regime needed to be established and put in place before the industries passed into the private sector. The legislation enacted before each utility privatization, beginning with the Telecommunications Act 1983 and including the Gas Act 1986 and the Electricity Act 1989, set out legislative provisions to deal with any of the variety of regulatory problems that might be encountered in the future.

The new regime established a single regulator for each utility, independent of the political process. This independence was facilitated by the regulator being appointed by the Secretary of State for a set period of time, usually five years. The regulator in turn was able to establish a separate office and appoint his or her own staff. In the case of gas the regulatory office was called the Office of Gas Supply (Ofgas); for electricity it was called the Office of Electricity Regulation (Offer).

Measures were put in place to help ensure a transparent and relatively predictable regulatory system. First, the discretion of the regulators was constrained by their general duties and powers set out in the relevant acts of parliament. Second, the regulated companies were given a clear idea of the rules under which they were operating since each had a licence setting out their obligations and constraints. Third, appeals against the regulator's decisions were to the Monopolies and Mergers Commission in terms of suggested modifications to the licence, including changes to the price control formula, and to the courts in respect of other decisions.

Thus, the key features of the new regime sought to achieve what most economists consider to be the highly desirable separation of policy from regulation, and the day-to-day management of the utilities from both.

However, concerns were expressed in some quarters that the regulators were too 'unaccountable'. Some commentators were concerned about a relative lack of accountability to Parliament. Others were concerned that, though the regulators act as quasi judges with the courts or the MMC acting as courts of appeal, they do not adopt the kinds of legal processes that are found in the judicially based regulatory systems in North America. Others expressed unease about the power of a single regulator. In effect, what these commentators were questioning was the very basis of new-style British regulation, which was crafted in the light of previous

UK experience when the utilities were nationalized and in the light of US experience.

The new style regulatory system was designed to provide a better middle way between these two systems – more independent of the political process and more open than regulation of the public corporations under nationalization, but more flexible and less costly than the US system and better able to promote competition and protect customers' interests as a result.

Under nationalization the UK utilities were subject to considerable direct government intervention, including in the day-to-day management of the public corporations. The resulting inefficiencies were well documented. In addition, the industries were regulated by civil servants entirely behind closed doors who rarely explained their actions in any detail.

By contrast the US has a judicial system, based on rules, very full disclosure of information, and lengthy public hearings followed by detailed reasoning explaining the decisions made. Thus it is an open, independent process. But it is not one that necessarily best serves customers. It is relatively inflexible, costly and lengthy and tends thereby to play into the hands of the incumbent monopolists who are often better able to afford to delay and incur the expense of lengthy courtroom hearings with expensive lawyers in attendance.

Inevitably both politicians and regulators in the UK have reacted to criticisms about the 'accountability of the regulator'. The changes have been largely incremental, intended to strengthen the UK regulatory system rather than replace it.

As mentioned earlier, some commentators, while supporting the principle of independent regulation, have queried whether the process is sufficiently accountable in the legal sense. These critics appear to hanker not for a return to the UK government's 'hands on' approach to regulation as experienced under nationalization, but a move to the US legal style. They have complained, for example, that it is difficult to challenge the reasonableness of the regulator's decisions through appeals to the courts, because the regulators do not put out sufficient information upon which their decisions are based, and do not set out in sufficient detail the reasoning behind their decisions.

There was probably substance in these accusations in the past. But the regulators themselves have responded in a positive way to such criticisms by changing the 'custom and practice' of regulation.

All the regulators now publish numerous and detailed consultation papers to encourage debate and the involvement of all relevant parties. They also put out detailed 'decision documents' setting out the reasons for their decisions, to provide the basis of legal challenge and more generally to give those concerned a clearer understanding of the 'rules of the game'.

However, Parliament also responded to the accusation of a lack of openness on the part of regulators and took the power in the 1995 Gas Act to require the gas regulator to give reasons for decisions. Now the Utilities Act 2000 will require openness in respect of both electricity and gas regulation.

More significantly, under the Utilities Act 2000 the regulation of the gas and electricity industries is being brought together. At the same time the single gas and electricity regulators are being replaced by a multimembered Gas and Electricity Markets Authority.

In response to growing convergence of the two industries – both at the wholesale end where around a third of generation is now gas fired, and at the retail end, where many suppliers offer 'dual fuel' products – steps had already been taken ahead of the Utilities Act to bring the gas and electricity regulatory offices together. The first significant step towards effective integration was the appointment of Callum McCarthy as gas regulator and electricity regulator as from the beginning of 1999. Until the Utilities Act 2000 became law the regulator continued to act under fuel-specific legislation, the Gas Act 1986 (as amended by the Gas Act 1995) and the Electricity Act 1989. The director general had concurrent powers in respect of both fuels with the DGFT under competition legislation, including the new Competition Act 1998.

Also during 1999 the Office of Gas and Electricity Markets (Ofgem) was formed by combining the functions of the former Office of Gas Supply (Ofgas) and the Office of Electricity Regulation (Offer). Steps were taken to relocate all the functions at one location in London and a new divisional structure was put in place, such that Ofgem was organized to address issues across both gas and electricity in new management divisions, rather than on separate industry lines.

Besides this divisional reorganization based on dual gas and electricity responsibilities, a new structure of corporate governance was put in place within Ofgem, based on an Advisory Management Board which had five independent non-executive members. The establishment of the Advisory Management Board was designed to ensure that regulation of gas and electricity draws on a full range of advice and experience and thereby lessens the emphasis on a single regulator.

Now, although the regulatory office will continue to be known as Ofgem, the Utilities Act 2000 is formally creating the Gas and Electricity Markets Authority to regulate both gas and electricity with five executive and six non-executive members.[6]

An independent 'dual fuel' consumer representative body is also being established – the Gas and Electricity Consumer Council (energywatch) to safeguard consumers' interests and complement the work of Ofgem.

The Utilities Act brings in new duties for the regulatory authority. It closely resembles the existing gas and electricity regulation by establishing as a principal objective the protection of the interests of consumers wherever appropriate by promoting effective competition, while having regard to a range of factors, including ensuring reasonable demand is met, and licence holders are able to finance activities that are the subject of regulatory obligations. The act also requires the regulator to have regard to the interests of certain categories of consumers such as those who are disabled and chronically sick, the elderly, people with low incomes and rural consumers. In addition, there is a new duty for the regulator to have regard to statutory guidance on social and environmental matters, which the Secretary of State has a duty to issue. Other new ministerial powers include a power to make charging schemes to achieve cross-subsidy of 'disadvantaged groups', power to impose requirements in relation to the efficient use of energy and power to impose obligations in relation to electricity from renewable generation.

CONCLUSIONS

It is likely that there will be a long-term need for gas and electricity regulation. The high and low pressure gas pipeline systems and the high voltage electricity transmission system and lower voltage distribution systems are likely to remain 'natural monopolies' for the foreseeable future. Moreover, while both the gas and the new electricity wholesale trading arrangements are market based, it remains the case that the inputs to and offtakes from both the gas and electricity transmission systems need to be kept in balance over a short time period (second by second in electricity) by a system operator, subject to regulation.

However, other services traditionally provided solely by the monopoly utilities, such as electricity generation and the retail supply of gas and electricity, are being provided in competitive markets. Indeed additional services, such as metering and gas storage are being 'unbundled' from the 'natural monopoly' and introduced to the disciplines of competition. It is effective competition that eventually provides the best 'uncoupling' of policy, regulation, and the commercial management of utility businesses. Then services such as gas and electricity supply can be treated like any other product or service and subjected only to general competition legislation.

One of the most innovative aspects of the UK regulatory system established in the 1980s is its emphasis on the promotion of competition by the utility regulators. The emphasis on competition is retained in the Utilities Act 2000, but additional social and environmental objectives have been added, and the single regulators for gas and electricity have given way to the establishment of a multiperson authority. It remains to be seen whether these changes mark a significant departure or the continued evolution of the regulatory regime.

NOTES

1. RPI−X, where RPI is the change in the retail price index.
2. The price controls were removed when intended.
3. The remaining price controls were removed in April 2002.
4. Known as 'Gate Closure'. Reduced to one hour in 2002.
5. The new trading arrangements were introduced in March 2001.
6. The functions of the Director General of Gas Supply and Director General of Electricity Supply were transferred to the authority on 20 December 2000.

REFERENCES

MMC (1988), *Gas: A Report on the Matter of the Existence or Possible Existence of a Monopoly Situation in Relation to the Supply in Great Britain of Gas through Pipes to Persons other than Tariff Customers*, London, UK: Monopolies and Mergers Commission, Cm 500 (www.competition-commission.org.uk).

MMC (1993), *British Gas plc: Volume 1 of reports under the Gas Act 1986 on the conveyance and storage of gas and the fixing of tariffs for the supply of gas by British Gas plc*, London, UK: Monopolies and Mergers Commission, Cm 2314 (www.competition-commission.org.uk).

NAO (1999), *Office of Gas Supply: Giving Customers a Choice – Introduction of Competition into the Domestic Gas Market*, London, UK: HC 403, National Audit Office (www.nao.gov.uk).

Offer (1998), *Review of Electricity Trading Arrangements: Proposals*: Birmingham, UK: Office of Electricity Regulation (www.ofgem.gov.uk).

Ofgem (1999), *The New Electricity Trading Arrangements and Related Transmission Issues Proposals on Licence Changes: A Consultation Document*, London, UK: Office of Gas and Electricity Markets (www.ofgem.gov.uk).

Ofgem (2000), *Review of British Gas Trading's Price Regulation: Final Proposals*, London, UK: Office of Gas and Electricity Markets (www.ofgem.gov.uk).

OFT (1991), *The Gas Review – Summary Review*, London, UK: Office of Fair Trading, OFT055.

2. Yardstick competition and comparative performance measures in practice

Catherine Waddams Price

INTRODUCTION[1]

One of Colin Robinson's prophetic roles has been in advocating privatization, especially in the energy sector, where others thought it infeasible. In 1994 Colin Robinson stated that 'no other major country [other than Britain] seems ready to go as far in breaking down the state gas and electricity monopolies which for so long have dominated markets at the expense of consumers' (Robinson, 1994, p. 19). One tool for controlling privatized companies with market power is to compare the performance of different companies, either for regulators to use some form of comparative regulation between monopolies, or to provide additional information for consumers as they are offered choice in previously monopolized markets. Such comparisons can therefore be seen as a tool enabling the transfer of both intrinsically monopoly companies (mainly network companies) and potentially competitive markets (especially in energy) to the private sector. However, practical experience of using comparative performance as a direct regulatory tool is surprisingly sparse. The potential for using such tools can be divided into two aspects. The first is setting minimum standards of some kind; failure to meet these standards results in costs for the company concerned, either directly in the form of (regulator or government administered) fines, or indirectly through compulsory compensation to consumers. Such compensation is usually administered centrally, but in the US it is possible to include in this category prosecutions brought privately for compensation to consumers or other suppliers. In the UK such formal lists of service quality and compensation schemes were developed after privatization, to counteract the incentives for cutting quality introduced by price-cap regulation. Detailed practice varies, with compensation paid automatically in some cases (electricity), and in others only after it is triggered by affected consumers (railways). The appendix to this chapter lists details of performance measures in the UK gas, electricity, water, rail and postal industries. The introduction of competition into gas and electricity has led to new proposals in 2001, and new statutory arrangements, which are discussed below.

The second potential for comparative competition is the use of formal analysis to identify efficient practice, and to relate the price cap directly to the results of such analysis. In the UK this has been used partially to set the price caps of the water and sewerage and water-only companies, and some comparative analysis contributed to the current price caps set for the electricity distribution companies. A new system of reward for performance is being introduced within the current price cap for UK electricity distributors. In the US the price caps for local exchange carriers have been automatically adjusted according to the company's recent performance (Norsworthy and Tsai, 1998). The most established use of comparative analysis in energy regulation is probably for Norwegian electricity companies, but even here there is only three years' experience. The Dutch regulator has proposed new price caps based on comparative productivity analysis, but this has been subject to heated debate. Each of these schemes is described below. The New South Wales regulator has recently commissioned a comparative analysis of gas companies, with a view to using this information to regulate them. In this chapter, the next section describes the use of comparative efficiency analysis in UK regulation and some accounting issues which arose in the separation of distribution and supply costs; the subsequent section describes the Norwegian and Dutch schemes and the final section concludes.

UK EXPERIENCE

Use of Performance Measures

All the UK privatized industries have had measures of quality introduced since the flotation of their shares. In some cases these were introduced at the time of privatization, but many more have been added since, reflecting concern that the cost-reducing incentives of private ownership, enhanced by those of price-cap regulation, might lead to deterioration of quality. The problem arises only in markets with monopoly power. Where there is competition, suppliers will be able to offer a choice of quality as part of the marketing process. However, where there are networks, not only is there no choice of supplier, but there are often technical limitations to how far consumers can be offered a choice of quality. For example, pressure in water pipes, or reliability of gas supply, cannot easily be differentiated between different small consumers (though gas interruptibility is a well-established way of offering industrial consumers a trade-off between lower price and continuity of supply).

Standards may be set at a number of levels. They may be required, with failure to meet them resulting in some sort of penalty, either imposed by a regulation authority or court or government, or in the form of compensation to consumers. The difficulty with such rigid standards is that firms may put a great deal of effort into meeting the standard, but have little incentive to exceed them or to meet other aspects of quality which are not rewarded or measured. Assuming that higher quality is more costly, the regulator's choice of quality standards influences the price which consumers must pay, as well as the quality delivered. In determining this trade-off the regulator may rely on consumer surveys. Both Ofwat (Office of Water Services) and Ofgem (Office of Gas and Electricity Markets) conduct surveys of consumer preferences (for example, Ofwat, 1993; Ofgem, 2001a). However, the discretion of the two regulators varies, with water quality standards set by two separate external regulators (the Environment Agency and the Drinking Water Inspectorate). Ofwat also measures and rewards quality of service. One result of these different institutional arrangements has been a much more public debate about the quality–price trade-off for water than for energy. It is also likely that the trade-off achieved is itself different, following Baron's (1985) model. This indicates higher standards, higher prices and higher profits with separate regulators (water) than for an integrated decision process (energy). An alternative is to set targets and to reward companies on a sliding scale according to how well they perform.

Water

In the UK, performance measurement was first linked with regulatory controls in the water industry. The water industry in England and Wales consists of ten water and sewerage companies and about a dozen smaller water-only companies (there have been a number of mergers and take-overs within this group). The methodology used in the 1999 periodic review, which is in force from 2000 to 2005, is outlined in Ofwat (1998a).

Ofwat had commissioned a study to assess the possibility of analysing total efficiency across all cost categories. Despite the positive recommendation of the report (Bosworth et al., 1996) Ofwat rejected this type of data envelopment analysis, partly on the basis of lack of reliable data. Instead, efficiency savings were assessed in a number of phases. First, overall savings potential for the whole industry was considered 'taking account of its current performance and that of other industry sectors and the potential for future improvement' (p. 5). Then the comparative efficiency of the companies within the water industry was identified. The regulator separated expenditure into operating, capital maintenance and capital enhancement categories. Ofwat then further subdivided costs within each of these categories. In the final determinations Ofwat assumed average improvements in operating expenditure of 2.7 per cent per year (ranging from 7 to 22 per cent); in capital maintenance expenditure of 3 to 15 per cent over the whole period; and in capital enhancement of 7 to 24 per cent by 2004–05. Quality of service was dealt with separately (Ofwat, 1998b), and companies with very good records of service allowed up to 0.5 per cent higher prices; a similar reduction in price of up to 0.5 per cent was imposed on companies with poorer than average service records.

In comparing performance with the target set for the 1995–2000 price control period, Ofwat noted that operating expenditure had been reduced significantly below the targets. Trends in capital maintenance were less clear. As expected, these varied considerably from year to year, and seemed on average to be about at the level assumed in the price caps. Capital enhancement expenditure was well below that allowed for in the price caps, a common phenomenon where firms talk up the capital requirements at the price review, and find economies once the revenue has been determined. Comparing the results of the econometric models used in the various cost assessments, Ofwat noted considerable changes since the last review.

There were obviously some doubts about the robustness of the results, and some concerns that the separate analysis and identification of 'best practice' for each category of cost ignored the scope for substitution between heads of expenditure, and might be too harsh in its overall conclusions. Ofwat therefore made some allowance for the possibility that it was not appropriate to choose the lowest possible expenditure from each category and expect firms to achieve this low expenditure across the board. Nevertheless such separate analysis does make it very difficult to assess how much of the savings in one category is at the expense of higher costs in another, and the process may discourage companies from making appropriate trade-offs.

Having made its estimates of the lowest achievable costs in each category, Ofwat then calculated the extent to which each company could be expected to lower its costs towards this frontier, and used this in calculating the revenues allowable. Individual companies argued that they had particular reasons for having higher costs than others, and this element of judgement became very subjective. Many outside observers (and the stock market) believed that the price caps were unreasonably harsh (see comment by NERA [National Economic Research Associates], 1999, reported below).

The water regulator has also undertaken a number of comparisons of the performance of water companies in England and Wales with those overseas (see for example Ofwat, 2000). However, these merely seem to compare levels of cost in different (quite detailed) categories, rather than to perform analysis either of an econometric or data envelopment analysis type. It is not clear how Ofwat uses these comparisons, beyond an enhancement of their general understanding of cost drivers in the water industry. Water and sewerage companies are also set standards of performance (listed in the appendix) and are subject to fines and compensation requirements if they do not meet them.

Electricity Distribution Price Review

The energy regulator imposed new price controls on the 14 electricity distribution companies in Great Britain for the five years from April 2000. He also sought to identify companies which were at the efficiency frontier, and those that could be expected to increase their relative efficiency. However, the process was much less sophisticated than that used in the water case. Only one year's figures were used, with a composite figure for both costs and output. Output was constructed (with little justification provided) from weighting customer numbers by 0.5, with weights of 0.25 each for units distributed and length of network; the 14 observations of operating cost and composite output were then plotted (Ofgem, 1999). A view was taken on the fixed cost of operating a network (about £25 million per year), and Ofgem then judged two companies to have the lowest per unit costs (these were also the two largest companies as measured by the composite output measure, which suggests that a linear assessment may not have been appropriate). Two companies (both also quite large) seemed to have particularly high costs, with the other eight in between. This information was used to set the price caps for the companies, along with other judgements from management consultants who had visited the companies. Capital expenditure was modelled using a common formula for expected expenditure required according to new business and requirements for reinforcement.

Assessment of Ofwat and Ofgem Reviews

Both Ofwat and Ofgem were criticized for their use of comparative information in undertaking the 1999 price reviews. NERA (1999) criticized both regulators for their separation of capital and operating costs, and for the arbitrary way in which their reviews were conducted. In the Ofwat case they argued that the econometric analysis was too mechanical, was not based on sound economic reasoning, and was therefore over-responsive to modelling changes indicated by the data. In 1994 Ofwat had used data envelopment analysis to check their cost analyses, but this was not used in the most recent review. Ofgem's modelling had been even more arbitrary, using only one year's data, despite the availability of figures over a longer period. In particular the composite output variable was based on little evidence, and the results were very sensitive to the definition of this variable. NERA were acting for several of the companies, so they had a particular interest in emphasizing any harshness in the judgements (in fact the energy regulator's final rulings were somewhat laxer than his earlier proposals, perhaps in acknowledgement of these criticisms). Nevertheless there seems to be some truth in the accusation of arbitrariness, both in separating the different cost elements, particularly in water where they were further disaggregated, and in the particular modelling processes employed.

Electricity Distribution Information and Incentives Project

As part of the recent price review, the energy regulator has instigated the Information and Incentives Project (IIP), partly in recognition of the crudeness of the analysis undertaken on only one year's data for operating costs, and partly in response to concerns about quality incentives under price-cap regulation. The objectives of the project include 'striking an appropriate balance between incentives . . . to reduce costs and . . . to maintain or improve quality of supply and standards of service; encouraging companies to feel they are competing against each other . . . rather than merely beating a single target . . . reducing uncertainty around the price control review process' (Ofgem, 2000, p. 5). The timetable is to introduce a financial incentive which directly reflects quality of supply from April 2002, representing up to 2 per cent of revenues allowed under the price cap. The measures of service quality are defined as the percentage of customers experiencing supply interruptions; the average customer minutes lost per connected customer; and the response to telephone enquiries. The input measures are total customer numbers served, numbers affected by interruptions, reportable incidents, incident times and units of plant and equipment.

Separating Distribution and Supply in the Competitive Energy Supply Market

One issue which arose in the most recent review of electricity distribution was the allocation of costs to the distribution (monopoly) business and to supply which has been fully open to competition since 1999. The regional electricity companies were privatized in 1990 with the requirement that they accounted separately for these two activities, but there was considerable discretion on cost allocation, and clear incentives to allocate as many costs as possible to the monopolistic distribution business. These distribution costs formed the basis of prices which each company could charge to entrants in its region; the higher they were the less the incumbent needed to recoup on the supply side, and the higher its competitors' costs.

In conducting the review for the 2000–2005 period, the regulator found that the companies had indeed exaggerated their distribution costs. Ofgem reallocated over a fifth of costs from distribution to supply, ranging between companies from 13 to 38 per cent (Ofgem, 1999). The new Utilities Act will require full business separation between supply and distribution, though not necessarily separate ownership, but the reallocation illustrates the difficulty of regulating vertically integrated companies which are competing in markets where they own the infrastructure to which entrants require access.

One result of the separate licensing of electricity distribution and supply is the need to allocate quality measures which previously applied to an integrated process to each business. While the industries were being separated, the regulation of gas and electricity was integrated into a single body in 1999, so similar quality measures were adopted across both industries. The regulator decided to concentrate such quality measurement on the monopoly transportation and supply businesses, leaving supply measures to the competitive market once prices were deregulated (Ofgem, 2001b). Absolute price caps were removed from gas in April 2001 (but with restrictions on relative prices) and electricity prices were deregulated a year later. After this time the regulator will no longer formally measure performance. However, the consumer body, energywatch, has new powers and duties to collect and disseminate information. This will centre around consumer complaints, and may include some formal performance matrix for companies competing in the supply market. It remains to be seen how far such comparisons can be divorced from the distribution businesses which determine many aspects of quality experienced by consumers, especially in electricity. It has been seen that these distribution businesses are subject to separate formal regulatory quality requirements and incentives.

Railways and Telephones

UK railways are regulated by two bodies: the Strategic Rail Authority (SRA) licenses and regulates the train operating companies (TOCs), and the Office of the Rail Regulator controls the owner of the infrastructure, Network Rail. Since recent concern over safety, Railtrack's performance measures are predominantly on the input side, for example investment levels. Operators are measured primarily by measures of punctuality, and are set individual targets periodically. If they exceed these they receive money from the SRA, and if they fall short they pay the SRA (which invests the proceeds in improving railway services). This continuous system of penalty and reward avoids the arbitrary 'cut-off' incentives of fixed targets and penalties independent of degree of violation. Train operators are also required to pay compensation to passengers for certain specified delays, but this needs to be triggered by the passengers themselves (compared with most of the water quality service targets where compensation is paid automatically, and one of the standards is a requirement to inform customers of their compensation rights). Passenger user groups perform a similar role to that envisaged for energywatch in collecting and publishing information about the performance of individual TOCs.

ELECTRICITY REGULATION IN NORWAY AND HOLLAND

Norway

In January 1997 the Norwegian Water Resources and Energy Administration (NVE) replaced rate of return regulation for the monopoly distributors with a revenue cap which incorporated an efficiency incentive[2] (NVE, 1997). There are about 180 Norwegian distribution companies, owned by local authorities. The initial regulation period was for five years, until 2001, with the efficiency incentive based on performance in 1994–95. Two years before the start of the regulation period the regulator assesses cost inefficiencies which then form the basis for the revenue caps set by the regulator. A rate of return element remains, since at the end of each five-year cycle the achieved rate of return is compared with floor (and ceiling) levels, and if it falls outside this range (2 to 15 per cent), additional (or lower) charges can be levied in the next period. In the case of mergers between companies, the regulator uses a weighted average of their cost efficiencies to calculate the revenue cap to be applied to the new entity. One characteristic of the scheme is that a uniform cost of capital is used for the industry, and so does not differentiate between equity and debt, or take account of different financial structures of the various companies (Agrell et al., 1999). The inputs used to inform the analysis are labour, energy loss, transformers, lines, goods and services; outputs are energy delivered, number of consumers and line length. Other potential variables, such as the corrosion index, climatic index, maximum power and energy supplied to different consumer groups, were eliminated by a stepwise procedure (Kittelsen, 1999). The general productivity improvement, based on the Malmquist index, is currently set at 1.5 per cent per annum, and individual efficiency improvements range from 0 to 3 per cent per annum. It is estimated that 38.4 per cent of the distribution units' inefficiency will be eliminated in four years.

This is probably the longest-running scheme which incorporates comparative efficiency results directly into the price cap of companies, albeit with a rate of return element providing bounds for the outcome. Its establishment owes much to the existence of a large number of comparators, high-quality data, a reasonably homogeneous output, ability to measure quality and the use of complementary statistical tests and econometric analyses (Kittelsen, 1999).

Holland

Comparative performance regulation has been introduced more recently by the Netherlands Electricity Regulatory Service, DTe; it fixed prices for the use of the 22 electricity networks from 1 January 2000, following new legislation requiring the separation of distribution and retail businesses. The new prices were based on the statutory principle that charges in 2000 should be equal to those in 1996; these were to be the same nominal charges, unless companies could demonstrate that they had not been able to absorb inflation increases with productivity growth. From 2000, efficiency discounts were to be introduced. With respect to efficiency discounts the regulatory authority notes: 'The key issue is the comparison of efficiency between different companies. On the basis of this comparison, the potential efficiency improvements of individual companies can be determined and, thereby, the percentage by which their charges could be reduced' (DTe, 1999, p. 3). In August 2000 the efficiency discounts were announced, ranging from 0 to 8 per cent per annum, applicable over three years, together with general discounts of up to 2 per cent per annum. 'In the coming three years companies will be required each year to reduce the tariffs they charged for the use of their grid in the preceding year by the amount of the discount' (DTe, 2000, p. 1).

The discounts resulted from extensive analysis of data from the companies, analysing both the efficiency of the companies themselves, and incorporating a view from the minister of economic affairs which was designed to eliminate historic differences in tariff policies (DTe, 2000).

CONCLUSIONS

There is surprisingly little direct use of comparative performance or so-called yardstick competition in regulation, despite several studies which suggest their potential (Sulamaa, 1999, for Finnish electricity; see

Waddams Price, 2000, for a fuller survey of the UK experience). The UK
regulator has explored the use of comparative efficiency studies between
the local distribution zones of the transmission and distribution gas incumbent, but the incentives and usefulness for regulation are unclear when virtually all the units are owned by the same company. Regulators often use
some comparison between companies to inform their regulatory decisions,
but these have not often been incorporated in a purely mechanical manner.
The Norwegian electricity regulation scheme, the introduction of efficiency
discounts in Holland and the plans for incorporating quality of service in
UK electricity distribution prices are pioneers in this area. In general, yardstick competition is difficult to apply unless there are a large number of
units, and data are easily verifiable. Indeed, mechanical imposition of comparative performance measures with poor data may distort incentives, with
perverse results. However, even if these ideal conditions do not apply, comparative performance studies can be undertaken and are likely to be an
important part of the regulator's tools, providing valuable information
even where this cannot realistically be applied in an automatic fashion
directly to allowed prices. The challenge, as in all performance measurement, is not to distort the decisions of the providers, but to ensure that they
reflect consumer preferences both in *what* is measured and the *level* of
service standards set (including the associated costs of meeting). In that
way such techniques can become a useful adjunct to the deregulatory
process which Colin Robinson has done so much to advocate, rather than
a cost which the industries (and their consumers) have to bear.

APPENDIX: STANDARDS OF SERVICE ASSESSMENT IN UK REGULATED INDUSTRIES

This appendix reports the standards of service imposed by five UK regulators, namely, the Office of Gas and Electricity Markets (Ofgem), the Office
of Water Services (Ofwat), the Office of Telecommunications (Oftel), the
Strategic Rail Authority (SRA) and the Postal Services Commission
(Postcomm). One issue which arises in surveying these standards is the
extent to which they are applied to final services (for example, train operating companies or energy supply) rather than intermediate products such
as Railtrack or transmission and distribution pipes and wires. The variation between regulators is doubtless a combination of their own preferences and the history and development of the industry and its regulation.
The main focus of this appendix is on the energy sector.

Energy

Electricity distribution

Application of yardstick competition to electricity distribution is discussed in detail in the following chapter, but the main features are summarised here. The Information and Incentives Project, introduced in 2002, directly links revenue and standards of service, allocating up to 2 per cent of regulated revenue according to performance on three quality of service measures, namely the number of supply interruptions; the duration of those interruptions; and the quality of telephone response. At the same time Ofgem continues work on guaranteed and overall standards of other dimensions of performance. The tables below show the new standards of service introduced in April 2001 (Ofgem, 2001b).

Ofgem has imposed both guaranteed and overall standards of service on electricity distribution. The former apply across the industry and carry with them a package of compensation to which consumers are entitled in the event that they are not met. The latter vary from company to company. The need to separate the standards to license supply and distribution functions separately has led to the following categorization by Ofgem. Ofgem has consulted on appropriate changes to service standards, including a consumer survey.

Ofgem proposes that guaranteed standards be maintained for the monopoly parts of the network, but may not be appropriate for the supply sector (see below for current standards of service applying to the electricity supply business). Their proposals for electricity distribution are summarized in Tables 2A.1 and 2A.2.

Gas: proposed standards for gas transporters

These have developed on a somewhat more ad hoc basis than for electricity, as a combination of required and voluntary standards. Tables 2A.3 and 2A.4 summarize the Ofgem proposals for guaranteed and overall standards for all gas transporters. New standards of performance are being developed alongside the price control review, based on research of consumers' viewpoints.

Gas and electricity supply

Ofgem removed the specific supply-related standards in electricity when price controls were removed in 2002. In gas, voluntary standards continued also until price control was removed. A formal requirement on reconnection, following disconnection for debt, applies as a metering standard for suppliers. Standards just before price controls were removed from electricity supply are shown in Tables 2A.5 and 2A.6.

Table 2A.1   Guaranteed standards in electricity distribution (2001)

Service	Required performance	Payment
Responding to failure of a mains fuse	Within 3 hours weekdays, 4 hours weekends	£20
Restoring supplies after a fault	Within 18 hours	£50 domestic £100 non-domestic
	For each further 12 hours	£25
Estimating charges	5 days simple jobs, 15 days others	£40
Notice of supply interruption	5 days' notice	£20 domestic £40 non-domestic
Investigate voltage complaints	Visit 7 working days or substantive reply 5 days	£20
Making and keeping appointments	Am or pm, or timed if requested	£20
Notifying of payments owed under standards	Write and make payments within 10 working days	£20

Table 2A.2   Overall standards in electricity distribution (2001)

Service	Required performance
Min % supplies to be restored within 3 hours	85% to 95%
All supplies reconnected after fault	Within 18 hours
All voltage faults corrected	Within 6 months
Connecting new tariff premises	Undetermined
Respond to all customer letters	5 working days

Table 2A.3   Guaranteed standards for gas transporters (2001)

Standard	Performance level	Payment
Making and keeping appointments	Morning or afternoon	£10
Alternative cooking or heating facilities	For elderly, disabled, chronically sick, children	£20
Notification of planned work	10 days for service pipe 5 days for meter	£20 domestic, £40 non-domestic
Notifying of payments	10 working days	£20

Table 2A.4   Levels of overall standards for gas transporters (2001)

Standard	Performance level	Target (%)
Making and keeping appointments	Am or pm	97
Alternative heating/cooking	As above	100
Notification of planned work	As above	99
Telephone calls	Answered within 30 secs	98
Replies to correspondence	5 days	96
Gas emergencies	One hour for uncontrolled escapes;	98
	2 hours for controlled	99

Table 2A.5   Electricity supply: guaranteed standards (2001)

Service	Required performance	Payment
Providing supply and meter	Arrange appointment 2 working days domestic, 4 working days other	£20–£100
Responding to meter problems	Visit 7 working days or substantive reply 5 working days	£20
Responding to queries	Substantive reply and agreed refunds 5 working days	£20
Making and keeping appointments	Am or pm, or timed if requested	£20
Notifying of payments owed under standards	Write and make payments within 10 working days	£20
Respond to prepay meter faults	3 hours weekdays, 4 hours weekends	

Table 2A.6   Electricity supply: overall standards (2001)

Service	Required performance
Reconnection within 1 working day of pay or arrangement	100%
Visit to move meter when requested	15 working days
Changing meters for new tariff	10 working days
Firm meter reading for all consumers	At least once a year
Respond to consumer letters	10 working days

Metering standards

The metering standards for application to gas and electricity suppliers, and to distributors and Transco where applicable are summarized in Tables 2A.7 and 2A.8.

Table 2A.7   Guaranteed metering standards

Service	Required performance	Payment
Providing a meter	Arrange and keep appointment, 2 working days domestic, 4 non-domestic	£20–1000
Responding to meter problems	Visit 7 working days, substantive reply 5 working days	£20–100
Making/keeping appointments	Am or pm or timed	£20
Responding to prepayment meter faults	3 hours weekdays, 4 hours weekends	£20
Appointments for final meter readings	Am or pm (2 days' notice)	£20
Special meter readings	3 days of request, am or pm	£20
Notifying consumers of payments	10 working days	£20

Table 2A.8   Overall metering standards

Service	Required performance
Reposition meter	15 working days
Change meters for new tariff	10 working days
Non-estimated meter reading: annual for domestic, every 2 years for non-domestic	90%
Respond to prepayment meter faults 3 hours weekdays	98%
4 hours weekends	95%
Reconnection by end working day	24 hours

Water

Ofwat operates a guaranteed standards scheme (GSS). Failure to meet these standards results in compensation to the customer either automatically or when claimed, as illustrated in Tables 2A.9 and 2.A.10.

Table 2A.9   Water guaranteed standards scheme

Service	Requirement	Automatic (A) or Claimed (C)
Appointments	Keep am or pm appointment	A
Account queries	Reply within 10 working days	A
Written complaints	Substantive reply within 10 working days	A
Meter installations	15 working days	A
Planned interruptions	Warning	A
Planned interruptions	Restoration as specified	A
Unplanned interruptions	Restoration within GSS period	A
Low pressure	Meet pressure standard	C
Sewer flooding	Flooding incidents	A

Table 2A.10   Total water performance indicators

DG2	Properties at risk of low pressure
DG3	Subject to unplanned supply interruptions for longer than 12 hours
DG4	Population subject to hose-pipe bans
DG5	Properties subject to sewer flooding (once in 10 years)
DG6	Billing contacts not responded to (within 5 working days)
DG7	Written complaints not responded to (10 working days)
DG8	Bills not based on meter readings
DG9	Telephone calls not answered in 30 seconds

Railways

The public performance measure for each train operating company combines figures for punctuality and reliability into a single performance measure. Rail complaints are treated as a useful addition to the range of performance indicators. Unlike other 'system-based' measures, the number of complaints reflects direct feedback from passengers. Public performance measures present data on the proportion of trains which are more than 5, 10, 15 or 20 minutes late, and those which are cancelled. These result in incentive payments either to or from the TOCs, according to their performance against target. In the most recent report (SRA, 2002) the SRA reports that a net payment of £83 million was paid to the SRA for the period year ending 31 March 2002, compared with £102 million in the previous year. The SRA will reinvest sums received in the railways.

Telecoms

Oftel provides little information on specific standards required of BT. However, it does publish lists of complaints and enquiries, both in terms of total numbers, and directs enquirers to sites where total complaints received against each company are listed.

Postal Services

Quality in postal services has developed rather differently from that in other regulated industries. Consignia (as the Royal Mail was known) is still publicly owned, and regulation and targets have been imposed much more recently, so to some extent they reflect experience in other industries. In October 2002 the regulator, Postcomm (2002) issued a proposal for 'Price and Service Quality Regulation' whose title reflects the centrality of quality in the price review. Consignia had failed to achieve most of its main targets since 1996, and had fallen further behind in the most recent three years. This is in marked contrast to service quality in other regulated industries, where targets were routinely met and exceeded. The targets for the price review period (2003–2006) were broadly consistent with those set (but often missed) in the immediately preceding period. The regulator suggested that direct consumer compensation be used for some services, and that the price cap be linked to achieved service quality in others, but that automatic consumer compensation and penalties on allowed revenue were alternatives, and should not both be used for the same service.

Since this was the first introduction of a link between quality and the price cap, its impact was to be limited to one third of 1 per cent of revenue in the first instance, much lower than the 2 per cent exposure which water and electricity distribution companies were facing at the same time. Another characteristic of the post office targets was the introduction of additional targets to be met in each regional area 'to incentivise Consignia to deliver a uniform quality of service across the United Kingdom' (Postcomm, 2002, p. 86). The discussion paper emphasizes the regulator's commitment to a uniform geographic tariff, and here extends this uniformity to quality also. The main service targets included in the link to the price cap are summarized in Table 2A.11.

In addition, direct compensation is payable automatically to bulk users at the rate of 1 per cent of revenue for each percentage point of service failure; and to domestic or retail service users for individual failures or loss, if claims are submitted. Consultations on this price review were still ongoing at the time of writing.

Table 2A.11   Postal service standards

Service standard	Target (by 2006) %	Performance in 2002 %
1st class delivered next working day: nationwide	93.0	89.9
2nd class delivered within 3 working days	98.5	98.3
1st class delivered next working day: min in each postcode area	91.5	n/a
Parcels: delivered within 3 working days	90.0	81

Source: Postcomm, 2002.

NOTES

1. Funding from the Economic and Social Research Council (award R022250167) is grate-fully acknowledged. The chapter was updated and developed from a plenary address to the 6th European Workshop on Efficiency and Productivity Analysis in Copenhagen in October 1999, which was published in the *Revista de Economia del Rosario* (Waddams Price, 2000).
2. Details available on the NVE website www.nve.no.

REFERENCES

Agrell, P.J., Bogetoft, P. and Tind, J. (1999), 'Efficiency and incentives in regulated industries: the case of electricity distribution in Scandinavia', Copenhagen, Denmark: Paper presented to the 6th European Workshop on Efficiency and Productivity Analysis, October.

Baron, D.P. (1985), 'Noncooperative regulation of a nonlocalized externality', *Rand Journal of Economics*, **16** (4), 553–68

Bosworth, D., Stoneman, P. and Thanassoulis, E. (1996), *The Measurement of Comparative Total Efficiency in the Sewerage and Water Industry: An Exploratory Study*, Birmingham, UK: Office of Water Services.

DTe (1999), 'Electricity charges in 2000 almost 2% lower than in 1999. DTe realises savings of NLG 225', The Hague, Netherlands: Netherlands Electricity Regulatory Service, Press Release 99-010 (www.dte.nl).

DTe (2000), 'DTe makes known the planned efficiency discounts for the electricity grids', The Hague, Netherlands: Netherlands Electricity Regulatory Service, Press Release 00-002 (www.dte.ntl).

Kittelsen, S.A.C. (1999), 'Using DEA to regulate Norwegian electricity distribution utilities', Copenhagen, Denmark: Paper presented to the 6th European Workshop on Efficiency and Productivity Analysis, October.

NERA (1999), *Comparatively Poor? A comment on the Ofwat and Ofgem approaches to the assessment of relative efficiencies*, London, UK: National Economic Research Associates Topics 22 (www.nera.com).

Norsworthy, J. and Tsai, D. (1998), 'Performance measurement of price-cap regu-lation of telecommunications: using evidence from a cross-section study of US local exchange carriers', in Crew, M.A. (ed.), *Regulation under increasing competition*, Boston, USA: Kluwer Academic Publishers, pp. 105–36.

NVE (2002), www.nve.no/modula/mmodule-109/publisher_view_product.asp? iEntityid=3646, 28 October.

Ofgem (1999), *Review of Public Electricity Suppliers 1998 to 2000, Distribution Price Control Review, Draft Proposals*, London, UK: Office of Gas and Electricity Markets (www.ofgem.gov.uk).

Ofgem (2000), *Information and Incentives Project: Output Measures and Monitoring Delivery between Reviews*, London, UK: Office of Gas and Electricity Markets (www.ofgem.gov.uk).

Ofgem (2001a), *Experience of the Competitive Market: The Domestic Electricity and Gas Markets – Research Study Conducted for Ofgem by MORI*, London, UK: Office of Gas and Electricity Markets (www.ofgem.gov.uk).

Ofgem (2001b), *Guaranteed and Overall Standards of Performance – Final Proposals*, London, UK: Office of Gas and Electricity Markets (www.ofgem.gov.uk).

Ofwat (1993), *Customer Preferences and Willingness to Pay for Selected Water and Sewerage Services: A Summary Report to the Office of Water Services by the Flood Hazard Research Centre, Middlesex University*, Birmingham, UK: Office of Water Services (www.ofwat.gov.uk).

Ofwat (1998a), *Assessing the Scope for Future Improvements in Water Company Efficiency: A Technical Paper*, Birmingham, UK: Office of Water Services (www.ofwat.gov.uk).

Ofwat (1998b), *A Proposed Approach to Assessing Overall Service to Customers: A Technical Paper*, Birmingham, UK: Office of Water Services (www.ofwat.gov.uk).

Ofwat (2000), *Comparing the Performance of the Water Companies in England and Wales in 1998–99 with Water Enterprises in Other Industrialised Countries*, Birmingham, UK: Office of Water Services (www.ofwat.gov.uk).

Postcomm (2002), *Review of Consignia plc's Price and Service Regulation: Proposal for a Second Price Control*, London, October.

Robinson, C. (1994), 'Gas: what to do after the MMC verdict', in Beesley, M. (ed.), *Regulating Utilities: The Way Forward*, London, UK: Institute of Economic Affairs, pp. 1–19.

SRA (2002), *On Track*, London: Strategic Rail Authority.

Sulamaa, P. (1999), 'Technical efficiency of Finnish electricity distribution sector', Copenhagen, Denmark: Paper presented to the 6th European Workshop on Efficiency and Productivity Analysis, October.

Waddams Price, C. (2000), 'Efficiency and productivity studies in incentive regulation of UK utilities', *Revista de Economia del Rosario*, **3** (2), 11–24.

3. Yardstick competition and efficiency benchmarking in electricity distribution

Thomas Weyman-Jones

INTRODUCTION

The last decade has seen significant developments in the privatization, liberalization and deregulation of the electricity industry in many countries. One characteristic has been vertical deintegration and the separate regulation of distribution natural monopolies by some form of price capping combined with productivity benchmarking and yardstick competition. This chapter surveys some of the developments in this area. It focuses in particular on the theory of yardstick competition and the implementation of benchmarking using data envelopment analysis (DEA). Three ideas are examined in detail: the extent to which DEA-based yardstick competition has attractive incentive properties, the issue of scale economies and convexity assumptions in DEA, and the arguments for and against benchmarking and yardstick competition in general.

Colin Robinson (1999) has emphasized that increased competition should be a major instrument of energy policy, and nowhere has this been more successfully implemented than in the electricity industry, first in the UK and subsequently in the rest of Europe. Privatization, market liberalization and deregulation have characterized the last decade of the industry's development in the European Union with its many different versions of the UK model of competitive generation and supply together with incentive-based regulation of transmission and distribution.

The distinction between these reforms is well known. Privatization means sale to the general public of at least 50 per cent of the shares in a state-owned industry. The industry may, however, remain a monopoly subject to more or less prescriptive regulation. Liberalization consists of policy changes to reduce entry barriers to the new industry, together with the replacement of government funding of investment projects by reliance on the private capital market. Deregulation implies both relaxed conditions on obtaining licences to supply electricity and a switch from prescriptive regulation of the natural monopoly parts of the industry to incentive-based regulation.

It is most difficult to see how competition can be brought to bear in the regulated natural monopoly parts of the industry such as transmission and distribution. For this reason attention is usually directed to comparative performance of different regulated utilities, and comparative performance itself can be subdivided into productivity benchmarking and yardstick competition. Incentive regulation based on comparative performance is spreading worldwide having been pioneered in the UK price control reviews. This chapter examines the regulatory issues that have emerged in these price control reviews, particularly as applied to the distribution sector of the industry. The 14 electricity distribution companies in Britain have been the primary focus of the evolution of price-cap regulation and they have been regarded as test cases for electricity regulation around the world. Distribution of electricity is frequently organized through regional or national monopoly franchises and regulators are therefore naturally drawn to the idea of using yardstick comparisons in reviewing the price controls applying to such companies. In setting price caps, electricity regulators may wish to look outside the industry at national performance in multifactor productivity growth in order to determine the initial incentive mechanism, but sooner or later customer pressure is likely to draw attention to the performance of the companies themselves. Regulators must then be prepared to make efficiency and productivity comparisons among the companies and use these to determine how price caps will be adjusted.

This chapter begins with a brief review of the methods for making inter-firm comparisons followed by a section considering the theory of comparative performance regulation. The subsequent section evaluates data envelopment analysis, which has been widely used by regulators, followed by a section examining the difficulties of efficiency comparisons in practice. The penultimate section summarizes some case studies of electricity distribution, with the final section summarizing the discussion.

METHODS FOR MEASURING COMPARATIVE EFFICIENCY

The earliest approach to productivity measurement (that is, the rate of change of productive efficiency) was productivity growth accounting (PGA) (see O'Mahony, 1999 for an excellent example). PGA requires robust price data and assumes competitive markets – however, it is not demanding in its data coverage and makes simple technological assumptions. More recently research has concentrated on frontier efficiency measurement itself. The most important methods are non-parametric data envelopment analysis (DEA), corrected ordinary least squares regression analysis (COLS), stochastic data envelopment analysis (SDEA) and stochastic frontier analysis (SFA) all of which are now well known in the literature. Lovell (1993) provides a guide to all of the methods mentioned here.

The DEA method uses linear programming to construct piecewise linear segments of the efficient frontier directly from all of the observed inputs and outputs and assumes that all of the variation in the observations is due to inefficiency of some type or other. DEA makes no assumptions about the nature of the underlying technological relationships and requires only that the researcher specifies the relevant multiple inputs and outputs. DEA can be the most conservative in its data requirements and it has frequently been used by regulators in practice, especially in initial benchmarking exercises.

In the COLS method, observations on, for example, cost and outputs are used to fit a multiple regression that is constrained to pass through the most efficient observations. This is achieved by estimating the slope coefficients in the usual way but constraining the intercept so that all observations lie on or above the estimated frontier cost function. The regression methodology is well known and the data requirements are not excessive, but once again all of the observed variation is attributed to inefficiency.

Two methods which combine both stochastic error and inefficiency in measuring the variation in firms' performances are SFA and SDEA. The SFA method constructs the frontier by statistically fitting a line relative to the scatter of points, but assumes that some of the variation is due to random errors of measurement and the rest to inefficiency. The researcher is required to specify the underlying technology and the distribution functions of both the random error term and the inefficiency term. SFA seems clearly preferable in terms of not attributing all variation to inefficiency but this is offset by the restrictiveness of the assumptions needed to model the frontier itself, and it requires large amounts of data. A promising but largely unexplored development is chance-constrained SDEA[1] which combines few restrictive economic and statistical assumptions while still allowing for random errors and inefficiency. It too requires considerable amounts of data. DEA has been rather widely adopted as a method for making efficiency comparisons, so later in this chapter it is examined in more detail.

YARDSTICK COMPETITION MODELS FOR REGULATION

When the UK adopted price-cap regulation as its incentive mechanism for all privatized utilities,[2] its original proponents recognized that resetting the X factor at regulatory review raised complex issues of how closely it should be related to the utility's achieved performance without destroying incentives and how much it could be decoupled from that performance without raising populist objections. Beesley and Littlechild (1989) suggest that in large-scale network industries where regional natural monopoly characteristics are important it would be difficult to avoid relating the X factor to some measure of company performance, especially the rate of return on capital, and consequently yardstick performance measures would become extremely important. This is becoming widely recognized and electricity network regulatory statements in the Netherlands and Australia are two recent examples of similar analysis: DTe (1999) and IPART (1999).

Yardstick competition has been a well-established idea in the academic literature since Shleifer (1985); it requires that the regulator stipulate a price cap that is based on any cost information other than the firm's own chosen cost level. This information reflects both current marginal cost and potential cost reduction. The cost information of the 'shadow firm' associated with the firm under regulation may reflect the mean performance of other identical firms or that of any other firm with appropriate allowance for exogenous differences.

The timeline of a yardstick competition game is shown in Figure 3.1. It is worth noting that whereas in game theory the only interesting activity occurs after the firm agrees to participate, in regulatory practice the first stage in which a mechanism is designed that encourages firms to participate may take up the largest share of time and activity. Most regulated companies have regulatory compliance and affairs departments whose principal role is to engage with the office of the regulatory authority in this first stage of discovering a game-theory-based mechanism design in which the firm will wish to participate.

In Shleifer's (1985) model there are N identical firms each of which has an identical demand curve, $q(p)$, and each of which has the same marginal cost of production c_0, which can be reduced to a lower level c by investing in cost-reducing effort $R(c)$. There are two versions of the game in Shleifer's paper and the case illustrated here arises when there are no transfer payments and the regulator sets a price, p, which covers the average cost $A(c)$ corresponding to any observed marginal cost c. The average cost function satisfies the Ramsey property where λ is the marginal social utility of the breakeven constraint and ε is the price elasticity of demand:

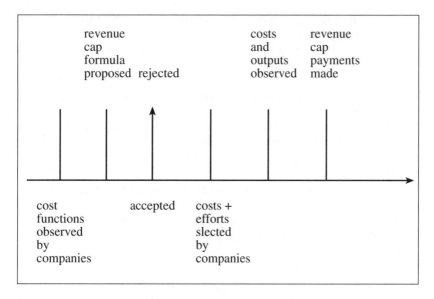

Figure 3.1 Timeline for yardstick competition game

$$p = A(c) \Rightarrow (p - c)/p = (-\lambda/1 + \lambda)(1/\varepsilon). \tag{3.1}$$

Shleifer then considers the situation in which the regulator cannot observe marginal cost but must commit to a pricing rule at the beginning of the game. The yardstick competition (*YC*) solution is to set the pricing rule for the typical firm as:

$$p_i = A(\bar{c}_i); \ \bar{c}_i = \sum_{j \neq i} c_j/N - 1. \tag{3.2}$$

The firm's price cap depends on the mean marginal cost for all the firms except itself observed after the regulator's commitment. As a result of this commitment by the regulator, Shleifer shows that the incentive-compatible first-order condition for the firm in the asymmetric information game has the same structure as the first-best condition in the case of fully observable costs, namely, that the additional profit arising from selling another unit at a lower price equates to the marginal expenditure of investing in cost reduction:

$$-q(p_i) - R'(c_i) = 0. \tag{3.3}$$

In this setting Shleifer asks what level of marginal cost c_i will the firm choose? His central proposition is twofold:

- a symmetric Nash equilibrium occurs where each firm chooses the first-best efficient marginal cost level, c^*;
- there is no other asymmetric Nash equilibrium in which any firm chooses a higher marginal cost $c_i > c^*$.

There appear to be four critical assumptions in the Shleifer model:

1. The regulator must commit to the YC pricing rule and be able to offer a credible threat of implementing the rule.
2. The regulator must ignore participating firms' complaints after the game's outcome.
3. The characteristics used to differentiate firms must be exogenous.
4. There should be no possibility of collusion – and to ensure this the regulator must be able credibly to threaten punishment and there must be a sufficiently large number of comparator firms to make cheating easy and collusion difficult to sustain.

Although Shleifer's (1985) paper is the classic theoretical basis for the field there have been further developments and among the most notable of these has been a series of papers by Peter Bogetoft and others, see especially Bogetoft (1997) and Agrell et al. (2000). In these papers the authors explore the relationship between yardstick competition and the use of DEA, which has been one of the most widely used methods of comparative efficiency measurement among regulated utilities. This section presents a simplified summary of the spirit of the Bogetoft models rather than a detailed analysis. The timeline for Bogetoft's regulatory principal–agent game is essentially similar to that of Shleifer but a different range of possibilities is explored. Among n different utilities the typical firm is observed to have input expenditures of wx, where x is a vector of inputs and w is a vector of input prices, a vector of outputs y and possibly a vector of non-controllable inputs z. These data are verifiable in the sense that the regulator can measure and check the data on outputs, input expenditures and non-controllable inputs. The regulator contracts with the firms at the beginning of the game to pay a revenue cap b according to a formula that depends on the observed costs and outputs of the firms.

The utility (but not the regulator) knows the minimal cost of using current technological possibilities to produce the outputs given the inputs, input prices and non-controllable inputs:

$$C(y|z, w) = \min_{x}\{wx : x \text{ and } z \text{ can make } y\} \qquad (3.4)$$

The firm (or the managers) can choose a degree of slack, s, which is also unknown to the regulator, so that the actual cost experienced by the firm is:

$$C(y|z, w) + s. \tag{3.5}$$

The regulated firm's *ex ante* utility is assumed to depend on the difference between (i) its allowed revenue cap b and its actual verified input expenditure wx, plus (ii) a fraction ρ of the difference between the expenditure on inputs and the cost (including slack) of producing its output target:

$$U = b - wx + \rho[wx - C(y|w, z) - s] \tag{3.6}$$

where the strict inequalities $0 < \rho < 1$ are satisfied. The slack is consumed by the firm in converting inputs into outputs using the available technological possibilities. The restrictions on the marginal utility of the slack, ρ, ensure that at the margin the firm prefers to increase profit rather than to consume slack although both yield positive utility. The regulator is unaware of the minimal cost function, but knows or estimates the firm's marginal utility of slack, and endeavours to minimize the informational rent paid to each regulated firm through the revenue cap.

Bogetoft and his associates show that generally an optimal (individually rational and incentive-compatible) revenue cap contract which will minimize the amount of informational rent to be paid to the firms takes the following form for each firm:

$$b = wx + \rho(C^* - wx), \text{ that is, } b = \rho C^* + (1 - \rho)wx \tag{3.7}$$

where C^* is a 'best-practice cost norm' or 'minimal extrapolation cost standard' set to act as a benchmark for the firm in question. In other words the firm is paid its observed input cost plus a proportion of the difference (positive or negative) between a benchmark of the cost of meeting the firm's observed output level and its observed input cost. This benchmark is 'the maximal cost of producing the firm's outputs that is consistent with the a priori assumptions about possible cost structures and the realised production plans [costs and outputs] of the other firms' (Bogetoft, 1997, p. 285). The role of the benchmark is to provide an upper bound on the costs of the firm so it is essential that it at least exceeds the minimal technological cost of production:

$$C^* \geq C(y|w, z). \tag{3.8}$$

To ensure that the informational rent required to encourage participation and correct revelation of costs is minimized, the benchmark should reflect the cost that would be observed if some other frontier-efficient firm were to supply the output of the firm in question. Clearly too low a benchmark C^*

will discourage the firm from participating in the regulatory game. On the other hand too high a benchmark will lead to inefficiently high payments to the firm. Consequently it is required that C^* is the *least upper bound* of the possible values of the cost of production. Without knowing the minimal technological cost of production, the regulator has to find the least upper bound of the set which contains this unknown function. The observed input expenditures, outputs and non-controllable inputs of the firms that are subject to the yardstick competition can provide information about this least upper bound. In particular, Bogetoft suggests that DEA-based models can provide the basis for estimating the required least upper bound to reflect the behaviour of the companies involved.

However, for incentive reasons Bogetoft argues that the benchmark should exclude the cost and output of the firm in question from the reference set for which the frontier is calculated. In this respect his suggestion replicates the DEA model of Andersen and Petersen (1993) which was initially suggested as a way to rank firms all of which are efficient according to the standard DEA model. In general, however, these arguments provide both a model of yardstick competition and an analytical justification for using the DEA frontier efficiency measure. Bogetoft argues that, in the presence of significant uncertainty about the technology on the part of the regulator, the DEA-based cost norm has several advantages:

1. it requires very little a priori technological information;
2. it allows flexible non-parametric modelling of multiple output and multiple input production processes; and
3. it is essentially conservative in determining the informational rents.

For these reasons and because DEA is widely used by regulators it is necessary to consider the method of DEA-based calculations in some detail and this is done in the next section of the chapter.

COMPARATIVE EFFICIENCY MEASUREMENT USING DEA-BASED METHODS

Regarding DEA as a model for estimating a production possibility set, the underlying assumptions can be set out as follows (see Lovell, 1993 and Bogetoft, 1997). Suppose there is a theoretical production possibility set T relating an input x to an output y and which is defined simply as the possible set of (x, y) pairs:

$$T = \{(x, y) : x \text{ can make } y\}. \tag{3.9}$$

It is necessary to estimate this set empirically from the collection of n observations on the input and the output of a collection of firms or decision-making units. The empirical estimate is T^*:

$$T^* = \{(x, y) \text{ constructed from } x_j, y_j, j = 1 \ldots n\}. \quad (3.10)$$

T^* is estimated as the smallest set containing the observed points and fulfilling certain assumptions, that is, the intersection of all sets containing the observations. One possible definition for the smallest set consists only of the observations and no other points: T_0^*

$$T_0^* = \left\{ (x, y) : x = \sum_{j=1}^{j=n} \lambda_j x_j, \quad y = \sum_{j=1}^{j=n} \lambda_j y_j, \quad \lambda_j \in \{0,1\}, \quad \sum_{j=1}^{j=n} \lambda_j = 1 \right\}. \quad (3.11)$$

This definition says that a point (x, y) is an element of T^* if and only if it is a combination of the observations where the weights in the combination (λ_j) are either 0 or 1 and add up to 1. This, however, is a rather restrictive definition and has the effect of ensuring that every observed point lies on the boundary or frontier of the production possibility set. Consequently the empirical set can be expanded by adding certain assumptions and these have the effect of making the empirical set contain the observations and other points.

A simple expansion of the smallest set arises in the next definition where inequalities replace the equations:

$$T_D^* = \left\{ (x, y) : x \geq \sum_{j=1}^{j=n} \lambda_j x_j, \quad y \leq \sum_{j=1}^{j=n} \lambda_j y_j, \quad \lambda_j \in \{0,1\}, \quad \sum_{j=1}^{j=n} \lambda_j = 1 \right\}. \quad (3.12)$$

This says that points with more input but the same output as an observed point, or less output but the same input as an observed point are also in the smallest set containing the observations. Figure 3.2 illustrates this with four observations (a, b, c and d) on the variables. It shows how this relaxation of the definition of T^* expands the definition of the smallest set, and shows that one of the observations now lies inside the efficient frontier. T_D^* is the free disposal hull (FDH) efficient frontier suggested by Tulkens (1993). It consists of the segmented line: $Xaa'bb'cc'$ in Figure 3.2 and the production possibility set is estimated by the area on and to the right of this frontier. The points a, b and c are still on the frontier while d lies inside the frontier. The efficiency of the point $d = (x_d, y_d)$ in the figure can be measured by the radial contraction in input needed to reach the frontier. This is the ratio: PR/Pd. Consequently, input-orientated FDH efficiency θ_d^{FDH} is the solution of the problem:

$$\min \theta_d^{FDH} \text{ s.t. } \theta_d^{FDH} x_d \geq \sum_{j=1}^{j=n} \lambda_j x_j, \quad y_d \leq \sum_{j=1}^{j=n} \lambda_j y_j, \quad \lambda_j \in \{0,1\}, \quad \sum_{j=1}^{j=n} \lambda_j = 1. \quad (3.13)$$

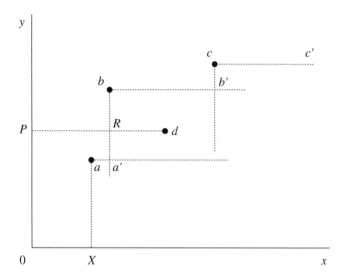

Figure 3.2   Free disposal hull frontier

A further expansion of the smallest set containing the observations can be obtained by relaxing the constraints on the weights to allow them to take values between 0 and 1. Each relaxation of the assumptions includes more points in the empirical estimating set and this has the consequence of potentially lowering the measured efficiency of any of the actual observations since the frontier may be moved further away (and certainly cannot be moved nearer to the observations). However, each relaxation of assumptions on the weights from this point on is also equivalent to adding the assumption that the empirical production possibility set T^* is convex. This happens because although each new set contains points which are not convex combinations of observations, these points are convex combinations of other points in the set being defined. In fact, the first expansion considered does contain convex combinations of observations:

$$T_{VRS}^* = \left\{ (x, y) : x \geq \sum_{j=1}^{j=n} \lambda_j x_j, \quad y \leq \sum_{j=1}^{j=n} \lambda_j y_j, \quad \lambda_j \geq 0, \sum_{j=1}^{j=n} \lambda_j = 1 \right\}. \quad (3.14)$$

This has the effect of adding regions aba' and bcb' to the estimated production possibility set now shown as $Xabcc'$ in Figure 3.3. The input-orientated technical efficiency of point d is now given by PQ/Pd and can be obtained from the DEA model:

$$\min \theta_d^{VRS} \text{ s.t.} \theta_d^{VRS} x_d \geq \sum_{j=1}^{j=n} \lambda_j x_j, \quad y_d \leq \sum_{j=1}^{j=n} \lambda_j y_j, \quad \lambda_j \geq 0, \sum_{j=1}^{j=n} \lambda_j = 1. \quad (3.15)$$

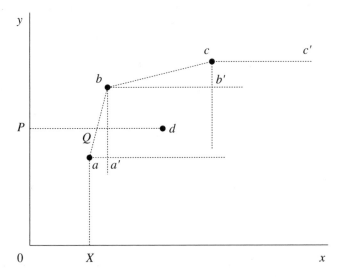

Figure 3.3   Convex DEA frontier

This can be interpreted as a variable returns to scale model but there is some controversy about this. A further relaxation of the estimating set allows any scaled-down observation also to be a member of the smallest set containing the observations:

$$T_{NIRS}^* = \left\{ (x, y) : x \geq \sum_{j=1}^{j=n} \lambda_j x_j, \quad y \leq \sum_{j=1}^{j=n} \lambda_j y_j, \quad \lambda_j \geq 0, \sum_{j=1}^{j=n} \lambda_j \leq 1 \right\}. \quad (3.16)$$

This is referred to as the non-increasing returns to scale estimating set. It corresponds in Figure 3.4 to adding the area $0baX$ to the definition of the smallest set containing the observations which is now shown as $0bcc'$. There is a corresponding measure of the efficiency of point d under the assumption of non-increasing returns to scale, θ_d^{NIRS}, represented by the ratio PS/Pd.

Finally the constraints in the estimating set can be relaxed further simply to permit non-negative weights:

$$T_{CRS}^* = \left\{ (x, y) : x \geq \sum_{j=1}^{j=n} \lambda_j x_j, \quad y \leq \sum_{j=1}^{j=n} \lambda_j y_j, \quad \lambda_j \geq 0 \right\}, \quad (3.17)$$

with corresponding efficiency of point d, θ_d^{CRS}. In Figure 3.4 the area on and to the right of $0be$, which is a convex cone, is now defined to be the smallest set containing the observations. The DEA model categorizes the scale efficiency of a point such as d as follows:

$$\text{scale efficiency} = \theta_d^{VRS}/\theta_d^{CRS};$$

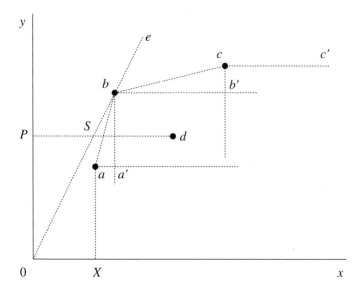

Figure 3.4   DEA frontiers with non-increasing returns (0bc) and constant returns (0be)

and

$$\theta_d^{NIRS} = \theta_d^{CRS} < \theta_d^{VRS} \Rightarrow IRS; \quad \theta_d^{CRS} < \theta_d^{VRS} = \theta_d^{NIRS} \Rightarrow NIRS. \quad (3.18)$$

This describes the FDH or DEA estimating set based on the observations (and the corresponding efficiency measure), T_k^*, where k stands for: $k =$ *FDH, VRS, NIRS, CRS*. Note that each of the DEA calculations maintains the assumption of convexity on the smallest set containing the observations. To see this, compare the different estimating sets in Figure 3.4. These are: DEA–*VRS*: *Xabcc'*; DEA–*NIRS*: 0*bcc'*; and DEA–*CRS*: 0*be*.

Each of these sets is convex because each contains a convex combination of any two of the points defined to be in the set, though in the case of *NIRS* and *CRS* the points may not be convex combinations of actual observations. This emphasizes the fact that DEA assumes the convexity of the estimating set and consequently that the frontier is the boundary of a convex set. This assumption is fundamental, of course, because DEA is based on the argument that the efficient frontier should be constructed from combinations of the observations even where such points represent hypothetical rather than actual firms. It is the FDH model which restricts the frontier to be drawn only from actual observations. As a result the FDH estimating set is not necessarily convex.

So far only the properties of the empirical estimating set based on the observations have been looked at. But what are the implications of imposing similar assumptions on the unknown theoretical production possibility set? The properties used have been: *disposability, variable returns to scale, non-increasing returns to scale, constant returns to scale* and *convexity*. Applied to the theoretical production possibility set these are:

$$T\{(x, y): x \text{ can make } y\} \qquad (3.19)$$

1. Disposability of T: $(x, y) \in T,\ x' \geq x,\ 0 \leq y' \leq y \Rightarrow (x', y') \in T$
2. T displays constant returns to scale: $\{(x, y) \in T \Rightarrow \alpha(x, y) \in T,\ \alpha \geq 0\}$
3. T displays non-increasing returns to scale: $\{(x, y) \in T \Rightarrow \alpha(x, y) \in T,\ \alpha \in [0,1]\}$
4. T displays variable returns to scale: $\{(x, y) \in T \Rightarrow \alpha(x, y) \in T,\ \alpha = 1\}$
5. T is convex: $(x, y) \in T,\ (x', y') \in T \Rightarrow \alpha(x, y) + (1 - \alpha)(x', y') \in T,\ \alpha \in [0,1]$

The last property is not strictly necessary for the definition of the theoretical production possibility set T. This can be illustrated with Figures 3.5 and 3.6 which show theoretical non-convex and convex production possibility sets in the case of one input and one output. These sets are defined by points on and right of the solid curve. It helps to remember here that

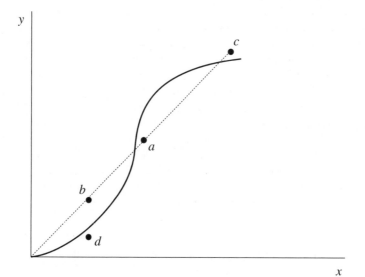

Figure 3.5   Non-convex production possibility set T^N

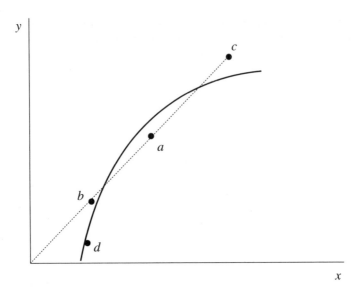

Figure 3.6   Convex production possibility set T^C

local returns to scale can be measured by the elasticity of output with respect to input: $E_{yx} = xMP/y$, where MP is the marginal product. Locally increasing, constant and decreasing returns to scale are given by $E_{yx} > 1$, $E_{yx} = 1$ and $E_{yx} < 1$, respectively. However, the returns to scale properties described above for T refer to global measures.

In Figures 3.5 and 3.6 the same four points: *a*, *b*, *c* and *d* are identified. Suppose we want to ensure that variable returns to scale are possible – perhaps in order to afford the companies the benefit of not penalizing them for scale inefficiency. Looking at property (4) above it can be seen that variable returns to scale means that arbitrary rescaling of point *a* either up or down will not necessarily yield another point in the production possibility set. For example, neither points *b* nor *c* are in the production possibility sets: T^N in Figure 3.5 and T^C in Figure 3.6. Under variable returns the possibility that any multiple of point *a* is not in T must be allowed. However, the two figures show sets with different boundary shapes, one being non-convex and the other being convex. Convexity of the theoretical production possibility set is not essential to the existence of variable returns to scale. Nevertheless DEA cannot help us to estimate the set T^N since DEA imposes the assumption of convexity on all of the empirical production possibility sets: T^*_{CRS}, T^*_{NIRS} and T^*_{VRS}. DEA can only help us to estimate T^C.

How serious is this assumption of convexity imposed on T^* by DEA?

Opinion is divided. Consider the danger of assuming that the true production possibility set is convex. In both Figures 3.5 and 3.6, points a and d are each in the sets T^N and T^C. However, in Figure 3.5 there are combinations of a and d (points on a straight line joining a and d) which are not feasible input–output combinations because they lie outside T^N. This is not the case in Figure 3.6. As long as a and d are in T^C, any points on the straight line joining a and d must also be in T^C and serve as possible comparators. Consequently DEA will assume the feasibility of unobserved technological choices which may not be justified if the theoretical production possibility set takes the non-convex rather than convex form.

There is another way of putting this. Comparing the frontiers in Figures 3.5 and 3.6 it can be seen that in the non-convex case MP is at first increasing and then decreasing, while in the convex case MP is always decreasing. Decreasing MP and convexity go together in this simple case. However, both MP properties are compatible with increasing returns to scale, $E_{yx}>$ 1. Strictly, therefore, theory does not require convexity of the theoretical production possibility set, although it is assumed by DEA methods for the empirical production possibility set. Petersen (1990) raises the question: what about having a non-convex empirical production possibility set but convex isoquants? Is it possible to apply DEA to this situation? In general the answer seems to be that this is not possible, certainly in the case of multiple inputs and outputs (Bogetoft, 1996). To remove convexity of the production possibility set and still have practicable estimating procedures it appears that convex isoquants have to be abandoned as well. But this leaves only the FDH model to work with. This is only one of the problems concerning the choice of benchmarking method and there are several others which also need to be considered.

It was seen earlier that the essence of Bogetoft's argument is that to encourage participation in the regulatory game the agent must be offered a contract based on an upper bound of the possible costs he or she could incur, but to minimize information rents the principal will seek a least upper bound to the set of possible costs. Within the range of comparative efficiency models it is possible to discover some that are nested and some that are not. This allows the researcher to examine different least upper bounds for the cost set under different assumptions. Begin with the basic distinction between parametric and non-parametric models. Parametric, that is, regression-based, models assume that each company uses the same underlying technology represented by the production function.[3] Within this group stochastic frontier models allow some of the variation in cost to be random while COLS models attribute all of the variation to inefficiency. Consequently, in this case the relationship between the minimal cost extrapolation or least upper bound of the relative frontier cost levels is

$C^{COLS} \leq C^{SFA}$. This means that the efficient benchmark for cost performance in the COLS model is at a lower total cost level than the efficient benchmark for the stochastic frontier cost model. However, since non-parametric models allow each company to have a different technology, it is clear that parametric and non-parametric models are not nested even when one is deterministic and the other is stochastic: C^{DEA}, C^{SFA} cannot be unambiguously ranked before calculation. In practice it is often the case that SFA methods find it difficult to discover widespread inefficiency in a sample. This is chiefly because the sample must be large enough to be able to test for significantly skewed regression residuals and to measure the effect of the inefficiency in causing the residuals to be skewed.

Within DEA-based models variable returns to scale possibilities allow some of the variation in cost to be attributable to inefficient scale rather than pure technical inefficiency so that nesting is possible on the basis of scale assumptions. This means that the efficient frontier cost benchmark is at a lower overall level for constant returns to scale models than for variable returns to scale models: $C^{DEA-CRS} \leq C^{DEA-VRS}$.

It is, however, possible to obtain a larger least upper bound to the frontier costs by using as an alternative to the conventional DEA methodology the free disposal hull (FDH) method described earlier. The DEA technical efficiency scores (θ) that arise from relaxing assumptions can be ranked as follows:

$$0 \leq \theta^{DEA-CRS} \leq \theta^{DEA-VRS} \leq \theta^{FDH} \leq 1 \qquad (3.20)$$

and consequently obtain the nested frontier costs:

$$0 \leq C^{DEA-CRS} \leq C^{DEA-VRS} \leq C^{FDH} \qquad (3.21)$$

so that FDH will always show companies in at least as good a light and usually better than DEA under variable returns to scale, and this in turn is at least as good as and usually better than DEA under constant returns to scale.

Supporters of the FDH methods do not recognize the validity of the DEA comparison of actual companies with hypothetical input–output combinations, and seek to compare efficiency scores of an observed firm only with other observed firms. Desprins et al. (1984, p. 264) put the case for this approach on two grounds: it rests on the weakest assumptions regarding the production set, and identification of dominating observations reveals an information set of direct use for managers. The assumptions required are simply input and output disposability (that is, the firm can reduce slack or unused inputs or use them to expand outputs without using up other additional resources). No assumption is made regarding the nature of the returns to scale. Nevertheless the method is controversial in the context of identifying potential efficiency gains. Some contrasting views illustrate the issue. The first can be stated thus: we should seek the frontier which shows the firm in the best light: 'evaluation of a given unit under the most favourable conditions has been claimed as one of the advantages of DEA' (Petersen, 1990, p. 313). This suggests that the tightest envelopment surface is to be preferred, and this is the FDH frontier. The second argument is that we should seek potential efficiency gains for firms:

> [A]t the heart of the method [DEA] is the assumption that we may interpolate between any number of units within the comparator set to construct efficient units which could have existed in principle even if not observed in practice. This way an efficient boundary of units are created, some observed some not, and then the distance of a unit from the boundary gives us a measure of its efficiency. (Thanassoulis, 1999, p. 42)

This suggests that convexity is an important comparator property for identifying potential efficiency gains, hence the DEA frontier is preferred from this point of view. There is a deeper incentive issue here. Since the cost frontiers have nested properties, companies will always have an incentive to skew the choice of efficiency comparison method towards the one which shows them in the best light. The closer the envelopment that can be ensured then the greater the incentive for a company to choose an idiosyncratic technology which may not be replicated by others. This incentive applies to all companies so that efficiency comparisons which are restricted to actual observations are an encouragement to companies to differ as widely as possible from one another. Strategic behaviour may be generated by the choice of efficiency measurement technique. An intermediate view is offered by Bogetoft (1996): 'On the one hand, we want to keep convexity whenever reasonable, and on the other hand, we must allow that not all technologies are convex' (p. 462).

It is possible to read into actual regulatory decisions the views of the players in the process. For example, the Dutch regulator specifically resisted the use of the FDH model using arguments based on the importance of allowing for potential competition (DTe, 2000). The key argument was that ignoring potential comparators would cause the regulator to lose credibility with consumer groups. In contrast, at least one US regulatory commission has indicated a reluctance to compare a regulated company with anything but other actual companies. By ignoring potential combinations of efficient companies the FDH frontier implies that market entry or performance is not feasible at that combination. However, in the context of a group of regulated monopolies, customer groups are unlikely to believe this, and rival companies certainly will not.

Energy in a competitive market

When stochastic models are considered, the SDEA approach will always permit a closer envelopment of the data than the deterministic model so that $C^{DEA-CRS} \le C^{SDEA-CRS}$. However, it is not possible to argue which relaxation will have the greater effect compared to deterministic constant returns to scale DEA – stochastic DEA or non-convex DEA – so that C^{FDH}, $C^{SDEA-CRS}$, for example, are not nested costs. As well as the choice of technique, other factors such as sample size and model specification also affect the minimal extrapolation costs. These are summarized in Table 3.1.

Table 3.1   Factors affecting data envelopment

Efficiency study context	Companies loosely enveloped = low mean efficiency	Companies closely enveloped = high mean efficiency	Regulatory credibility	Comment
Scale	CRS	VRS→FDH	VRS yes, FDH no?	Potential comparators
Sample size	Large	Small	Want large comparator set	Data comparable?
Number of variables	Low	High	Put a limit on the dimensions of comparison	Companies say their operations are all different
Stochastic	No	Yes	Data availability limited	Some limits needed on efficiency differences

BENCHMARKING VERSUS YARDSTICK COMPETITION

Up to this point the discussion has treated benchmarking and yardstick competition as equivalent terms, but it makes sense to be more precise in the usage of these words. The regulatory exercise in the Netherlands has drawn one distinction along the following sequential lines (DTe, 2000).

- Firms are *benchmarked against one another* to determine an efficient frontier, and then given different cost reduction targets to ensure that each catches up with the frontier over time.
- Subsequently, all of the firms in the group may be given the same cost reduction frontier, for example, the rate of total factor productivity

growth in the economy as a whole, in order to implement *yardstick competition.*

However, an almost exact reversal of the terminology perhaps makes more sense, as the following suggests:

- *Benchmarking* is the exercise of setting a regulatory target in which each company is rewarded or penalized according to whether it meets or fails to meet the target.
- *Yardstick competition* is a mechanism in which the set of regulatory firms are able to earn a reward in proportion to the amount by which each exceeds or falls short of the performance of the others.

The advantage of using this latter distinction is that the *competition* aspect of yardstick competition is emphasized in the second mechanism, while the first mechanism of benchmarking emphasizes that the regulator has adopted an absolute or exogenous standard that does not depend on the application of the superior information of the firms. Staying with this analytical distinction, it turns out that regulated firms have often expressed a strong preference for abandoning yardstick competition and concentrating on the activity of meeting a benchmark performance set by the regulator – for example, see the discussions about incentivizing capital expenditure plans initiated in the Information and Incentives Project (IIP) of Ofgem (2000, 2001). There is a clear rationale for this from the firms' point of view which reflects the insights of the Shleifer and Bogetoft papers. In the asymmetric information game between a regulator and the regulated companies any incentive mechanism must de-couple the firm's own statement of its costs from the incentive payment it receives. Consequently a regulated firm can expect to be compared with a performance criterion into which it has no input itself. The Shleifer and Bogetoft mechanisms follow the game theory literature in comparing each firm against the other regulated firms serving the same or closely located markets. However, regulated firms themselves are frequently on record as preferring that the regulator should set a minimum performance benchmark and reward, or not penalize companies that outperform this standard. Using the Bogetoft framework the revenue cap for the typical firm in our definition of benchmarking is:

$$b_i = wx_i + \rho_i(C^* - wx_i) \qquad (3.22)$$

where C^* is a cost benchmark or fixed budget. This could be set exogenously by the regulator. The firm minimizes cost but earns informational rents in excess of those resulting from the optimal rent-minimizing yard-stick competition mechanism because it is competing against the regulator's badly informed benchmark target rather than against the observed behaviour of other participating firms. The optimal yardstick competition mechanism preferred by Shleifer and Bogetoft therefore uses a cost norm based on observed performances by the firms involved instead of the exogenous benchmark. To minimize the rents paid to the firms it is a best-practice or frontier cost norm, that is, a least upper bound on the unknown costs.

Regulated firms are not slow to recognize that their informational advantages make it easier to meet exogenous benchmarks than to compete against other well-informed firms. Consequently, regulated firms, if offered the choice, generally prefer exogenous benchmarking to yardstick competition – the former offers more scope to extract informational rent. The arguments used by regulated firms in this respect are illuminating and are well demonstrated in the consultation documents for the Ofgem IIP exercise, Ofgem (2000, 2001). Firms usually state that it is essential for the regulator to set a benchmark otherwise they will have no idea how to plan for improved performance. Moreover, firms' managers will often claim that their shareholders will be less tolerant of their performance if it is second best in a yardstick competition mechanism, than if it is one of a large group that meets an exogenous benchmark. Consequently it is often easier to obtain agreement on participation in a regulatory game at the first stage of the game's timeline if benchmarking is used rather than yardstick competition. Of course, this easier initial agreement is associated with larger informational rents to the regulated firms. Referring back to Figure 3.1 it can be seen once again that in practice the first stage in the timeline – obtaining the firms' participation – may be the most time consuming.

The arguments so far emphasize the benefits of yardstick competition, but there have been criticisms of the mechanism as well. For example, Shuttleworth (1999) reflects a variety of industry objections to some of the major regulatory benchmarking exercises which have been implemented. Shuttleworth's first point reflects a problem arising if the regulator separately benchmarks different components of cost – notably operating and capital expenditures (OPEX and CAPEX). Since there is potentially a trade-off between the two reflecting the ability of the firm to substitute variable inputs for capacity, it is important to keep all of the firm's cost performance under balanced review. He adds the fundamental principle that benchmarking and yardstick competition should be as objective as possible, using publicly available data and mechanistic rules. Shuttleworth argues that these precepts have not been adopted in some UK regulation where the data have been manipulated and the rules interpreted in a way that relies too heavily on the subjective interpretations of the regulator. Shuttleworth also sees problems in compelling firms to compete with an efficient benchmark while simultaneously insisting on them earning no more than a normal rate of return on capital. He argues that regulators who adopt an unquestioning attitude to efficiency measurement may be unwilling to accept that any variation in performance could be due to factors other than inefficient behaviour. Finally he questions whether benchmarking enthusiasts take sufficient notice of the need to maintain the financial viability of the regulated company. Shuttleworth's objections to regulatory comparisons, which lead him to advocate abandoning the procedure, are based on the difficulties of implementation rather than principle.

Bös (1991) is one of the earliest critics of yardstick competition. He argues in the context of the Shleifer model that 'the fascinating clarity and straightforwardness of yardstick regulation is flawed if the actual application is considered' (p. 82). He offers four principal objections. First, the model assumes that the firms have the same characteristics. Although Shleifer suggested a regression-based approach to correcting for heterogeneity among the comparators, this solution may be very imperfect if the regression has low explanatory power. DEA approaches, however, do allow for differences in the exogenous operating characteristics of different firms through the use of non-discretionary inputs and outputs. The effect is to add constraints to the problem so that if a particular firm is penalized by its operating characteristics compared with the rest of the industry then it obtains a closer envelopment (higher efficiency score) than in the absence of the constraints. Bös's second argument notes that the Shleifer model excludes information asymmetry relating to demand but this too is an area where the regulator may be poorly informed. The third argument points out that the solution assumes that the regulator is able to commit himself or herself not to support the firm if it is threatened with bankruptcy. However, the ability to commit in this way is often ruled out in the legislation setting up regulatory offices, and the commitment is difficult to sustain with any credibility. Finally, the model assumes no collusion among the firms, but this may be very unrealistic when dealing with a group of newly privatized utilities used to working together prior to privatization.

Nevertheless, the benchmarking approach is favoured by regulators because it is an attempt to overcome the problem of asymmetry of information and the lack of incentive mechanisms in purely prescriptive procedures such as cost of service or rate of return regulation. As with any form of regulation, comparative efficiency measures can be applied sensitively or naively and it is clear that their incentive properties are so theoretically attractive that regulators will be reluctant to ignore them.

CASE STUDIES OF COMPARATIVE EFFICIENCY AMONG ELECTRICITY DISTRIBUTION UTILITIES

Having established the choice of frontier and the measurement method, the next step is to consider the variables involved. It is critical that the regulator and the companies achieve consensus on what a regulated company looks like in terms of the range of outputs and the controllable inputs. The regulator will need to rely on company data so the companies must feel an incentive to provide data that reflect what their business is about and that will yield incentive mechanisms to which they can respond. The essential data include outputs and inputs that all the players recognize as wide ranging and meaningful. Whether or not these have measurable market prices will determine the sort of frontier that is constructed. Some features will be outside the companies' control. By adding uncontrolled factors into the measurement activity as additional constraints, their adverse effect on the companies' performance is alleviated. This is because each company's relative efficiency is measured as its minimum distance from the frontier. Adding constraints to reflect uncontrolled factors has the effect of raising the apparent frontier closer to the company's actual position, thereby increasing its measured efficiency. The regulator must exercise judgement and deploy incentives where there is doubt about the extent to which a factor such as quality of supply or response to adverse weather is outside a company's control or is part of its regulated economic activity.

To convey some idea of the range of variables and methods used in benchmarking studies, Table 3.2 is a non-exhaustive summary of some recent studies from the academic research literature. A wide-ranging survey is provided by Jamasb and Pollitt (2000).

The models generally use as outputs a subset of the variables: energy distributed in kilowatt hours (kWh), numbers of customers (*ncust*), maximum demand (*maxdd*) on the system in kilowatts. Inputs may be in physical terms: number of employees, length of network, numbers or capacity of transformers, or in real financial terms: operating expenditures and capital used. There are variables which reflect the operating characteristics of the utilities but which may be outside their control: customer density, market structure and so on.

Not all models use the same production specification. For example, network length has been used as an input in some studies, as a measure of the uncontrolled operating characteristics of the network in others, and even as an output in the Ofgem study of 1999. This last study differed from much of the usual practice in defining a composite firm size variable to represent the output variables driving operating cost.

It can be seen from Table 3.1 that the sample sizes used in comparative

Table 3.2 *Some comparative efficiency studies*

Study	Outputs	Inputs	Note
Hjalmarsson and Veiderpass (1992)	kWh (lv and hv), *ncust* (lv and hv)	Lines, transfer capacity, employees	DEA, Sweden
Salvanes and Tjøtta (1994)	kWh, *ncust*	Prices of labour and energy	Translog cost function, Norway
Burns and Weyman-Jones (1994)	kWh, *ncust, maxdd*	Lines, transfer capacity, employees	Density and structure controls, DEA – Malmquist panel England and Wales
Pollitt (1995)	kWh (by volt), *ncust*, service area, *maxdd*	Employees, transfer capacity, lines	DEA and OLS for US and UK 1990
Burns and Weyman-Jones (1996)	kWh, *ncust, maxdd*	Prices of labour and capital	Density and structure controls, SFA panel UK
Zhang and Bartels (1998)	*ncust*	Lines, transfer capacity, employees	DEA – 3 countries with bootstrapping
Khumbakar and Hjalmarsson (1998)	Quality adjusted hedonic output index	Transfer capacity, employees	SFA translog hedonic input requirements function
Førsund and Kittelson (1998)	Distance, kWh, *ncust*	Labour hours, losses, materials ($), capital ($)	DEA – Malmquist panel Norway
Tilley and Weyman-Jones (1999)	kWh, *ncust, maxdd*, quality of supply	Labour (real $), capital stock (real $)	Density and structure controls, DEA – Malmquist panel UK
Ofgem (1999)	Composite size (function of lines, *ncust*, kWh)	Base operating cost	UK panel for 1997, adjusted regression

Notes:
lv = Low voltage
hv = High voltage

57

efficiency studies naturally reflect the number of regulated utilities in any given regulatory jurisdiction. The Bogetoft model showed that the number of comparators was important for determining the size of the bench-marked revenue cap. However, having a large number of comparators will affect the measured scale efficiency of the companies in the industry.

CONCLUSIONS

The overwhelming conclusion to emerge from this survey of comparative efficiency issues in electricity distribution is that the process has very attractive incentive properties but it is fraught with difficulty. The chapter began by looking at yardstick competition models and arguing that there is a fundamental principle in the theoretical literature. This says that a regulator should establish an upper bound for the allowed costs of the company being regulated. The upper bound should be generous enough to encourage participation and incentive compatibility but not so generous that excessive informational rents are earned by the company on the basis of its superior knowledge of its costs. Consequently the regulator must search for a least upper bound to the company's costs. Such a least upper bound is offered by observing the comparative performance of other companies engaged in the same industry.

Among the ways of constructing a least upper bound on costs based on observation of companies, frontier methods are an obvious and attractive solution. The chapter considered the arguments for and against different frontier methods in terms of their nesting properties. Issues concerning DEA frontier estimation received particular examination because this approach has been used by several regulators in recent years. Opinion is divided on the theoretical properties of DEA, partly because it compares actual companies' performances with potential performances without the guarantee that the benchmarks are theoretically feasible. Regression-based methods including SFA do this as well of course. In practice this difficulty may be overstated and the alternative of solely comparing actual observations not only may have the effect of making all companies look equally efficient, but also may offer incentives to adopt idiosyncratic technologies in order to eliminate comparators.

The practical issues were illustrated in the context of a variety of case studies. Finally the chapter examined the arguments for and against yard-stick competition in general. The fundamental dilemma remains: it has strong incentive properties but is sensitive to the choice of variables, measurement techniques and sample size. It offers fertile ground for both further research and strategic behaviour.

NOTES

1. SDEA converts stochastic linear programmes into deterministic non-linear programmes by assuming that the measurement errors are normally distributed and using certainty equivalents (Lovell, 1993, pp. 35–6).
2. RPI–X, where RPI is the change in the Retail Price Index.
3. The assumption may be relaxed in random parameters models but the nesting effect is not clear.

REFERENCES

Agrell, Per J., Bogetoft, P. and Tind, J. (2000), 'Multi-period DEA incentive regulation in electricity distribution', Hawaii, USA: INFORMS Conference Paper (and *Journal of Productivity Analysis*, forthcoming).

Andersen, P. and Petersen, N.C. (1993), 'Procedure for ranking efficient units in data envelopment analysis', *Management Science*, **39** (10), 1261–4.

Beesley, M. and Littlechild, S. (1989), 'The regulation of privatized monopolies in the United Kingdom', *Rand Journal of Economics*, **20** (3), 454–72.

Bogetoft, P. (1996), 'DEA on relaxed convexity assumptions', *Management Science*, **42** (3), 457–64.

Bogetoft, P. (1997), 'DEA based yardstick competition: the optimality of best practice regulation', *Annals of Operations Research*, **73**, 277–98.

Bös, D. (1991), *Privatization: A Theoretical Treatment*, Oxford, UK: Clarendon Press.

Burns, P. and Weyman-Jones, T. (1994), *Regulatory Incentives, Privatization and Productivity Growth in UK Electricity Distribution*, London, UK: CRI Technical Paper 1, Centre for the Study of Regulated Industries, Chartered Institute of Public Finance and Accountancy (IPFA).

Burns, P. and Weyman-Jones, T. (1996), 'Cost functions and cost efficiency in electricity distribution: a stochastic frontier approach', *Bulletin of Economic Research*, **48** (1), 44–64.

Desprins, D., Simar, L. and Tulkens, H. (1984), 'Measuring labor-efficiency in post offices', in Marchand, M., Pestieau, P. and Tulkens, H. (eds), *The Performance of Public Enterprises*, Amsterdam, Netherlands: North-Holland; London, UK: Elsevier, pp. 243–67.

DTe (1999), 'Price cap regulation in the electricity sector: information and consultation document' (unauthorized translation), The Hague, Netherlands: Netherlands Electricity Regulatory Service (www.dte.nl).

DTe (2000), *Guidelines for Price Cap Regulation of the Dutch Electricity Sector in the period from 2000 to 2003*, The Hague, Netherlands: Netherlands Electricity Regulatory Service (www.dte.nl).

Førsund, F.R. and Kittelsen, S.A.C. (1998), 'Productivity development of Norwegian electricity distribution utilities', *Resource and Energy Economics*, **20** (3), 207–24.

Hjalmarsson, L. and Veiderpass, A. (1992), 'Efficiency and ownership in Swedish electricity distribution', *Journal of Productivity Analysis*, **3**, 7–23.

IPART (1999), *Regulation of Electricity Network Service Providers: incentives and principles for regulation*, Sydney, Australia: Independent Pricing and Regulatory Tribunal of New South Wales, Discussion Paper DP-32 (www.ipart.nsw.gov.au).

Jamasb, T. and Pollitt, M. (2000), *Benchmarking and Regulation of Electricity Distribution and Transmission Utilities: lessons from international experience*, Cambridge, UK: DAE Working Paper 0101, Department of Applied Economics, University of Cambridge.

Khumbakar, S. and Hjalmarsson, L. (1998), 'Relative performance of public and private ownership under yardstick competition: electricity retail distribution', *European Economic Review*, **42** (1), 97–122.

Lovell, C.A.K. (1993), 'Production frontiers and productive efficiency', in Fried, H., Lovell, C.A.K. and Schmidt, H. (eds), *The Measurement of Productive Efficiency*, Oxford, UK: Oxford University Press, pp. 3–67.

Ofgem (1999), *Distribution Price Control Review Draft Proposals*, London, UK: Office of Gas and Electricity Markets (www.ofgem.gov.uk).

Ofgem (2000), *Information and Incentives Project: output measures and monitoring delivery between reviews, final proposal*, London: UK: Office of Gas and Electricity Markets (www.ofgem.gov.uk).

Ofgem (2001), *Information and Incentives Project: incentive schemes*, London, UK: Office of Gas and Electricity Markets (www.ofgem.gov.uk).

O'Mahony, M. (1999), *Britain's Productivity Performance 1950–96: An International Perspective*, London, UK: National Institute of Economic and Social Research.

Petersen, N.C. (1990), 'Data envelopment analysis on a relaxed set of assumptions', *Management Science*, **36** (3), 305–14.

Pollitt, M. (1995), *Ownership and Performance in Electric Utilities*, Oxford, UK: Oxford University Press.

Robinson, C. (1999), 'Utility regulation in Britain: the state it's in', Oxford, UK: Third International Conference of the British Institute of Energy Economics.

Salvanes, K.G. and Tjøtta, S. (1994), 'Productivity differences in multiple output industries: an empirical application to electricity distribution', *Journal of Productivity Analysis*, **5**, 23–43.

Shleifer, A. (1985), 'A theory of yardstick competition', *Rand Journal of Economics*, **16** (3), 319–27.

Shuttleworth, G. (1999), *Regulatory Benchmarking: a way forward or a dead-end?*, London, UK: NERA Energy Regulation Brief, National Economic Research Associates.

Thanassoulis, E. (1999), 'DEA and comparative efficiency', *The Utilities Journal*, **2** (August), 40–42.

Tilley, B. and Weyman-Jones, T. (1999), 'Productivity growth and efficiency change in electricity distribution', Oxford, UK: Third International Conference of the British Institute of Energy Economics.

Tulkens, H. (1993), 'On FDH efficiency analysis: some methodological issues and applications to retail banking, courts and urban transit', *Journal of Productivity Analysis*, **4**, 183–210.

Zhang, Y. and Bartels, R. (1998), 'The effect of sample size on the mean efficiency in DEA with an application to electricity distribution in Australia, Sweden and New Zealand', *Journal of Productivity Analysis*, **9** (3), 187–204.

4. The Swiss electricity industry and the regulation of distribution prices

Massimo Filippini and Jörg Wild

INTRODUCTION

The deregulation of the electric power sector was introduced in England and Wales in 1990. Switzerland is probably going to take a similar step in the next few years with the introduction of a new Swiss electricity market law.[1] As in other countries, the reform of the Swiss electricity market is certainly not a removal of all regulatory interference with the electric utility. The new market law will introduce market competition in two activities of the electricity supply business (generation and sales), but the transmission and distribution activities, which remain natural monopoly activities, will still need regulation. For the transmission and distribution activities, economic theory requires the regulation of network access prices. In fact, most countries – with Germany as a prominent exception – implemented access price regulation as part of the deregulation process.

Access price regulation is a difficult task. On the one hand, prices should be set in a way that enables network operators to cover their costs and gives sufficient incentives for investment. On the other hand, price regulation should give incentives for the efficient operation of the networks. Unfortunately, in reality there exists a fundamental conflict between these two regulatory goals: a guaranteed recovery of all costs tends to destroy efficiency incentives, because network operators are able to pass on all their costs to final consumers. Whereas incentive-orientated regulation mechanisms – for example, price-cap regulation – emit strong incentives for cost reductions and efficiency improvements, they do not guarantee the recovery of all costs.

The aim of this chapter is to present the most important elements of the new Swiss electricity market law and to suggest a methodology to regulate the access prices based on the yardstick competition concept, introduced by Shleifer (1985). The chapter is structured as follows. In the next section a short survey of the Swiss electricity industry is presented followed by a section that outlines the key elements of the new Swiss electricity market law. In the subsequent section an application of the yardstick competition concept for the regulation of access prices in Switzerland is proposed. The last section contains the concluding comments.

THE SWISS ELECTRICITY INDUSTRY[2]

Switzerland is a modern federal state with a population of about 7 million people.[3] The federal government is responsible for foreign policy, defence, pensions, post, telecommunications, railways, national highways and currency. Whatever is not specifically in the hands of the federal government is, in principle, the responsibility of the 26 cantons. This includes schooling, roads, hospitals, taxation systems and electric utilities. Each canton comprises many municipalities, which not only implement such cantonal directives as civil law and schooling, but also collect their own income taxes and choose which basic utilities to provide, such as water and electricity. Because Switzerland is a federal state, it is the municipalities or the cantons and not a central government that own the public utilities that generate, transmit and distribute electricity. At the time of writing, the cantons and municipals hold more than 70 per cent of the total capital invested in the electricity industry, whereas less then 30 per cent is owned by private investors.

Market Structure

The Swiss electricity industry is composed of about 1,200 utilities, with about 90 per cent of them publicly owned distributors that provide power to their communities exclusively. About 140 of them also generate power, but generally, the amount of generated power is small and is determined by the ability to exploit favourable hydroelectric power generation possibilities. There is great divergence in size and activity among these utilities. The smallest ones sell not more than 0.1 GWh and the largest ones sell over 10,000 GWh, which is still only about one-fifth of the sales of the average regional electricity company in the UK. Moreover, in Switzerland, the average number of persons served by an electric utility is approximately 6,000, whereas in England and Wales it is about 1.8 million. However, the largest 100 utilities in Switzerland account for 75 per cent of total electricity sales to end-users whereas the smallest 980 or so utilities account for the remaining 25 per cent.

The municipal and regional electric utilities purchase power mainly from seven utilities, the so-called '*Ueberlandwerke*', which form the backbone of the industry. These larger vertically integrated companies provide most of the generated electricity. Some of them are also involved in the distribution of electricity to final consumers. Moreover, these dominant companies own and control the national grid, which is planned and used in close cooperation. To meet short-term needs for power and to sell surplus production, they organized a kind of power exchange market among themselves based on short-term bilateral trade. Since 1998, prices of this short-term trade have been published in the Swiss Electricity Price Index (SWEP). The SWEP indicates prices in the short-term Swiss–European electricity spot market. It is calculated on working days for working days and applies to the peak hour (11 am to 12 noon).

Electricity production in Switzerland consists of roughly 60 per cent hydro and 40 per cent nuclear. About 80 of the largest power plants (hydro and nuclear) are organized as joint ventures (*Partnerwerke*) of the seven *Ueberlandwerke* and some of the largest utilities owned by the cantons (see Table 4.1). This form of co-ownership was a successful way of sharing the risk of the long-run investments, which characterized the hydropower sector.

Table 4.1   Structure of the Swiss electricity industry

Utility type	Number of utilities
Ueberlandwerke (generation and transmission)	
with distribution	3
without nameable distribution	4
Distributors	
without generation	~940
with generation	~140
(*Partnerwerke*) generators	~80

Due to the fact that most of hydro capacity consists of storage and pump storage power stations, Switzerland has developed a position as European electricity peak producer and trader. Electricity is mainly imported from France and exported to Italy, principally during the times of peak demand. In total, the electricity trade volume corresponds to almost 170 per cent of domestic consumption.

The latest developments show the beginning of a consolidation phase. Cooperative agreements among several private and public utilities brought forth the new companies Axpo (utilities in eastern Switzerland), Swiss Citypower (utilities in major cities) and Avenis (utilities in western Switzerland), with a pre-deregulation market share of approximately 20 per cent each. So far, none of these cooperative agreements has resulted in a merger.

Regulation Structure

In Switzerland, the federal government, the cantons and the municipalities exercise jurisdiction over the activities of the electricity industry. The federal government has authority to license and regulate the construction and operation of all nuclear power plants, the construction of trans-regional grids and the exploitation of water resources for hydroelectric power generation. The cantons and municipalities regulate the activities of regional private and public electricity utilities. Only broad generalizations about their operations can be made because the cantonal and municipal authorities regulate these utilities in different ways. Some cantons regulate all utilities, while others limit jurisdiction to private utilities and leave regulation of local public or private utilities to local municipal government. Regulations on the canton and municipal levels govern entry, quality and condition of service, including the obligation to serve all customers in the assigned service area. Furthermore, electricity price changes by private electric utilities have to be approved by the Federal Price Surveillance Authority, whereas electricity price changes by public electric utilities must be approved by either the cantonal or the municipal public utility commission. In these cases, the intervention of the Federal Price Surveillance Authority is not always required.

Concerning electricity distribution, the main policy options employed on the cantonal and municipal levels are the provision of electricity by a regulated public monopoly and the provision of electricity by a privately owned but regulated monopoly franchise. In exchange for guaranteed service to all customers, public and private electric utilities receive an exclusive territorial franchise. Thus, these utilities operate as local monopolies in their legally defined service territories and are protected from competition from other utilities offering the same service elsewhere. Of course, with the introduction of the new Swiss electricity market law, this situation will partially change.

In practice the municipalities have the following two options when deciding how to provide their communities with electricity. The first option consists of the attribution of the exclusive territorial franchise to a private utility, while the second one involves the attribution to a local or cantonal public utility. This self-governing process in the organization of the distribution of electricity at the municipal level can explain the high number of municipal electric utilities in Switzerland. With the introduction of the new electricity market law the municipalities will still have the possibility of deciding which utility will have the right to operate the distribution network on their territory.

THE NEW SWISS ELECTRICITY MARKET LAW (EML)

After a long period of talks and different legislative proposals, in December 1999 the Swiss parliament adopted the new Swiss electricity market law. With the introduction of the law, the electricity sector of Switzerland will be reformed by moving from regulation to liberalization of some parts of this industry. All customers will have the free choice of energy supplier, hence introducing competition in energy generation and sale activities. Dispatching, transmission and distribution, on the other hand, will continue to be a natural monopoly.

The main characteristics of the EML include:

1. A system of regulated third party access to the networks and therefore, wholesale and retail competition.
2. Organizational unbundling of electricity transmission at the extra-high-voltage level and other activities. As part of the regulatory reform, the high-voltage transmission grid will be disinvested by the seven firms (*Ueberlandwerke*), which today control the national grid. The national grid will be organized as a private company with the function of an independent system operator (ISO).
3. Separate accounting for generation, distribution/retail supply and non-electricity activities.
4. The creation of a new institution, the Arbitration Commission, as an independent agency with responsibility for supervising transmission and distribution tariffs.
5. A system based on bilateral contracts freely negotiated between buyers and sellers; therefore, a system without an ISO that operates a centralized spot market.
6. Power exchange with other countries based on the adoption of a reciprocity clause. However, a safeguard clause in the law ensures that access to the grid can be refused to suppliers from countries with less liberalized electricity.

The EML stipulates a gradual market liberalization over six years. During an initial phase of three years, about 100 electricity consumers with a demand of over 20 GWh per annum can buy electricity from the producer of their choice. Additionally, distributors are allowed to procure from the market 20 per cent of their electricity sales to non-eligible customers. This results in a 30 per cent market opening. During the second phase, about 250 consumers with a demand of over 10 GWh per year have market access, and distributors may buy 40 per cent of their sales from the competitive market, which corresponds to a market opening of 50 per cent. After six years, the electricity market will be fully open to competition, which goes beyond the requirements of the EU electricity market directive.

The access to the transmission and distribution network will be organized subject to a regulated third party access (TPA) model with point-of-connection ('postage stamp') network prices. All transmission and distribution network owners will have the obligation to provide non-discriminatory access to the network. The transmission grid will be operated by one independent grid company, which will be privately owned with the condition that the majority of capital be held by Swiss parties. At the same time, the distribution grid operators will only be required to keep separate accounting for distribution activities on the one hand and sales or production activities on the other.

The EML will regulate the transmission and distribution prices with an approach that is principally based on rate-of-return (ROR) regulation. The ROR regulation allows the utility to set prices that cover its operating and capital costs as well as a return on capital. Moreover, Article 6 of the law states that transmission and distribution prices should reflect costs of an efficiently operated network company. Therefore, this article of the law contains some elements of the ROR regulation as well as elements of yardstick regulation.

The EML sets up a new institution, the Arbitration Commission, as an independent agency with nominated experts. This commission will carry out the regulation of TPA and access prices. It has the authority to check distribution and transmission prices, and it decides on disputes concerning provision of access. Supplementing the Arbitration Commission, the Price Surveillance Authority also has some competence with respect to prices that have been fixed or approved by local authorities.

To deal with stranded investments, for a period of ten years the federal state can grant loans at its cost of capital to hydroelectric plants that have difficulty realizing required amortization. In exceptional cases, loans can be granted for the maintenance of hydroelectric plants, if this significantly improves the economic and environmental situation of the plant. These loans should be reimbursed as soon as the company's financial situation allows. Renewable energy (under 1 MW; hydro under 500 kW) can benefit from an exemption of network charges for a ten-year transition period. The costs of the network owners will be financed by a supplement on the transmission price.

A YARDSTICK COMPETITION CONCEPT

This section presents a summary of a yardstick competition concept suggested by Filippini and Wild (2001) that might be used by the Arbitration Commission to regulate (or control) access prices of the 1,000 or so distribution network operators.

Shleifer (1985) proposed yardstick competition in terms of price to regulate local monopolies producing a homogeneous good. The regulated price for the individual firms depends on the average costs of identical firms. Shleifer shows that under ideal circumstances it is the dominant strategy for each firm to choose the socially efficient level of cost reduction. Yardstick competition can also be used to set the informational basis for a more effective price-cap regulation because it reduces the informational asymmetries between firms and regulator regarding costs. It has the additional advantage of taking into account general shocks that might cause problems in a pure price-cap regulation.

The yardstick competition concept can also be applied to firms that are producing under different environmental characteristics. For the electricity distribution utilities these environmental characteristics could be the customer density, the share of unproductive land, the share of customers living in rural areas and so on. To correct the yardstick for the heterogeneity in the environmental characteristics, the regulator can use the results of the empirical estimation of a multivariate average cost function. In this case the observable environmental characteristics are included as explanatory variables in the cost model to correct for cost differences that are only due to the heterogeneity of output. Therefore, to implement the idea of yardstick regulation in the electricity distribution sector using the approach suggested by Shleifer (1985), it is necessary to estimate a network cost function that includes as explanatory variables the output, the factor prices and some environmental characteristics. However, only those environmental factors that cannot be altered by the distribution utilities must be incorporated in the cost model.

In the empirical literature on electricity distribution, most studies estimate cost functions, which also include the expenditure for purchasing electricity.[4] However, since the regulator is only interested in network costs, it is important to separate costs of network operation and costs for purchasing electricity and only consider the former, as suggested by Filippini and Wild (2001).

The average cost model used by Filippini and Wild, which also includes in the model some service area characteristics as explanatory variables, is:

$$AC = AC\,(Y,\,PL,\,PC,\,HGRID,\,LVSH,\,AVGL,\,LF,\,CD,$$
$$AGSH,\,FOSH,\,UPSH,\,OTSH,\,T), \tag{4.1}$$

where

AC = average cost per kWh;

Y = output represented by the total number of kWh transported on the medium-voltage grid;

PL = price of labour;

PC = price of capital;

$HGRID$ = dummy variable to separate distribution utilities that are also operating a high-voltage grid;

$LVSH$ = share of electricity that is delivered on the low-voltage network;[5]

$AVGL$ = average consumption per low-voltage customer;

LF = load factor;

CD = customer density measured in customers per hectare of settlement land;

$AGSH$ = share of agricultural land;

$FOSH$ = share of forestland;

$UPSH$ = share of unproductive land with respect to the total size of the service area;

$OTSH$ = variable used to control for outputs other than the distribution of electricity that are included in the accounting data of electric utilities; and

T = time variable to capture the shift in technology representing a change in technical efficiency.

Filippini and Wild used a panel of 59 Swiss utilities to estimate this model. They found a rather high explanatory power of the model with over 80 per cent of the variation of average costs explained by the model. Moreover, all of the explanatory variables were found statistically significant and with the expected sign.

The two most important results concerning the regulation of access prices found in the Filippini and Wild study are:

1. The majority of the electricity distribution utilities do not reach the minimum efficient scale. Thus, in the Swiss electricity distribution sector there are non-exploited economies of scale. This situation of scale inefficiency clearly has an impact on the level of the access prices.
2. The heterogeneity factors included in the cost model have a significant influence on the cost of the distribution network. Average distribution costs are high if:

*   the share of low-voltage customers is high,
*   the average consumption per customer is small,

- the load factor is small (that is, strong demand fluctuations over time),
- shares of farm, agricultural and unproductive land are high, and
- customer density is low.

Therefore, by applying a concept of yardstick regulation the Swiss regulator should consider the impact on costs of the environmental factors. For illustrative purposes the econometric results reported by Filippini and Wild are used to estimate the average distribution costs for utilities of different sizes and with different environmental conditions. Table 4.2 shows the results of this simulation exercise.

Table 4.2   Predictions of average cost for electricity distribution (high, medium and low voltage) in Swiss cents per kWh, 1996 prices

	Small network, median output (100 GWh)	Medium network, average output (250 GWh)	Large network, efficient scale (1000 GWh)
Simple environmental conditions (all heterogeneity variables set to 1. or 3. quartile value)	6.9	6.1	4.2
Average environmental conditions (all heterogeneity variables set to median value)	9.0	8.2	6.3
Difficult environmental conditions (all heterogeneity variables set to 1. or 3. quartile value)	11.5	10.8	8.8

The table presents the calculated average costs for small, medium-sized and large utilities, respectively. Moreover, three environmental conditions are identified that could characterize the production process of the distribution utilities: simple, average and difficult conditions, respectively. The results reported in Table 4.2 confirm that with an increase in the size of the utility, the average costs decrease (scale effect). Moreover, utilities operating in areas with difficult environmental conditions show higher average costs than those operating in areas with simple conditions. The average costs in areas with difficult conditions are twice as high as costs in areas with simple environmental conditions.

The results reported in Table 4.2 might be very useful in applying a yardstick regulation approach. Of course, in the estimation of individual utility prices for the implementation of the yardstick regulation only those environmental factors that cannot be altered by the distribution utilities should be considered. In the model employed by Filippini and Wild, the factors not under the control of the network operator are:[6] the pattern of land use (settlement, farming, forest and others), the population density, the costumer structure (industrial, commercial, resident) and the average demand per customer category.

The firm size (output) and the load factor are under the control of the network operators and, therefore, should not be considered in the estimation of the individual prices. For instance, utilities may change their firm size through mergers with other adjacent utilities. This point is very important in Switzerland, because most utilities do not reach an efficient scale. In cases where individual benchmark prices vary with the firm size, utilities will not have the proper incentives to reduce scale inefficiency. To improve the scale efficiency in the Swiss electricity distribution sector, the regulation authority should utilize the individual prices of a large utility as a benchmark.

A similar argument can be used for the load factor. Generally, a better load management (that is, smoothing of the demand fluctuations over time through a peak load pricing strategy) will, *ceteris paribus*, decrease capital cost per kWh and, therefore, increase the efficiency of the utility. Of course, the incentive to decrease the distribution costs through a peak load pricing policy disappears as soon as the individual load factors are considered in the calculation of the individual benchmark prices.

SUMMARY AND CONCLUSIONS

This chapter has investigated the possibility of implementing a yardstick regulation concept of access prices in the framework of the new Swiss electricity market law. This new law will gradually push competition to the level of smaller and smaller customers, until all customers will have the option of choosing their electricity supplier. A more important issue for this chapter is that the new EML will open the transmission and distribution grid to third parties under non-discriminatory and transparent prices (third party access principle).

It has been suggested in this chapter that the TPA principle should be implemented using the yardstick regulation method proposed by Shleifer (1985). Basically, this method proposes to calculate individual benchmark access prices using the econometric results of the estimation of an average cost function. Moreover, this average cost function should include as explanatory variables some environmental characteristics variables.

In the second part of the chapter, a short overview of an empirical application of the yardstick competition concept for the Swiss electricity distribution sector was presented. This application shows that the idea of yardstick regulation proposed by Shleifer (1985) could be an interesting and powerful tool in the implementation of the new electricity market law.

NOTES

1. This chapter focuses on the regulation of distribution prices in Switzerland. It was written before the first proposed electricity market law was put to popular referendum in September 2002 and rejected. The Swiss government will prepare, in all probability, further proposals in the not too distant future.
2. For a more detailed presentation of the Swiss electricity sector, see Filippini (1997), Mutzner (1997) and IEA (1999).
3. Swiss electricity demand is about 50,000 GWh, which is equivalent to one-sixth of UK demand.
4. See Neuberg (1977) and Pollitt (1995) for the estimation of average cost functions and Roberts (1986), Nelson and Primeaux (1988), Salvanes and Tjøtta (1994), Burns and Weyman-Jones (1996), Filippini (1996), Hayashi et al. (1997) and Filippini (1998) for the estimation of total cost functions.
5. This variable considers the differences among the utilities in terms of customer structure.
6. Admittedly, the network operators may have an influence on the demand and, perhaps, the location choice of industry customers, via the network prices. But these influences may be ignored due to the rather inelastic demand and due to the fact that only very few industries in Switzerland have energy cost shares over 3 per cent of total cost.

REFERENCES

Burns, P. and Weyman-Jones, T.G. (1996), 'Cost functions and cost efficiency in the electricity distribution: a stochastic frontier approach', *Bulletin of Economic Research*, **48** (1), 41–64.

Filippini, M. (1996), 'Economies of scale and utilization in the Swiss electric power distribution industry', *Applied Economics*, **28** (5), 543–50.

Filippini, M. (1997), *Elements of the Swiss Market for Electricity*, Heidelberg, Germany: Physica.

Filippini, M. (1998), 'Are municipal electricity distribution utilities natural monopolies?', *Annals of Public and Cooperative Economics*, **69** (2), 157–74.

Filippini, M. and Wild, J. (2001), 'Regional differences in electricity distribution costs and their consequences for yardstick regulation of access prices', *Energy Economics*, **23** (4), 477–88.

Hayashi, P.M., Goo, J.Y.-J. and Chamberlain, W.C. (1997), 'Vertical economies: the case of the U.S. electric utility industry, 1983–87', *Southern Economic Journal*, **63** (3), 710–25.

IEA (1999), *Energy Policies of IEA Countries, Switzerland 1999 Review*, Paris, France: OECD/International Energy Agency.

Mutzner, J. (1997), *The Swiss Electricity Supply Industry: Development and Structure*, Zurich, Switzerland: VSE/UCS.

Nelson, R.A. and Primeaux, W.J. Jr (1988), 'The effects of competition on trans-
    mission and distribution costs in the municipal electric industry', *Land
    Economics*, **64** (4), 338–46.
Neuberg, L.G. (1977), 'Two issues in the municipal ownership of electric power dis-
    tribution systems', *Bell Journal of Economics*, **8** (1), 302–23.
Pollitt, M.G. (1995), *Ownership and Performance in Electric Utilities*, Oxford, UK:
    Oxford University Press.
Roberts, M.J. (1986), 'Economies of density and size in the production and deliv-
    ery of electric power', *Land Economics*, **62** (4), 378–87.
Salvanes, K.G. and Tjøtta, S. (1994), 'Productivity differences in multiple output
    industries: an empirical application to electricity distribution', *Journal of
    Productivity Analysis*, **5**, 23–43.
Shleifer, A. (1985), 'A theory of yardstick competition', *Rand Journal of Economics*,
    16 (3), 319–27.

5. Efficiency and performance in the gas industry

David Hawdon

INTRODUCTION AND OUTLINE

Perhaps the most obvious characteristic of the gas industry is its rapid growth during recent years. Production of gas worldwide rose by almost 5 per cent between 1998 and 1999, with Russia, Algeria, Norway and Argentina experiencing the most rapid change (IGU, 2000a and 2000b). Output of the North Sea producers (Great Britain, Norway and the Netherlands) has expanded by over 77 per cent during the last decade, supplying large importers such as Germany, Italy, France, Belgium and Spain. International trade has grown as consumption in the leading importers – America, Japan and Germany, and the Asian-Pacific area – has increased rapidly in recent years. These developments point to the success of gas in displacing other fuels in the energy mix, and represent not merely an economic response to relative price changes but in addition a fundamental switch in taste towards less-polluting fuels. Particularly significant has been the growth in markets in power generation, co-generation, transport (sales to natural gas vehicles), cooling and dehumidification (especially in Asian markets).

On the policy front, the impact of regulatory reform has been important particularly throughout North America and Europe.[1] The deregulation of the electricity sector and its opening to market trading has tended to work in favour of gas as older, less flexible power stations are phased out, and nuclear expansion slowed and in some cases reversed. Countries most recently affected here are Belgium, Canada, Finland, Germany, Hungary, the Netherlands and, outside of Europe, in Korea.

The aim of this chapter is to assess the efficiency and performance of a wide range of gas industries using recently published country-level data on essential outputs and inputs. Detailed individual country studies of efficiency have been carried out before by Price and Weyman-Jones (1996) and by Kim and Lee (1995). Neither of these attempted to compare the national industry with international experience. More recently Yunos and Hawdon

(1997) and Kim et al. (1999) have attempted international comparisons for electricity and gas, respectively. Yunos and Hawdon focused particularly on developing countries while Kim et al. examined the performance of gas companies in North America, Europe, Japan and Korea. The analysis in this chapter gives a wider coverage based on over 30 countries in order to attempt a balanced assessment of factors affecting efficiency.

GAS POLICY DEVELOPMENTS

Significant policy developments affecting the gas industry since the mid-1980s have included the privatization, liberalization and deregulation of national gas markets, and the reduction of trade barriers within important multinational groupings. The process commenced in the United States, was followed in the United Kingdom and currently dominates the debate over gas policy in the European Union (EU) as well as in other countries.

In the United States, reform was precipitated by the impact of falling oil prices during the 1980s on a market which had become locked into high-price, long-term contracts for gas. The US Federal Energy Regulatory Commission (FERC) decision to release distributors from take-or-pay provisions in 1984 led to the stranding of many gas pipeline contracts. In 1992, pipeline companies were required to unbundle transportation, storage and open access. The resulting upsurge in competition, and development of spot markets led to significant falls in the price of gas. This makes the US experience a powerful model in favour of more competitive markets elsewhere.

The UK gas market has also liberalized significantly. Between privatization in 1986 and the passing of the 1995 Gas Act, the industry regulator, the Office of Gas and Electricity Markets (Ofgem) (and before that the Office of Gas Regulation, Ofgas),[2] has sought to introduce competition into the gas market. The 1995 Act opened up the UK retail market to competition in a process which was completed by May 1998. This was followed by the commencement of gas storage auctioning in 1999, the development of new gas capacity, balancing and trading arrangements involving an on-the-day commodity market (OCM) and most recently by the auctioning of entry and exit capacity. Regulation of prices is still significant, however, as indicated in discussions over Transco's price control for the period from 2002 to 2007.

Although energy, including gas, was not part of the original policy ambit of the EU, significant intervention began in the early 1990s with the price transparency directive of June 1990, followed in May 1991 by the directive covering the transit of natural gas via grids. More important was the adoption on 22 June 1998 of the directive on the interior gas market (European Commission, 1998). Although the directive took effect on 10 August 2000, various member countries had already begun to open their markets. Some countries (the UK, Belgium, Finland, Ireland, Italy and Spain) have already implemented the directive at least in part (European Commission, 2000). Others like Austria, Denmark, France, Germany, Luxembourg, Sweden and the Netherlands are moving towards implementation while Greece and Portugal have still to begin the process. The effectiveness of the directive is likely to be variable because of lack of agreement on access charging and unbundling. Most producers are reluctant to separate transportation, storage and trading activities as the UK has done. Lack of agreement on access to upstream pipeline networks could significantly slow access to cheapest sources of gas. Although the Commission anticipates that 77.9 per cent of the 15-member market will be open by 2000, 90 per cent by 2008 and 91.4 per cent 'later', a large variation in implementation (from 33 to 100 per cent) is anticipated.

The development of trade in gas within Europe was already apparent from the opening of the interconnector between the UK and Belgium in October 1998. The 1998 Gas Directive provides further stimulus to this process. Pipeline owners are required to give access to third parties to the extent that capacity is available. Although owners can refuse to provide access on a number of grounds including public-service obligations, or serious economic and financial difficulties with take-or-pay contracts, it is likely that the directive will promote significant extra competitive pressures on operators.

DISTINGUISHING FEATURES OF THE GAS INDUSTRY

In seeking to understand developments in the gas industry, it is important to recognize some special features of the gas industry (Newbery, 2000). These include:

- opaque and ill-defined costs,
- production determined by geology which influences exploration, production and pipeline investment and operating costs,
- producers' preferences for guaranteed markets/long-term contracts/ high prices to recover investment costs together with a tendency to desire vertical integration, and
- consumer preference for long-term security of supply.

All of the above factors constitute barriers against efficiency improvements in the gas industry. That European countries have been able to overcome some of these barriers is due to a unique set of circumstances including the expansion of offshore supplies in Europe, the availability of gas from Russia following the collapse of its domestic economy post-cold war, the extension of international pipeline systems, investment in liquefied natural gas (LNG) terminals to ensure diversity of supply sources, removal of discriminatory access to third party pipeline networks, and the opening of the electricity market to gas. One of the purposes of this chapter is to establish whether these conditions have led to improved levels of efficiency.

MEASURING THE EFFICIENCY OF THE GAS INDUSTRY

The efficiency literature distinguishes between technical and allocative efficiency (Fare et al., 1994). Technical efficiency concerns the relationship between inputs and outputs such that a firm is efficient if it achieves maximum output for given inputs or minimum input utilization for given outputs. Allocative efficiency assumes technical efficiency, and compares alternative positions in terms of relative prices, either of inputs or outputs. In attempting to measure the efficiency of the gas industries of various countries, gas consumption or sales are used as a measure of output. This ensures that the focus is on the downstream element of the gas industry which handles imported as well as domestically produced gas. Gas production (the upstream part of the industry) has a very different structure to the publicly owned or regulated downstream industry and it is that latter part which is of interest. Gas production is carried out by a mixture of oil and gas companies, often large multinational oil producers. The analysis is confined to gas from its entry into the bulk transmission system, through the local distribution networks to the final consumer.

An important feature of this part of the gas industry is that it is multi-product in that gas is supplied under different conditions to different types of consumers. Household, industrial, commercial and power station customers have very different load and other characteristics, and can be supplied on either continuous or interruptible bases. At the same time, availability of gas is important to consumers. Finally, regulatory authorities prefer that industries supply as many potential customers as possible. Thus at a minimum, sales and numbers of customers should be taken as separate outputs when considering the efficiency and performance of the gas industry.

Two major inputs into gas transmission and distribution are the labour force involved in gas industry activities and the capital services of the pipe-line system which connects producers to consumers. The labour force requires specialist skills in gas supply and engineering, as well as non-specific skills in sales and administration. The services of a pipeline system depend on a wide variety of factors, including pipeline diameter and length, inlet and outlet pressures and the availablity of compressor equipment to regulate operating pressures. Other factors affecting supply include the availability of storage capacity for seasonal and other top-ups to regular supplies. The gas network functions in a fairly complex way to deliver gas to users.

The environment in which the gas industry functions varies considerably from country to country, in terms of the terrain over which gas is trans-ported, the geographic density of customers, and their economic character-istics. While this is easily recognized, treatment of such individual circumstances can be affected by strategic considerations. Producers have an interest in stressing the uniqueness of the conditions of supply since regula-tory concessions often flow from such recognition. Any such concessions may, however, be welfare reducing as they remove pressure on producers to improve efficiency in the absence of properly functioning competitive markets. It is sensible to adopt a cautious approach to the inclusion of envi-ronmental variables and incorporate them only when the evidence is clear.

The same cautious approach should be displayed towards potential economies of scale arguments. One of the major arguments used in favour of public ownership is that a single producer would enjoy the benefits of large-scale production. This argument is taken to justify the absence of competition for the incumbent firm. In practice, as electricity industry experience has shown, the opportunities for profitable operation on a small scale are often considerable once appropriate incentives are in place.

DATA AND METHODOLOGY

In order to test whether changes in regulatory regime, levels of cost-reducing investment and other factors have impacted on the performance of the gas industry, a frontier estimation technique is used to estimate a model with the following outputs and inputs:

Outputs: Gas consumption, numbers of customers
Inputs: Employment, pipelines

Previous work on efficiency estimation has used either stochastic frontier methods (SFA) or data envelopment analysis (DEA) techniques. SFA has

a number of well-known advantages – parameters of economically meaningful production functions can be estimated, scale effects can be identified
and, at least in the panel variants of this approach, individual efficiencies
can be identified (Kalirajan and Shand, 1999).

On the other hand, satisfactory estimates can only be obtained from relatively large data sets because the number of parameters is often large. At a
deeper level, assumptions have to be made both about the functional form,
which can be tested, and about the distribution of two types of error – the
divergence of observations from the efficient frontier and the usual stochastic error term found in econometric investigation – which cannot. Again the
stochastic models are not able to cope satisfactorily with multiproduct firms.

DEA on the other hand can cope relatively easily with multiple outputs
and inputs. In addition, DEA requires minimal assumptions regarding the
structure of production, and places no restriction on the functional form
relating inputs to outputs. It produces detailed information on the efficiency of the unit not only relative to the efficient frontier but also to specific efficient units which can be identified as role models or comparators.
It identifies slack in specific inputs so that sources of inefficiency can be
analysed. A major shortcoming of DEA has until recently been its failure
to deal effectively with the stochastic element of efficiency estimation. This
is because DEA is based on an optimization procedure which uses linear
programming techniques to locate those producers who combine given
inputs most efficiently to produce relevant output. These methods are sensitive to inaccuracies in input values and may yield alternative optimal solutions even when data are accurate. In the latter case, the efficiency estimates
are not affected, only the identification of comparators. The sensitivity to
data is a more fundamental problem and places a considerable onus on care
in data selection so that meaningful results can be obtained. The bulk of
previous DEA studies have lacked estimates of the uncertainties surrounding individual efficiencies or the impacts of specific variables.

Recently, however, considerable advances have been made in the incorporation of uncertainty in DEA. Banker (1993) showed both that DEA is
a maximum likelihood estimator of efficiency and that the estimates are
consistent (that is, the bias decreases as the sample size increases). He also
suggested various tests for differences of efficiency estimates between
models, including the Kolmogrov–Smirnov test and the *t*-test for nested
models. These tests have been explored in some depth using Monte Carlo
methods by Kittelsen (1999a) who has investigated the sensitivity of DEA
estimates to the following problems:

1. The property that the greater the number of restrictions placed on the
    model, the higher the measured efficiency values will be.

2. The known bias in DEA efficiency estimates. This bias arises because DEA indicates that certain units are 100 per cent efficient (the comparator set) and yet the probability of a unit being exactly 100 per cent efficient is zero. The extent of the bias, which is upward, will vary with the sample size but could be quite important for small samples.

3. The fact that the efficiency values are dependent because they are calculated in relation to the most efficient units in the data set. This makes it difficult to satisfy the assumption of independently distributed units which lies behind many statistical tests.

Kittelsen (1999b) finds that dependency and bias work in opposite directions with a tendency to cancel each other out. Thus it is possible to use the tests recommended by Banker. The *t*-test can be used when 'bias is low due to large samples, low dimensionality (numbers of outputs and inputs), and inefficiency distributions that are dense at the frontier. If bias is somewhat higher, the . . . Kolmogrov–Smirnov test is better' (Kittelsen, 1999b, p. 49).

The Kittelsen approach is a general to specific method of testing nested models (see Kittelsen, 1999a). Taking any two sets of efficiency estimates, for example one with and one without a specific input variable, the Kolmogrov–Smirnov (KS) test checks the computed maximum absolute difference between the cumulated distribution function of the two sets of estimates. This is defined as $D = \sup_E \{S_0(E) - S_1(E)\}$ where S_0 and S_1 are the relevant cumulated distributions of measured efficiencies. The *t*-test is the familiar *t*-test for the equality of group means and is distributed with $(n_0 + n_1 - 2)$ degrees of freedom where n_0 and n_1 are the sizes of the samples. The KS test allows for the entire distribution of efficiencies while the *t*-test is a test of average impacts. It can be applied because the distribution of the sample means will be approximately normal in large samples by the central limit theorem.

That the various DEA models are nested is clearly seen from the specification of the VRS model as the general model:

$$F(y|\text{VRS}) = \{x: y \leq zM, zN \leq x, \ \Sigma z_j = 1\}, \quad z \in \mathcal{R}^J, y \in \mathcal{R}^M. \quad (5.1)$$

The CRS model is obtained by removing the last constraint, $\Sigma z_j = 1$.

$$F(y|\text{CRS}) = \{x: y \leq zM, zN \leq x\}, \quad z \in \mathcal{R}^J, y \in \mathcal{R}^M. \quad (5.2)$$

The other models are formed by successively reducing the number of *y*s and *x*s.

RESULTS

Although data on gas production and prices are relatively abundant, very little material is available on productive inputs and costs for the purpose of international comparisons. This study uses data made available from the International Gas Union on 61 countries including developed and developing countries. Unfortunately, no split is available for the different functions carried out within the industry such as transmission, distribution or storage. Thus the results on efficiencies provide only a broad-brush comparison and they will need to be supplemented by further investigations at a more disaggregated level (see Kim et al., 1999) for an example of a firm-by-firm comparison focusing on Japan).

Countries were included if data were available on two outputs – consumption (*CONS*) and customer (*CUST*) numbers; two inputs – employees (*EMP*) and length of pipelines (*PIPES*); and four environmental variables – share of gas in total energy (*SH*), growth in demand (*RF*), reform in terms of privatization or deregulation (*REFORM*), and responsiveness to the European Union Gas Directive (*DIR*). Of the original 61 countries, some were excluded as clear outliers. These included both the United States and Russia, whose gas industries were many times the size of any other developed country. Venezuela was excluded because of concerns about the data. Ultimately, 33 countries were considered suitable for inclusion.

The most general model involved all eight variables and an assumption of variable returns to scale. DEA efficiency estimates were made for this most general model. Then assumptions are changed and variables removed from the model either singly or in groups and the significance of these changes tested using the KS test and the *t*-test described above. The null hypothesis of zero difference in efficiency measurements between the nesting and the nested model is used to justify exclusion (null hypothesis accepted) or inclusion (null hypothesis rejected) in the model. For example, the full VRS model yielded average measured DEA efficiencies of 0.869. Nested within this model is the less restrictive constant returns to scale (CRS) model found by dropping the VRS assumption. In the CRS model with identical variables, the average efficiency is found to be 0.798 but the difference in efficiencies is not sufficient to reject the null hypothesis on both the KS test and the *t*-test (see Table 5.1). In this instance, CRS is accepted as the basic model.

The model is then tested to see whether it is multiproduct by removing variable Y_{CUST} from the data set. This is rejected by both the KS test and the *t*-test but only at the 5 per cent level. Since the two tests are conservative in tending to over-reject, Y_{CUST} is not removed. Retention of Y_{CUST} supports the use of the multiproduct model.

Table 5.1   Tests for gas efficiency model

H_0: Exclude	Change in mean	KS test	t-test	Conclusion
VRS	0.0710	0.1818	1.3553	Accept CRS
Y_{CUST}	0.1580	0.2424*	2.2507*	Reject exclusion
X_{DIR}	0.0200	0.0909	0.3475	Accept exclusion
$X_{REFORM+DIR}$	0.0700	0.2121	1.1220	Accept exclusion
$X_{RF+REFORM+DIR}$	0.2180	0.3636**	3.3115**	Reject exclusion
$X_{REFORM+DIR}$	0.0500	0.2102	0.7942	Accept exclusion
$X_{RF+REFORM}$	0.1480	0.2727*	2.0880*	Reject exclusion
$X_{SHARF+REFORM+DIR}$	0.0340	0.1337	0.7488	Accept exclusion
$X_{PIPES+EMP}$	0.1020	0.2424*	1.5212	Reject exclusion
Critical 5%*		0.2310	1.6924	
1%**		0.2770	2.4448	

Exclusion of the EU directive is accepted by both tests, as is the exclusion of the combination of *REFORM* and *DIR*. However, when *RF* is added to the group, both the KS test and the *t*-test are significant at the 1 per cent level, suggesting that one out of the group is significant. The next test suggests that *REFORM* is not the significant variable when made conditional on *DIR*. On the other hand, *RF* conditional on *REFORM* and DIR is significant at the 5 per cent level so that *RF* should be retained in the analysis. The *SH* variable, measuring the importance of gas in the energy mix, is not seen as significant and may safely be left out of the model. Finally a test of exclusion of *PIPES* as an input is rejected at the 5 per cent level by the KS test but is accepted by the *t*-test. Since the KS test is superior for small samples, it is concluded that *PIPES* should be included in the model.

Although the data set is small and relates to only one year, a few conclusions can be drawn. First, a multiproduct two-input production process model is not rejected by the data. Second, there is some evidence that efficiencies are significantly affected by rising/falling gas sales. It is not unreasonable to suppose that investment in an expanding market includes cost-saving improvements which would be difficult to justify during periods when contraction occurs. On the other hand, neither of the policy-related variables seems to have had any significant effects. The EU directive does not appear yet to have stimulated any marked productivity improvements in affected countries even though freeing of trade is one of its objectives. More importantly, the various market reforms taken as a group do not seem to have had any measurable effect either. This is probably because of the diversity of types of reform which a more sensitive set of measurements

Energy in a competitive market

might have distinguished. Interestingly, however, high efficiency scores were obtained by some reforming countries, for example, Great Britain (GB), and these were maintained consistently across all models.

One problem with the DEA analysis so far is that it has ignored dynamic considerations. Sengupta (1995) has pointed out that the actual input–output combination observed at any one time may not be optimal because adjustment processes are taking place. Thus units which appear optimal on DEA measurement may in fact prove to be inferior in the long run once factors are fully adjusted. Sengupta gives two reasons for this: 'first . . . capital inputs have a multiperiod dimension, since they generate outputs in future periods . . . current input (DEA) thus biasing efficiency comparisons against capital-intensive processes. Secondly, DMUs may take more than one time period to adjust their decision variables' (Sengupta, 1994, p. 119). Further, 'the DMU may be efficient for some of the time and inefficient for other times' (p. 120). Sengupta developed his ideas in the framework of a log linear production function which is not employed here. Instead the dynamic effects are tested by including a quadratic term in the change in X_{PIPES} between 1997 and 1998 (ΔX_{PIPES}) in the production frontier.

The results are somewhat inconclusive (see Table 5.2). Clearly, adding a variable to the minimal DEA model improves the average efficiency result

Table 5.2   Tests for dynamic effects

H_0: Exclude	Change in mean	KS test	t-test	Conclusion
$\Delta PIPES$	0.1270	0.2549*	1.9747*	Inconclusive
$X_{PIPES97}$	0.0000	0	0	Accept exclusion
Critical 5%*		0.2310	1.6924	
1%**		0.2770	2.4448	

(from 0.669 to 0.796) as would be expected. Neither the KS test nor the t-test are passed at the 1 per cent level of significance, although both are significant at the 5 per cent level. This suggests that dynamic effects, while they cannot be ignored, may be difficult to isolate. It is noteworthy that including the lagged value of pipelines ($X_{PIPES97}$) in the model did not make any difference to measured efficiencies. Lack of data prevented further analysis of dynamic effects at this stage of the research.

In general, measured efficiencies are as expected. In the countries of the EU, they range from 1 (GB, Ireland and the Netherlands) to 0.444 but are higher on average than for the set as a whole. The most efficient region was the Japan/Asia/Australia (JAA) group with Australia, Japan, Korea, Malaysia and Thailand all achieving unit scores. By contrast the lowest efficiencies were recorded in other European countries, although Hungary, Ukraine and Poland were above average. Both Canada and Iran had above average efficiencies. (Table 5.3 gives the efficiency scores for all 33 countries in the sample.)

Marginal products (per 100 extra units of the factor) are given in the second and fifth columns of Table 5.4. They show higher than average

Table 5.3   Measured efficiencies using input-orientated DEA model

Country	Code	Efficiency
Algeria	AL	0.410
Australia	AU	1.000
Austria	A	0.497
Belgium	B	0.764
Bosnia-Herzegovina	BAH	0.567
Bulgaria	BU	0.287
Canada	C	0.775
Czech Republic	CAR	0.408
Denmark	D	0.543
Estonia	E	0.427
Finland	IF	0.782
France	F	0.627
Germany	G	0.569
Great Britain	GB	1.000
Hungary	H	0.966
Iran	IRA	0.721
Ireland	I	1.000
Italy	IT	0.622
Japan	J	1.000
Korea	K	1.000
Latvia	L	0.585
Lithuania	LI	0.148
Malaysia	M	1.000
Netherlands	N	1.000
New Zealand	NZ	0.458
Poland	P	0.686
Romania	R	0.310
Spain	S	0.903
Sweden	SW	0.444
Thailand	T	1.000
Tunisia	TU	0.390
Ukraine	U	0.824
Yugoslavia	Y	0.352

Source: IGU and author's calculations.

Energy in a competitive market

Table 5.4   Factor productivity and slacks

Country	Employees			Pipelines		
	MP_{CONS}	MP_{CUST}	Slack	MP_{CONS}	MP_{CUST}	Slack
Algeria	0.0	0.0	11,120.7	18.0	46,339.0	0.0
Australia	14.2	63,210.1	0.0	0.0	0.0	0.0
Austria	17.1	71,138.1	0.0	1.0	4,948.1	0.0
Belgium	14.1	59,514.6	0.0	1.0	4,178.6	0.0
Bosnia-H'vina	0.0	0.0	63.3	7.0	56,699.5	0.0
Bulgaria	14.8	38.1	0.0	1.0	4.6	0.0
Canada	18.7	31,008.0	0.0	0.0	0.0	38,826.5
Czech Rep	8.6	58,937.6	0.0	0.0	0.0	2,660.8
Denmark	8.5	15,334.9	0.0	19.0	35,083.3	0.0
Estonia	11.3	65,753.3	0.0	0.0	0.0	105.7
Finland	41.7	9,449.5	0.0	2.0	463.9	0.0
France	7.9	63,664.8	0.0	0.0	0.0	4,925.1
Germany	10.0	52,599.4	0.0	0.0	0.0	7,262.3
Great Britain	6.9	41,058.1	0.0	3.0	20,508.5	0.0
Hungary	0.0	0.0	7,782.0	8.0	55,230.7	0.0
Iran	11.4	28,934.6	0.0	7.0	19,262.9	0.0
Ireland	12.4	29,869.6	0.0	0.0	0.0	0.0
Italy	6.2	38,649.0	0.0	0.0	0.0	0.0
Japan	0.0	0.0	0.0	2.0	20,929.3	0.0
Korea	4.0	43,489.8	0.0	0.0	0.0	0.0
Latvia	0.0	0.0	1,031.4	6.0	56,183.5	0.0
Lithuania	10.5	71,604.5	0.0	0.0	0.0	0.0
Malaysia	0.0	0.0	0.0	2.0	72.3	0.0
Netherlands	0.0	0.0	0.0	0.0	0.0	0.0
New Zealand	35.9	38,532.0	0.0	2.0	2,978.1	0.0
Poland	0.0	0.0	13,111.7	3.0	57,962.1	0.0
Romania	0.0	0.0	3508.7	26.0	26,884.6	0.0
Spain	12.3	78,667.9	0.0	0.0	4,288.1	0.0
Sweden	31.6	46,933.6	0.0	2.0	3,440.9	0.0
Thailand	5.8	1.4	0.0	0.0	0.0	0.0
Tunisia	48.9	46,238.8	0.0	0.0	0.0	944.3
Ukraine	0.0	0.0	15,687.6	8.0	49,340.9	0.0
Yugoslavia	12.7	21,716.6	0.0	2.0	3,920.2	0.0

Note: MP_{CONS}: PJ/100 employees, PJ/100 pipelines, MP_{CUST}: Cust/100 employees, Cust/100 pipelines; PJ = Petajoules.

marginal products (MP_{CONS}) per employee in the EU, Africa, Iran and Canada. GB's marginal product by contrast is quite low, suggesting that the industry has exhausted any potential size advantages. On the other hand GB seems particularly productive in terms of customers per employee, generating 33 per cent higher than world levels. This lends some support to the view that one of the effects of privatization has been to reduce quality (customer service) as firms have focused on cost reduction. However, Austria, Spain, Sweden, France and Germany have even higher marginal product per customer (MP_{CUST}) and in their cases the reason must lie elsewhere than in reform. Pipeline productivity shows a different pattern: highest marginal productivities are found for other European countries (Bosnia, Hungary, Poland and Latvia having particularly high MP_{CUST}) suggesting potential for expansion in terms of new customers in these countries. In terms of sales, pipelines are most productive in North Africa and Iran, indicating less mature markets than in Europe and JAA.

The existence of slack in factor utilization indicates potential for relatively painless efficiency improvements. Labour slack is particularly high in Africa and in other European countries, areas characterized by significant state control of enterprises. By contrast labour slack is non-existent throughout the EU, Canada and JAA. Slack in pipeline utilization has a rather different implication. Spare pipeline capacity provides extra security in the system and can substitute for scarce storage resources. It can be helpful in the development of markets. Within the EU, France and Germany have slack pipeline capacity suggesting that one of the conditions for market liberalization is met there. On the other hand, some results are difficult to interpret. Canada, for example, has the largest amount of slack in pipeline utilization, and yet is reasonably efficient on other criteria.

CONCLUSIONS

Often empirical work in economics is hindered by lack of appropriate statistical information. This is particularly so in the gas industry where vital information relative to the restructuring of the industry is often unavailable because of the tradition of bilateral negotiations between government agencies and large state-run companies that has dominated this sector in the past. Even in the era of privatization, the persistence of monopoly has, until recently, hindered the release of information on which yardstick evaluation of comparable activities can be made. This is one aspect of the 'legacy of monopoly' as Colin Robinson has called it (Robinson, 1994, p. 14). This chapter has made use of recently available data which provide a snapshot from which relative efficiency estimates can be made. Some results are surprising – the lack of clearly defined economies of scale, for instance. Some are less so – the inability to detect significant dynamic processes in gas production/distribution. Nevertheless the analysis does lend support to the notion that the reforms introduced in GB and intended in the rest of the EU are associated with high levels of technical efficiency, good utilization of labour and levels of underutilization of capital sufficient to support the development of competitive markets.

NOTES

1. Colin Robinson detected the beginnings of a Schumpeterian 'gale of creative destruction' in the UK in 1994 (Robinson, 1994).
2. Ofgem is an amalgamation of Ofgas and Offer (Office of Electricity Regulation).

REFERENCES

Banker, R.D. (1993), 'Maximum likelihood, consistency and data envelopment analysis: a statistical foundation', *Management Science*, **39** (10), 1265–73.

European Commission (1998), *Directive 98/30/EC of the European Parliament and of the Council of 22 June 1998 concerning common rules for the internal market in natural gas*, Brussels, Belgium: Directive 98/30EC.

European Commission (2000), *An overview of the state of implementation of the EU Gas Directive*, Brussels, Belgium: May (98/30/EC).

Fare, R., Grosskopf, S. and Lovell, C.A. (1994), *Production Frontiers*, Cambridge, UK: Cambridge University Press.

IGU (2000a), *Natural Gas in 1999*, Denmark: International Gas Union Press Release 23 May.

IGU (2000b), *Panorama of the Gas Industry in the IGU Countries: Statistics Data 1999*, Denmark: International Gas Union.

Kalirajan, K.P. and Shand, R.T. (1999), 'Frontier production functions and technical efficiency measures', *Journal of Economic Surveys*, **13** (2), 149–72.

Kim, T.Y. and Lee, J.D. (1995), 'Cost analysis of gas distribution industry with spatial variables', *Journal of Energy and Development*, **20** (2), 247–69.

Kim, T.Y, Lee, J.D., Park, Y.H. and Kim, B. (1999), 'International comparisons of productivity and its determinants in the natural gas industry', *Energy Economics*, **21** (3), 273–93.

Kittelsen, S.A.C. (1999a), *Monte Carlo simulations of DEA efficiency measures and hypothesis tests*, Oslo, Norway: Memorandum 9/1999, Frisch Centre/ Department of Economics, University of Oslo.

Kittelsen, S.A.C. (1999b), *Stepwise DEA: Choosing variables for measuring technical efficiency in Norwegian electricity distribution*, Oslo, Norway: Foundation for Research in Economics and Business Administration (SNF).

Newbery, D.M. (2000), *Privatization, restructuring and regulation of network utilities*, Cambridge, MA, USA and London, UK: MIT Press.

Price, C.W. and Weyman-Jones, T. (1996), 'Malmquist indices of productivity change in the UK gas industry before and after privatization', *Applied Economics*, **28** (1), 29–39.

Robinson, C. (1994), 'Gas: what to do after the MMC verdict', in Beasley, M.E. (ed.), *Regulating Utilities: The Way Forward*, London, UK: Institute of Economic Affairs, pp. 1–19.

Sengupta, J. (1994), 'A model of dynamic efficiency measurement', *Applied Economics Letters*, **1** (7), 119–21.

Sengupta, J. (1995), *Dynamics of Data Envelopment Analysis: Theory of Systems Efficiency*, London, UK: Kluwer Academic Publishers.

Yunos, J.M. and Hawdon, D. (1997), 'The efficiency of the National Electricity Board in Malaysia: an inter-country comparison using DEA', *Energy Economics* **19** (2), 255–69.

6. UK coal in competitive energy markets

Mike J. Parker

INTRODUCTION: LONG-TERM TRENDS[1]

Over the 1980s and 1990s, a substantial body of literature was devoted to the effects of policies of UK governments to liberalize the operation of energy utilities by the promotion of competition and privatization. While these developments were to have an impact on the UK coal industry, the case of this particular industry is distinctive, not least because of the importance of politics. This was an industry whose deteriorating fortunes were the outcome of the complex interaction of politics and economics, often in ways unexpected by the players involved.

However, the decline of the UK coal industry and, in particular, its deep mines, also needs to be set in a longer-term context (as illustrated in Table 6.1). UK coal *consumption* fell by more than 70 per cent between 1960 and 2000.

By the time Margaret Thatcher came to power in 1979, the coal industry had lost the whole of its market in gas production and most of its sales in the industrial and domestic markets as a result of competition from oil and gas, technical changes, the decline of the 'smokestack' sector and domestic clean air legislation, with these losses only partly offset by substantial gains in power generation.

Table 6.1 UK coal consumption (m. tonnes)

	Power stations	Other markets	Total
1960	53	147	200
1970	77	80	157
1980	90	33	123
1990	84	24	108
2000	46	13	59

Source: Various issues of the *UK Digest of Energy Statistics (DUKES)*.

Table 6.2   UK coal output (m. tonnes)

	Deep mines	Opencast, etc.	Total
1960	189	9	198
1970	137	10	147
1980	112	18	130
1990	73	20	93
2000	17	14	31

Source: Various issues of the *UK Digest of Energy Statistics* (*DUKES*).

The fall in UK coal output between 1960 and 2000 was even more marked: total output fell by over 80 per cent and deep-mined output by more than 90 per cent (see Table 6.2). In absolute terms, the fall in deep-mined output in the two decades before the advent of Thatcherite administrations was similar to that experienced in the last 20 years. Thus the nationalized monopoly, the National Coal Board (NCB), inherited by Margaret Thatcher in 1979, was no stranger to the adverse effects of market forces and competition from other primary fuels, or to the problems of reducing deep-mined output, with associated colliery closures and manpower rundown.

However, the period from 1980 to 2000 was very different from the previous 20 years, when, in percentage terms, the *rate* of deep-mine contraction more than doubled and, whereas up to 1980 deep-mined output represented 90 per cent or more of coal supplies to UK markets, by 1990 this share had fallen to 68 per cent and, in 2000, to 30 per cent.

THATCHERITE 'POLITICAL AGENDA' FOR COAL

Whatever the underlying trends were, the arrival of Margaret Thatcher's government in 1979 represented a radical turning point in UK coal policy. It is clear that, from the outset, there was a Thatcherite 'political agenda' for coal comprising two main elements: first, the need permanently to break the power of the National Union of Mineworkers (NUM) to 'hold the country to ransom' and, second, radically to change what was seen as the inefficient way in which the NCB was operated in the public sector, by turning the industry into a viable commercial enterprise (although the policy on ultimate privatization took some time to evolve).

As circumstances turned out, these two essential elements in coal policy tended to be mutually reinforcing. The aim of permanently breaking the power of the NUM entailed a large reduction in the two-thirds dependence of the electricity industry on UK deep-mined coal which, because of the absence of realistic alternative markets, in turn involved a large reduction in output; and the objective of fully commercial operations under increasingly unfavourable market conditions pointed not only to lower output but also to the need for large increases in productivity and, hence, very large reductions in colliery manpower.

By 1997, it appeared that the Thatcherite 'political agenda' for coal had been totally achieved. Compared with 1979, deep-mined output had fallen from 108 million tonnes to 30 million tonnes and, even more spectacularly, manpower had fallen from 233,000 to 12,000. Moreover, both output and manpower were still on a downward trend. The share of deep-mined coal in the fuelling of power stations (the original basis of NUM power) had fallen from 70 per cent to less than 20 per cent. Finally, NCB/British Coal had been privatized and was operating with profits of £200 million a year without overt subsidy. Some have seen this as a clear case of cause and effect; in other words, that the outcome was due almost entirely to the exercise of political will. But this is much too simple.

It is not the intention here to describe, in detail, the interaction of politics and economics in the UK coal industry over the last 20 years, but rather to ask a somewhat more limited question: how far was the rapid decline of UK deep-mined coal over the last 20 years due to Thatcherite liberalization through greater exposure of the industry to market forces in a competitive market framework and the greater disciplines arising from coal privatization?

DEFEAT OF THE GREAT STRIKE

The first Thatcherite government of 1979–83 made no progress with its 'political agenda' on coal. Initially, the approach was to impose tough 'cash limits' in the NCB. But this immediately faced the board with the problem that the only way to comply with this remit was to accelerate the reduction of uneconomic, surplus production by pit closures. The NCB's attempts to deal with this dilemma led to strike threats from the NUM and government capitulation in February 1981. The result was a stay on the additional closures and a substantial increase in government funding. This impasse in coal policy was not broken until the defeat of the great strike of 1984/85, which owed more to the folly of the NUM leadership than to careful planning by the government.

Leaving on one side the controversies surrounding the origin, conduct and ending of the great strike, the totality of its defeat was of great significance in the conduct of the coal industry's affairs. Effective resistance to large-scale colliery closures and manpower rundown was removed. Indeed, the whole programme of liberalization and privatization, both in the coal industry itself and in the electricity industry, would not have developed as it did without the defeat of the great strike.

AMBIGUOUS LINKS WITH 'FREE MARKET FORCES'

Notwithstanding the scale of the NUM's defeat in 1985, Margaret Thatcher proceeded with considerable caution in the aftermath of the strike. Power station coal stocks were rapidly rebuilt and the finances of British Coal (as the NCB had become) were so organized that the large-scale government 'restructuring' grants and generous redundancy schemes encouraged the 'voluntary' reduction of manpower without any significant protest against the loss of over 100,000 jobs between 1985 and 1990.

But there was also careful management of the market for UK coal in order that contraction might take place in an orderly fashion. There was no sense in which Margaret Thatcher can be said to have exposed the coal industry to 'free market forces'. Within a year of the end of the great strike, OPEC (Organization of Petroleum-Exporting Countries) oil prices collapsed, making fuel oil, once again, a considerable threat to British Coal's markets at a time when a rapid development of international trade in power station coal, at falling prices, was also very evident. The government's response was to curb the power of the electricity industry to buy cheap oil and imported coal by brokering a series of 'joint understandings' between the nationalized Central Electricity Generating Board (CEGB) and British Coal, which safeguarded the bulk of BC sales in return for below-inflation constraints on price increases. Moreover, this policy was followed (but in a contractual form) even when the electricity industry had been privatized, right up to 1998. And, because the prices of international coal continued to fall in 'real' terms, and faster than BC's costs (notwithstanding very large increases in productivity), the effect of this policy was to create a hidden subsidy to BC's deep mines paid by the electricity consumer rather than the taxpayer. Yet, given the unexpected severity of the external market pressures on British Coal, such a policy was seen as a necessary mitigation of market forces to maintain contraction of deep-mined output and manpower at a politically acceptable rate.

The first Thatcher government had attempted to erode the power of the NUM by initiating a large programme of pressurized water reactor (PWR) stations. This was an almost total failure. In spite of a decade of strong

government advocacy, only one PWR (Sizewell B) was built, and not commissioned until 1994. The advent of electricity privatization exposed the
commercial and financial risks of nuclear power and effectively removed
the threat to coal of *new* nuclear stations (although the performance of
existing stations greatly improved under the stimulus of privatization and
liberalization of the electricity market). However, privatization of the
electricity industry did give rise to a new threat to UK coal: a large programme of new combined cycle gas turbine (CCGT) stations, known col-
loquially as the 'dash for gas'.

Yet it would be difficult to claim that the 'dash for gas' was a result of the
operation of 'free market forces'. Rather, it was the unexpected result of
complex interaction of the side-effects of the way in which the gas and
electricity industries were liberalized, privatized and regulated. The liberalization of the gas market effectively destroyed the monopsony buying position of British Gas in the North Sea which, in the circumstances of the
early 1990s, led to increased availability of natural gas which needed a new
large and secure market. This new market for gas appeared in the electricity market as a result of the structure of privatized generation (a duopoly
whose dominance could only be reduced at that stage by the introduction
of new CCGT plant promoted mainly by regional electricity companies
and oil companies) and the high *prices* established for contracts for coal-
based generation (which was regulated on the basis of price rather than
cost). The outcome was a very rapid growth in the applications to build new
gas-fired plant. The Major government readily gave the required consents,
even though, by general acknowledgement, most of the new CCGTs had
total costs (including capital charges on new capital) in excess of the *avoid-
able costs* at existing coal stations. If this was a market, it was a very dis-
torted one.

COAL PRIVATIZATION

In other privatizations, there is much evidence that the introduction of
competition, on the ending of nationalized monopoly through privatization, has been instrumental in improving performance and reducing costs.
In the case of British Coal, improved performance proved to be a *precon-
dition* rather than the result of privatization. In its latter years, the task for
BC was to establish a tenable balance between supply and demand in a
rapidly falling market (as a result of the 'dash for gas' and the Major government's decision to allow the privatized generators rapidly to close down
their large coal stocks) and to reduce costs sufficiently to enable the buyers
of BC assets (particularly of deep mines) to make reasonable profits at

prices and volumes already agreed in the government-brokered contracts with the generators. After privatization, the profits of RJB Mining (which took over nearly all BC's deep-mined capacity) depended almost entirely on the price premia (against imported coal) embedded in the inherited contracts. Little further improvement was made in labour productivity.

As New Labour was to discover, once the inherited contracts (and their price premia) came to an end in March 1998, most of the profit of the privatized deep mining disappeared. The privatized coal industry, far from being self-reliant and free of political complication, once again was seen petitioning for government intervention, first for a moratorium on new CCGTs and, later, for direct subsidies to avoid politically sensitive closures.

Coal privatization, as such, made little difference, for good or ill, to the fortunes of the coal industry's deep mines; by the end of 2000, output had virtually halved since privatization. To see why this was so, it is necessary to look at the fundamentals.

ADVERSE ECONOMIC FUNDAMENTALS

Increasingly, the true market value of UK coal has been set by the price of imported power station coal (after adjustment for inland transport costs). At year 2000 money values, this price fell from about £3/GJ before the great strike to less than £1/GJ by the year 2000. Even with a huge programme of high-cost colliery closures and a fivefold increase in labour productivity, the costs of most remaining deep mines could not be brought down to a *sustainably* profitable level. Indeed, even if the market distortions of the 'dash for gas' had been avoided, and there had been instead a free market in imported coal, it is doubtful whether the output of deep-mined coal would have been any higher than it turned out to be.

Replacement capacity (necessary for any extractive industry) which required major capital projects on new mines or other larger developments, appeared uneconomic from the mid-1980s onwards. This was reflected in the rapid decline in the industry's capital investment. In the early 1980s, total capital investment was equivalent to some £15/tonne of deep-mined output (2000 money values), at a time when the major new capacity projects under 'Plan For Coal' were still in progress. Since privatization, this figure has fallen to around £2/tonne, a long way below the level required to sustain even the much-diminished level of output, so that further decline is now inevitable.

These fundamental underlying trends are also reflected in the assessment of remaining coal reserves. Effectively, only reserves accessible to existing mines have any real chance of being economic. (And the greater the economic pressures on the industry, the more selective will be the working of these remaining reserves.) Boyds, the American Consultants employed by the government in 1993, assessed the total at some 2,100 million tonnes, but put greater weight on a discounted figure of around 1,000 million tonnes (by excluding 'unclassified' reserves requiring major expenditure to access). International Mining Consultants (IMCL), in a report to government in March 1999, assessed reserves at some 600 million tonnes – reflecting colliery closures and output produced since Boyds had reported. More realistically, the IMCL figure might be discounted to 300 million tonnes. And in December 1999, the Department of Trade and Industry itself proposed a figure of 200 million tonnes. These assessments suggest a reserve/production ratio for deep mines of no more than 10/15 at the beginning of the twenty-first century.

CONCLUSION

In the case of the UK coal industry, it is difficult to disentangle the influences of politics and economics, and the impacts of market liberalization and privatization are by no means straightforward. But it is clear that economic fundamentals and the Thatcherite 'political agenda' for coal both pointed in the same direction (subject only to the dictates of political prudence), leading to the enormous contraction of a once great industry.

NOTE

1.   A detailed discussion of the interaction of politics and economics in the affairs of the UK
     coal industry since 1979, including issues referred to in this chapter, can be found in Parker
     (2000).

REFERENCE

Parker, M.J. (2000), *Thatcherism and the Fall of Coal*, Oxford, UK: Oxford University Press.

7. Economists and the oil industry: facts versus analysis, the case of vertical integration

Paul Stevens

INTRODUCTION

This chapter is a return to a theme developed some time ago by Stevens (1995). It concerns the way in which economists can or cannot illuminate the working of the international oil industry. Economics is about questions. There are two aspects. First is to ask a question about something very complicated and then use simple economics to make the answer understandable. This is a major contribution and simple economics can be an extremely powerful explanatory tool. Unfortunately, many economists are losing sight of this and take delight in increasing obscurity. The second aspect about questions and economics comes from the late Joan Robinson who used to remark, 'the function of economists is to make sure the right questions are being asked – any damn fool can provide the answers!'. In the context of this chapter, the questions concern the operation of the international oil industry.

Once the question has been posed, the next stage in the process is to look in the economist's proverbial tool bag. This contains a variety of concepts and ideas whose function is to provide an analytical framework to address the question.

However, there are two potential problems. The first is that the concepts may pull you in different and conflicting directions. The second problem (which is the focus of this chapter) comes from the old academic adage: 'never let facts get in the way of good analysis'. Too often economists have reached into their tool bags but then have completely ignored the facts of the context in which the questions were being asked. This has been a recurrent problem in energy economics, especially when it comes to considering the international oil industry. A large part of the problem arises because too few academic economists know anything at all about the international industry. Furthermore, they do not trouble themselves to find out. The classic example was the oil shocks of the 1970s and the rediscovery of the ideas of Harold Hotelling (Hotelling, 1931). Faced with a quadrupling of oil prices, too many economists simply looked into their tool bags and came out with Hotelling's ideas on exhaustible resources. They completely ignored the facts of what was going on, which had nothing whatever to do with resource scarcity or depletion. To compound the error they then failed to observe the first law of holes – 'when you are in one, stop digging'. They stubbornly kept ignoring the facts and continued to persist in using this tool for analysis. Hence the second oil shock of 1978–81 was equally misunderstood by most of the economics profession. As a result they moved further and further away from reality while giving moral support to those who continue to predict the imminent running out of oil reserves (Stevens, 2000).

A NEW ERA?

This chapter turns to a new area where this problem of 'ignoring the facts and getting on with the analysis' is re-emerging in a different context. The issue concerns vertical integration and the large oil companies, both private and national. Vertical integration is the state of affairs when different stages in the same value chain are somehow linked together. Economists have long had an interest in this concept and it has always been a topic of considerable interest for the oil industry. The economics literature on the oil business is full of discussions and descriptions of the fact that major oil companies have been characterized as vertically integrated. Over the years, much has been written on the reasons and the implications (De Chazeau and Khan, 1959; Bindemann, 1999).

Unfortunately, many authors neglect the simple fact that it is necessary to consider two different types of vertical integration. Furthermore, the distinction (while not being relevant before the second oil shock of 1979–81) has become increasingly important in ways to be explained. Two definitions are relevant. Financial vertical integration occurs where the same company owns different stages in the same value chain. Hence the company consists of a headquarters and a number of owned subsidiaries or affiliates. The company headquarters fulfils a capital budgeting role among the affiliates. By contrast, operational vertical integration is where these different affiliates take their inputs or send their outputs to other owned affiliates. When economists write about 'vertical integration' they imply (but do not make it explicit) that they are considering companies that are financially *and* operationally vertically integrated. However, and herein lies the problem, if a company is financially vertical integrated, while it may also use operational vertical integration, it may instead choose to use markets. Hence 'vertical integration' may only refer to financial vertical integration.

This distinction for the oil business is crucial. Before the second oil shock of 1978–81, the major oil companies were financially and operationally vertically integrated. There were a number of reasons why operational vertical integration was favoured (Hartshorn, 1980; Stevens, 1985). Oil markets were small and inefficient. There were very few players involved in arm's-length transactions with very poor market transparency. Hence the transaction costs in using markets were high. The best way to ensure maximum throughput (essential for healthy profitability given the high fixed costs of the industry) was to own and use owned crude or owned products. Operational vertical integration simply meant lower costs. However, there were other factors at work encouraging the companies to use operational vertical integration. It acted as a very significant constraint on competition by the creation of major barriers to entry. There were lots of tax games to be played by manipulating transfer prices between owned affiliates – the famous dictum of the 1960s was 'only fools and affiliates pay posted prices'. Finally, access to owned affiliates undoubtedly gave benefits from access to information in the different stages of the value chain plus certain synergies. The result of all this was that the majors had very high levels of financial and operational vertical integration. The distinction between the types of integration was irrelevant because there was no viable market alternative to operational vertical integration.

The process started to change with the nationalizations of the crude producing affiliates in the first half of the 1970s. De jure this meant the loss of much of the owned crude affiliates by the majors. However, de facto this was not the case. Many producer governments, having taken over the production decision, left the disposal of the crude with the former foreign companies. It was not until the second oil shock drove a wedge between the administered price and the spot price that producer governments took over crude disposal. This began the process of breaking the operationally vertically integrated chain (Hartshorn, 1993) and the development of markets. In addition to the older producer governments selling at arm's length, during the 1980s a whole group of new crude oil suppliers also emerged. This was the result of the high oil prices of the 1970s, the expectations of ever-higher prices in the first half of the 1980s and the drive by the majors to replace their lost sources of owned crude. These new players were not financially vertically integrated and so were forced to sell on an arm's-length basis. More players in the market, greater transparency, courtesy of the development of forward and futures markets in a world of an information technology revolution all led to the crude and product markets becoming more efficient. Suddenly, the transaction costs of using markets began to fall.

Companies that had been forced to use markets once the producer governments took over crude disposal now began to use markets through choice.

Through the 1980s and 1990s other factors also encouraged the major
private companies to move away from using operational vertical integration. Markets were becoming more competitive. Entry became easier as (for
example) the petropreneurs begin to emerge (Bleakely et al., 1997). Hence
barriers to entry were no longer a driver. The tax authorities got smarter;
hence there were fewer tax games to be played. Synergies could now be
achieved through strategic alliances and partnering. The collective result
was that the majors, while remaining financially vertically integrated,
replaced operational vertical integration with markets. For example, by the
1990s, in a company like British Petroleum less than 20 per cent of its
owned crude went (deliberately) through its own refineries.

During the 1980s another new trend emerged relevant to vertical integration and markets. The national oil companies of the oil producers led by
Venezuela and Kuwait started to become financially vertically integrated by
purchasing downstream assets – many of them following a portfolio shake-
out from the majors in the 1980s. However, against the trend followed by
the old majors, these new 'majors' chose to use operational vertical integration rather than markets. Several factors can be used to explain this. Many
in the producing countries simply did not realize the distinction between
financial and operational vertical integration. They thought the old majors
continued to be both operationally and financially vertically integrated.
Second, part of the motivation to move downstream was to try and lock in
markets for crude exports in an effort to counter the intense and growing
competition from non-OPEC states. Hence operational vertical integration
would guarantee dedicated market outlets. Finally, and this is perhaps more
controversial, operational vertical integration could help to deepen the
information asymmetries between principal and agent which was the key to
the rent-seeking behaviour which was pursued by many national oil companies (Van der Linde, 2000).

Hence by the 1990s, there are two types of major international oil
company – the financially vertically integrated private majors which use
markets and the national oil companies which are financially and operationally vertically integrated. This distinction is not yet registered in the
economics literature in general and the energy economics literature in particular.

The distinction matters for two reasons. Interest in vertical integration
has recently revived because the structure of oil companies has come under
great scrutiny in the last two years. For the private companies this scrutiny
has been because of the spate of mergers driven by concern over shareholder value in a declining industry (Stevens, 1999). For the national oil

companies, the scrutiny has been because of the moves to reform and restructure national oil companies. These in turn have been driven by concern over their efficiency and the validity of many of the decisions to vertically integrate financially. However, because of the changes with respect to vertical integration outlined above, the resulting studies now face serious constraints. In the past, studies of vertical integration were either times-series or cross-section studies. Now, neither method is valid. Different companies have different structures and therefore cross-section studies are extremely dangerous. The 'vertical integration' of the private companies is not the same as the 'vertical integration' of the national oil companies. Equally, company structure over time has changed; therefore time-series studies are extremely dangerous. The 'vertical integration' which ruled in the 1970s is not the same that rules today, at least for the private companies. Many researchers have yet to realize this problem.

The second reason the distinction matters is because by failing to make the distinction, a whole fascinating area of study is being ignored. There are two key questions that emerge once vertical integration is more carefully defined – the future of operational vertical integration and the future of financial vertical integration.

The future of operational vertical integration is both uncertain and important. The key lies in what the national oil companies might do. A consequence of the recent mergers has been divestiture of affiliates by the private majors. This has been especially noticeable in terms of their downstream assets. This divestiture has been driven by two factors. There has been forced divestiture to satisfy regulatory authorities to allow the mergers to go ahead – the Federal Trade Commission in the United States and the European Commission. In addition, the key reason for the mergers was to improve the average performance of the asset portfolio. This will involve selling lesser performing assets – most obviously in refining. Given this downstream selling, the question arises as to whether the national oil companies will take the opportunity to develop further their financial vertical integration by buying these downstream assets. If they do and maintain their use of operational vertical integration, this might reduce the efficiency of markets encouraging others to move back to operational vertical integration. On the other hand, if smaller petropreneurs buy the assets, this might increase market efficiency forcing the national oil companies to follow the private majors and switch to operational vertical integration. This process could be reinforced if the national oil companies are corporatized or even privatized. On the other hand, given the rise of paper barrel markets, do markets any longer need large numbers of buyers and sellers of wet barrels to maintain efficiency? Taking a longer time horizon, could governments begin to interfere in markets thereby reducing market efficiency? The joys of market forces are increasingly being questioned especially in a world of growing oil price volatility.

The second question of interest concerns the future of financial vertical integration. No oil company owns a drilling rig or a seismic team. Why should they own a refinery? The original logic behind financial vertical integration was that it was a necessary condition to be operationally vertically integrated. If this is the case, why has financial vertical integration survived in the majors if operational vertical integration has been disappearing? The question is particularly pertinent since it is becoming increasingly apparent that the poor financial performance of the majors and their inability to outperform the market is largely because of the poor performance of the downstream in general and refining in particular (API, 1999).

While there are explanations for the survival of financial vertical integration, they are far from complete, comprehensive or indeed in many cases convincing. It is possible that in the early 1980s the oil companies had more money than sense. One only has to consider the grandeur of some of the headquarters built by oil companies in this period – Standard Oil of Ohio's in Cleveland is a classic case. In such a world, arguably a few poorly performing refineries might be regarded as unimportant although during the 1980s many companies did begin to sell off older downstream assets (Lynch, 1995). Industrial inertia might also provide part of the explanation. However, in a world where maximizing shareholder value began to dominate corporate thinking this is an unlikely explanation by the 1990s. National oil company downstream investments outlined above were obviously a direct source of expansion for financial vertical integration. Some have also argued that being in the upstream and downstream provides a mechanism for hedging crude price risk. Lower crude prices hit upstream profits but in theory should increase refinery margins and hence downstream profitability. There are still some synergies from being in different stages. In certain highly specialized circumstances there are also tax games and information advantages, although these tend to be associated more with the ownership of transport infrastructure rather than refineries.

Why might this change? Continuing poor refinery profitability will provide a driver to divest. Arguably, as suggested above, in the post-merger world that began in 1998, the new companies will evaluate their asset portfolio. To maintain their average performance in line with the market they will sell marginally performing assets, the majority of which will be refineries. Who will buy remains a key question for the future of financial vertical integration. The national oil companies themselves are coming under scrutiny, especially their downstream acquisitions. For example, Hugo Chavez in Venezuela in his election campaign promised to force PDVSA to divest itself of all its overseas assets. Something that (at least at the time of writing) has yet to happen. Similarly in Kuwait, the National Assembly has been highly critical of KPC's investments abroad. Such pressures could at the very least inhibit further financial vertical integration and could actually reverse the trend. For example, Kuwait has now stopped all its refinery acquisitions in Europe from refining, using them only as storage depots to service their gas station chain.

CONCLUSION

All these are interesting questions. The answers will determine the future structure of both oil companies and oil markets. Economists and others, if they neglect the facts, are in great danger of either missing these debates or (arguably even worse) intervening in an extremely unhelpful way.

REFERENCES

API (1999), *Economic State of the US Petroleum Industry*, Washington, DC, US: American Petroleum Institute Research Papers.

Bindemann, K. (1999), 'Vertical integration in the oil industry: a review of the literature', *Journal of Energy Literature*, **5** (1), 3–26.

Bleakely, T., Gee, D.S. and Hume, R. (1997), 'The atomization of big oil', *McKinsey Quarterly*, No. 2, 122–43.

De Chazeau, M.G. and Khan A.E. (1959), *Integration and Competition in the Petroleum Industry*, New Haven, US: Yale University Press.

Hartshorn, J.E. (1980), 'From multinational to national oil: the structural change', *Journal of Energy and Development*, **5** (2), 207–20.

Hartshorn, J.E. (1993), *Oil Trade: Politics and Prospects*, Cambridge, UK: Cambridge University Press.

Hotelling, H. (1931), 'The economics of exhaustible resources', *Journal of Political Economy*, **39** (2), 137–75.

Lynch, M.C. (1995), 'Shoulder against shoulder: the evolution of oil industry strategy', *Journal of Energy and Development*, **19** (1), 15–56.

Stevens, P.J. (1985), 'A survey of structural change in the international oil industry 1945–84', in Hawdon, D. (ed.), *The Changing Structure of the World Oil Industry*, London, UK: Croom Helm, pp. 18–51.

Stevens, P.J. (1995), 'Understanding the oil industry: economics as a help or a hindrance', *Energy Journal*, **16** (3), 125–39.

Stevens, P.J. (1999), 'Oil company mergers: why and to what effect?', *Pipeline*, Issue 22, 14–16.

Stevens, P.J. (2000), 'Introduction', in Stevens, P.J. (ed.), *The Economics of Energy*, Cheltenham, UK: Edward Elgar, pp. lix–lxviii.

Van der Linde, C. (2000), *The State and the International Oil Market: Competition and the Changing Ownership of Crude Oil Assets*, Boston, US: Kluwer Academic Publishing.

8. The economics of field cluster developments in the UK continental shelf

Alexander G. Kemp and Linda Stephen

INTRODUCTION

The UK North Sea is now in its mature years. Oil production has peaked. Gas production will continue to grow for another few years on the basis of fields under development, but thereafter decline is very likely. The average size of discovery has been falling for many years, and over the last few years the exploration success rate and the exploration effort have been lower than in earlier periods.

There is, however, a substantial inventory of undeveloped discoveries. The industry is currently seriously examining for development over 50 'probable' fields as well as over 70 incremental investment projects in mature fields. A further 278 discoveries containing information on their possible size, type (oil, gas, condensate), and location by block number are in a database constructed by the present authors.

Most of these undeveloped discoveries are quite small. On a stand-alone basis many are not economically viable. This leads to the notion that joint development of a group of fields might be viable where individual projects remain unattractive. Joint development could involve benefits from (a) economies of infrastructure cost sharing and (b) risk sharing. These subjects are investigated in this chapter.

INITIAL SCREENING OF POTENTIAL

It is likely that the most economical method by which new field developments can be undertaken is via the utilization of existing major infrastructure. This includes pipelines and processing facilities on platforms. Sometimes new fields can readily feed directly into such major infrastructure. This is shown schematically in the left-hand part of Figure 8.1. Joint

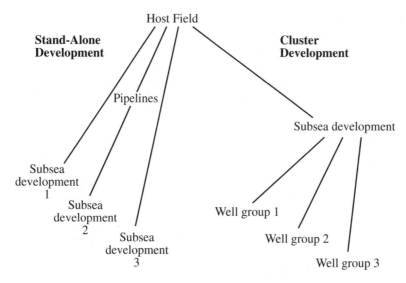

Figure 8.1   Individual and cluster development

development of fields could involve the use of some common infrastructure. This is illustrated in the right-hand part of Figure 8.1. The individual fields are tied into an infrastructure incorporating a manifold and associated facilities for communal use. There is then only one pipeline from the manifold infrastructure to the major infrastructure.

The next stage of the study was to undertake an initial screening of the potential in the UK continental shelf (UKCS) for cluster developments of the type described. The database outlined was utilized for this purpose. All fields for which no development plan has been determined were mapped with a view to determining whether a cluster on the lines discussed above was plausible. It is generally acknowledged that subsea tie-back developments are currently plausible up to distances of about 50 kilometres. The results of the mapping exercise are shown in Figures 8.2–5 for various basins of the UKCS. The data show for each basin (a) the number of fields in each cluster, (b) the maximum and minimum distances of individual fields from the hub of the cluster, (c) the aggregate reserves in each cluster, (d) the distance of the common manifold from the major infrastructure, and (e) the type of reserves (oil, gas or mixed).

In Figure 8.2a the results for the Southern North Sea (SNS) are shown. Twelve clusters were found with six involving five or more fields. The maximum reserves in any one cluster were around 170 million barrels of oil equivalent (mmboe). Four clusters had reserves below 50 mmboe.

In the results shown in Figure 8.2a there were some fields which were

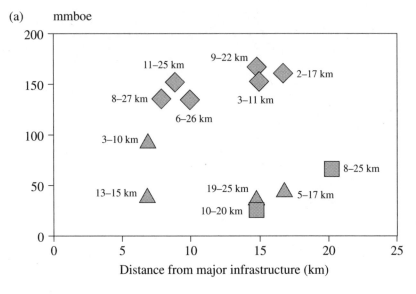

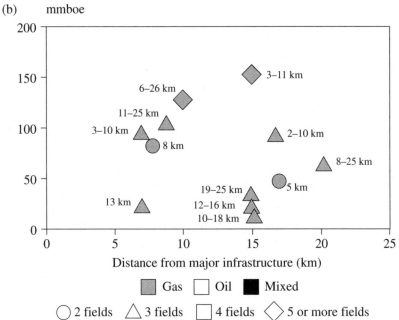

Figure 8.2   Possible cluster developments in SNS

individually closer to the major infrastructure than to the common manifold. A cluster development incorporating such fields can be perfectly rational from an economic perspective, but it is also possible that those fields would tie in directly to the major infrastructure. If such fields were excluded from the analysis the resulting clusters for the SNS would be as shown in Figure 8.2b. There are still 12 clusters, but the average size is somewhat less.

In Figure 8.3a the results for the Central North Sea (CNS) are shown. There are 24 clusters, of which three have reserves of 250 mmboe or more. The great majority are much smaller, however. Seventeen have reserves of 100 mmboe or less, and 11 have reserves of about 50 mmboe or less. When fields located nearer to major infrastructure than to the common manifold are excluded, the results are as in Figure 8.3b. There are still 24 clusters, but only two have reserves of 200 mmboe or more. Again there are 11 with reserves of about 50 mmboe or less.

In Figure 8.4a the results are shown for the Northern North Sea (NNS). There are 11 clusters of which two have reserves of about 200 mmboe or more. Six have reserves of just over 50 mmboe or less. When fields which are closer to existing major infrastructure than to the communal manifold are excluded, the results are as shown in Figure 8.4b. There are no clusters with reserves exceeding 200 mmboe, and six with reserves of 50 mmboe or less.

In Figure 8.5 the results are shown for West of Scotland (WOS). Although little infrastructure exists in this province from a purely geographic viewpoint there are as many as seven potential clusters, two of which have reserves exceeding 200 mmboe.

It is emphasized that the results of the mapping do not indicate anything concerning economic viability. This depends on several factors including not only oil and gas prices, but the costs of the field developments, the perceived reservoir risks, the processing facilities available on the host infrastructure, and the tariffs payable for these and the related transport facilities. The economic hurdle test will inevitably mean that many of the clusters identified above will probably not be viable. But there is enough evidence to support the view that the concept can be applied on a more widespread scale than has been the case to date.

POTENTIAL ECONOMIES OF SCALE FROM CLUSTER DEVELOPMENTS

Methodology and Data

It is clear that the employment of a common infrastructure (manifold plus pipeline) produces an economy of scale. The question which is now

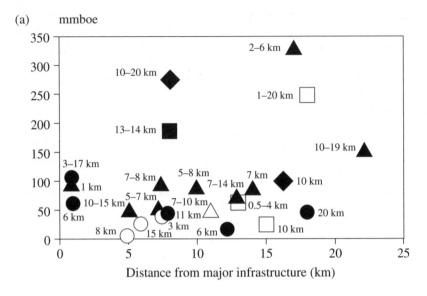

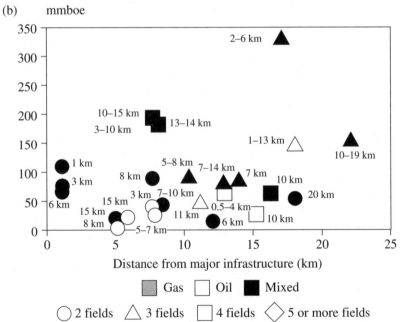

Figure 8.3   Possible cluster developments in CNS

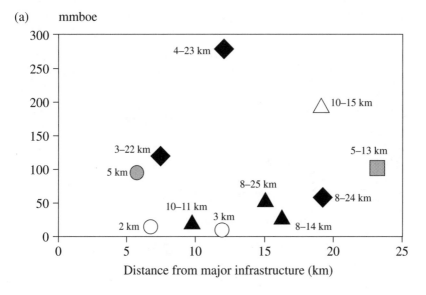

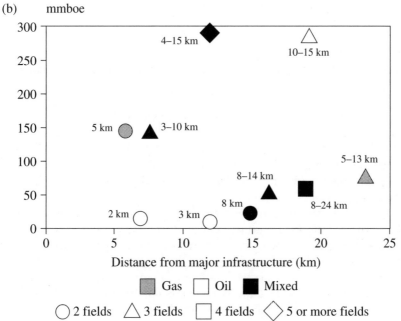

Figure 8.4 Possible cluster developments in NNS

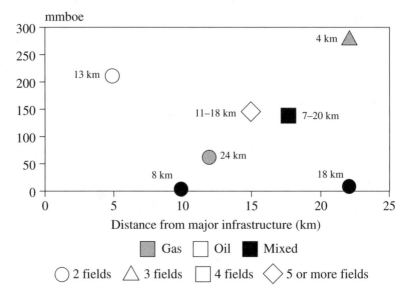

Figure 8.5   Possible cluster developments in WOS

investigated is whether the economy of scale is worthwhile and what difference it makes to the prospective returns compared to independent field
investments.

The procedure adopted was to examine the returns from a set of fields
typical of those available for development when developed (a) individually
and (b) as a cluster. Based on the findings of field reserve and possible size
of clusters in the previous section, five model fields were selected for analysis. When developed individually (but still linked to major infrastructure)
their investment, operating and decommissioning costs were estimated as
shown in Table 8.1.

The specific development, operating and decommissioning costs of these
fields when developed as part of a cluster were then estimated. The data are
shown in Table 8.2. The common infrastructure costs for three-field and
five-field clusters were then estimated. The results are shown in Table 8.3.
In obtaining these estimates use was made of data on the cost structures of
existing cluster developments. When these common infrastructure costs
had to be apportioned to fields, they were done so in relation to the total
reserves of the fields.

Deterministic financial modelling was employed to calculate the returns
to the fields when developed individually and as clusters. The results for
three-field and five-field clusters are shown. Comparisons are made with

Table 8.1   Deterministic assumptions for individual development

mmbbl	5	10	20	35	50
Devex $/bbl	10	8	7.5	6.5	5
Annual opex as % devex	8	9	9	7	7
Abandonment as % devex	10	10	10	10	10
First production	t 0	t 1	t 1	t 1	t 1
Tariff	£1.5/bbl	£1.5/bbl	£1.5/bbl	£1.5/bbl	£1.5/bbl

Table 8.2   Deterministic assumptions for cluster-type development

mmbbl	5	10	20	35	50
Devex $/bbl	8	4.5	4.5	4.5	4
Annual opex as % devex	8	9	9	7	7
Abandonment as % devex	8	8	8	7	7
First production	t 0	t 1	t 1	t 1	t 1
Tariff	£1.5/bbl	£1.5/bbl	£1.5/bbl	£1.5/bbl	£1.5/bbl

the sum of the returns to the fields in question when developed individually. The base price is $18 per barrel in real terms with sensitivities of $24 and $12. The results are shown in terms of net present values (NPVs) at various discount rates.

Results

In Figure 8.6 the comparative returns to the 10, 15 and 50 million barrels (mmbbl) fields are shown when developed individually and as a cluster under the $18 price. At 10 per cent discount rate the NPV for the cluster is over £100 million. With individual developments the combined return is less than £50 million. At 15 per cent discount rate the NPV for the cluster development is about £60 million, but only about £7 million for the sum of individual developments. At 20 per cent discount the NPV is plus £30 million for the cluster development, but minus £30 million for the individual developments.

From Figure 8.7 it is seen that at the $12 price the returns to the investments are generally negative irrespective of whether the fields are developed individually or as a cluster. The returns are much worse with individual development. From Figure 8.8 it is seen that at the $24 price the returns are substantially positive under both investment situations. The returns are significantly higher with the cluster developments.

Table 8.3 Common infrastructure of cluster

	Fields	Common infrastructure capacity	Common infrastructure devex	Common infrastructure annual opex	Common infrastructure decommissioning
3-field cluster	10, 20, 50 mmbbl	80	$1/bbl	2.5% of devex	17% of devex
5-field cluster	5, 10, 20, 35, 50 mmbbl	120	$0.8/bbl	2% of devex	18% of devex

Costs shared on a percentage of total reserves basis

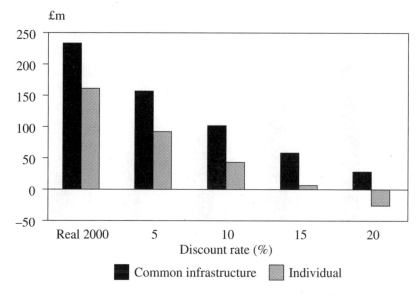

Figure 8.6   Post-tax NPV for three-field cluster (oil price $18/bbl)

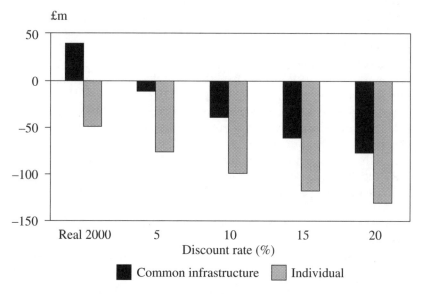

Figure 8.7   Post-tax NPV for three-field cluster (oil price $12/bbl)

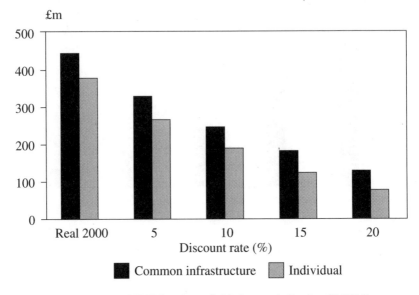

Figure 8.8   Post-tax NPV for three-field cluster (oil price $24/bbl)

Cost sensitivity is now considered. The results at $18 when field develop-
ment costs are increased by $1 per barrel are shown in Figure 8.9.
(Operating costs are also automatically increased because they are modelled in relation to investment costs.) It is seen that at 10 per cent discount
rate the NPV for the cluster development is plus £50 million while the sum
of the three individual developments is minus £20 million. At 15 per cent
discount rate the NPV is plus £8 million with the cluster development, but
minus £50 million with the three individual developments.

In Figure 8.10 the results are shown for the 5, 10, 25, 35 and 50 mmbbl
fields at the $18 price. At the 10 per cent discount rate the NPV with the
cluster development exceeds £150 million. For the five individual developments the NPVs run to £50 million. At the 15 per cent discount rate the
NPV for the cluster development is about plus £100 million. The individual developments produce a negative NPV. In Figure 8.11 the returns under
the $12 price are seen to be generally negative. In Figure 8.12 the returns
under the $24 price are substantially positive and are significantly higher
with the cluster development.

In Figure 8.13 the results of a cost sensitivity where field development
costs are increased by $1 per barrel are shown under the $18 price. At the
10 per cent discount rate the NPV for the cluster development is plus £80
million while for the sum of the individual field developments it is minus

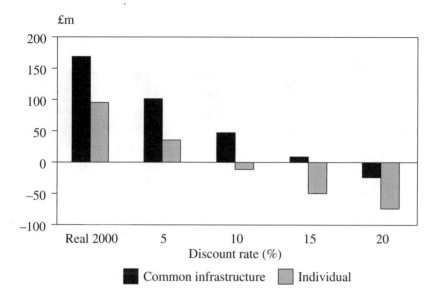

Figure 8.9   Post-tax NPV for three-field cluster field devex + $1/bbl (oil price $18/bbl)

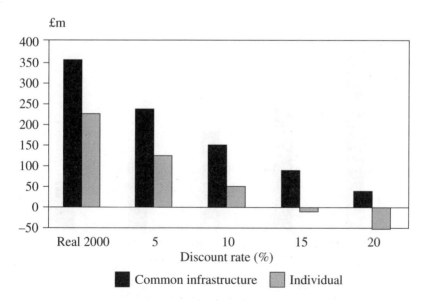

Figure 8.10   Post-tax NPV for five-field cluster (oil price $18/bbl)

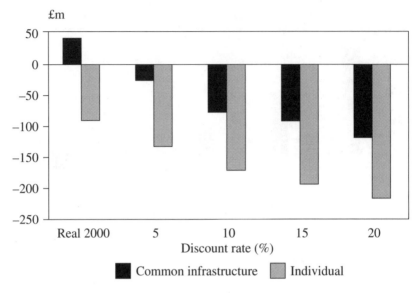

Figure 8.11   Post-tax NPV for five-field cluster (oil price $12/bbl)

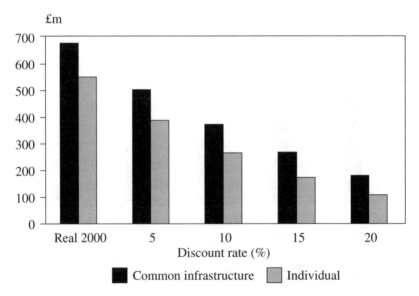

Figure 8.12   Post-tax NPV for five-field cluster (oil price $24/bbl)

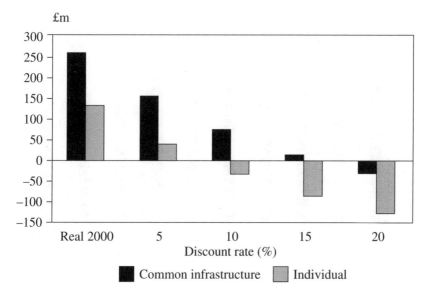

Figure 8.13   Post-tax NPV for five-field cluster field devex + $1/bbl (oil price $18/bbl)

£30 million. At the 15 per cent discount rate the NPV for the cluster development is plus £12 million, but minus £80 million for the sum of the five individual developments.

It was seen from Table 8.3 that the cost of the cluster common infrastructure depended on the capacity required. So far in the analysis all the fields have been developed simultaneously. The plateau production of all the fields overlaps, thus maximizing the required capacity for the combined reserves of the fields. The capacity cost could be reduced by staggering the development of the fields so that the plateau production from each did not coincide. Of course, if a field development is delayed, its NPV (to the original base year) is thereby reduced. The net effect of delaying the development of the 35 mmbbl field without any other changes is shown in Figure 8.14. In the left part of the figure the NPVs to the initial base year are shown for the five fields with delays introduced in the timing of the development of the 35 mmbbl field. The NPVs fall to a moderate extent. The next part of Figure 8.14 (with LC symbol) shows the returns when the reduced investment requirement for the common infrastructure is also included in the calculation. While this improves the return compared to the situation without the reduced investment cost, it remains the case that the 'early' development of all the fields is generally preferable at the 10 per cent discount rate despite the increased common infrastructure cost.

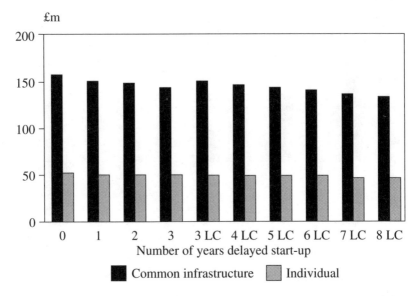

Figure 8.14   Post-tax NPV at 10 per cent for five-field cluster with delays for 35 mmbbl field (oil price $18/bbl)

In Figure 8.15 the results of the same exercise under the $12 price are shown. Generally delaying the development of the 35 mmbbl field reduces the losses (in NPV terms). In Figure 8.16 the results for the $24 price case are shown. They are consistent with those for the $18 case. The highest returns are obtained under the case where all fields are developed simulta-neously, despite the lower overall capital expenditure from delaying the development of one of the fields.

In Figure 8.17 the results for the case where field development costs are increased by $1 per barrel are shown under the $18 price case. The pattern of results remains the same as in other cases, with the most striking feature being the distinctly positive returns with the cluster development and neg-ative returns with individual field developments.

The main conclusions which can be drawn from the financial modelling are that under likely field development conditions in the UK North Sea, sig-nificant scale economies can be obtained from cluster developments com-pared to individual field developments. In some cases these benefits could be sufficient to produce positive returns where individual field develop-ments produce negative returns.

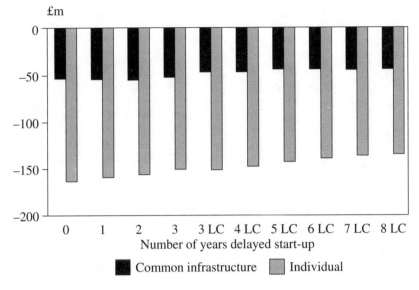

*Figure 8.15   Post-tax NPV at 10 per cent for five-field cluster with delays
for 35 mmbbl field (oil price $12/bbl)*

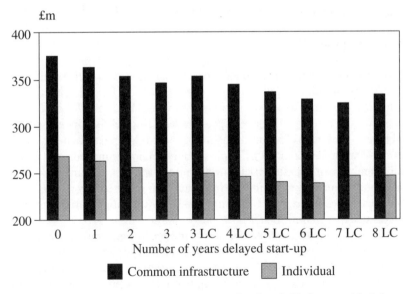

*Figure 8.16   Post-tax NPV at 10 per cent for five-field cluster with delays
for 35 mmbbl field (oil price $24/bbl)*

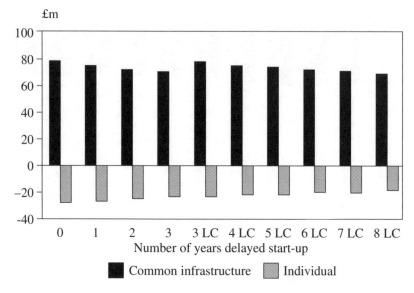

£m

Figure 8.17   Post-tax NPV at 10 per cent for five-field cluster with delays
for 35 mmbbl field devex + $1/bbl(oil price $18/bbl)

RISK SHARING WITH CLUSTER DEVELOPMENTS

Methodology and Data

A different possible benefit relates to the risk sharing which results from
investment in a cluster rather than individual fields. These benefits are con-
ceptually the same as those obtained from holding a portfolio of shares
compared to an individual one. The issue requiring detailed investigation is
whether in the realistic conditions of the North Sea these benefits of risk
diversification are substantial or not. Diversification reduces unique,
unsystematic, or specific risks, but not systematic risk. In principle diversification reduces risk rapidly at first and then more slowly as the size of
the portfolio is enlarged.[1] In the present study the oil price risk cannot be
diversified.

The approach adopted has been to conduct a comparative risk analysis
of the investments using the Monte Carlo technique. The key assumptions
are set out in Table 8.4. There are four stochastic variables, namely field
reserves, development costs, operating costs and oil price. The distribution
of field size is taken to be normal with a standard deviation (SD) of 30 per
cent of the mean. In addition minimum and maximum values are stipu-

Table 8.4   Assumptions for Monte Carlo analysis

Mean reserves (mmbbls)	5	10	20	35	50
SD 30%					
Minimum	0.5	1	2	3.5	5
Maximum	9.5	19	38	66.5	95
Mean devex ($/bbl)	8	4.5	4.5	4.5	4
SD 20%					
Minimum	3.2	1.8	1.8	1.8	1.6
Maximum	12.8	7.2	7.2	7.2	6.4
Annual opex (% of accum. devex)	8	0.09	0.09	0.07	0.07
SD 20%					
Minimum (%)	3	4	4	3	3
Maximum (%)	13	14	14	11	11
Mean oil price (real)	$18				
SD 40%					
Minimum	$8				
Maximum	$39.6				

lated. For field development costs the distribution is also taken to be normal with the SD equal to 20 per cent of the mean. Again, maximum and minimum values are specified. The distribution of field operating costs is also taken to be normal with the SD equal to 20 per cent of the mean. Minimum and maximum values are also specified. The oil price is taken to be mean reverting. The mean value is set at $18 (real terms) and the SD at 40 per cent of the mean. Minimum and maximum values are also specified.

To make meaningful comparisons of the risk position the distributions of the expected returns from cluster developments were compared with those from the individual fields. To the specific costs of the latter were added a share of the common infrastructure costs. This was related to the particular field's share of the total reserves of the member fields of the cluster. Emphasis was put on the distribution of NPVs. Risk in the statistical sense is often measured by the SD of the distribution. Because the mean values of the distributions of the NPV for the cluster will be much higher than those for the individual fields, meaningful comparisons cannot be made using this measure. Coefficients of variation can be used for this purpose and emphasis is given to these.

Results

In Figure 8.18 the distributions of NPVs at 10 per cent discount rate for the 10, 20 and 50 mmbbl fields are shown. The coefficients of variation are, respectively, 90, 73 and 66 per cent. In Figure 8.19 the results are shown at 15 per cent discount rate for the same three fields. The coefficients of variation are 126, 102 and 89 per cent. In Figure 8.20 the distributions of NPVs for the three-field cluster are shown. The coefficient of variation at 10 per cent discount rate is 50 per cent and at 15 per cent it is 61 per cent. The reductions in overall project risk as indicated by this measure are quite dramatic.

Risk is often considered in relation to the chance of making a loss. In the present context this is measured as the probability of the NPV being negative. The results of this calculation for the three individual fields and the cluster are also shown in Figures 8.18, 8.19 and 8.20. At 10 per cent discount rates for the 10, 20 and 50 mmbbl fields respectively, the probabilities are 13.5, 6.5 and 4.5 per cent. The probability of the cluster having a negative NPV is 1.5 per cent. At 15 per cent discount rate the probabilities of negative NPVs for the three fields are 22.5, 14.5 and 12.5 per cent. The probability of the cluster having a negative NPV is 3.5 per cent. The reduction in risk from the cluster development is quite noticeable.

Investors are also interested in upside potential. The Monte Carlo modelling obtained measures of this by calculating the probabilities of the internal rate of return (IRR) in real terms exceeding specified values. In Table 8.7 (below) the results are shown for IRRs of 20, 25, 40 and 50 per cent. For the 10 mmbbl field the respective probabilities are 67.4, 55.8, 23.6 and 11.2 per cent. For the 20 mmbbl field the probabilities are respectively, 70.7, 56.6, 17.2 and 7.6 per cent, and for the 50 mmbbl field they are 74.6, 58.4, 19.4 and 7.9 per cent. For the cluster development the corresponding probabilities of reaching the specified threshold returns are 76.6, 59.4, 14.6, and 4 per cent. These results indicate that the chances of the IRR exceeding 20 and 25 per cent are greater with the cluster development. For threshold IRRs of 40 and 50 per cent the probabilities are higher with the individual fields.

The analysis was repeated for the five-field cluster and its constituent fields. The results for the NPVs at 10 per cent discount rate for the five fields are shown in Figure 8.21. The coefficients of variations for the 10, 20, 50, 35, and 5 mmbbl fields are respectively 84, 68, 61, 75 and 201 per cent. For the five-field cluster the coefficient of variation is 47 per cent at 10 per cent discount rate (Figure 8.22). At 15 per cent discount the coefficients of variation relating to the five constituent fields are, respectively, 113, 92, 81, 100 and 348 per cent (Figure 8.23). The corresponding coefficient of variation

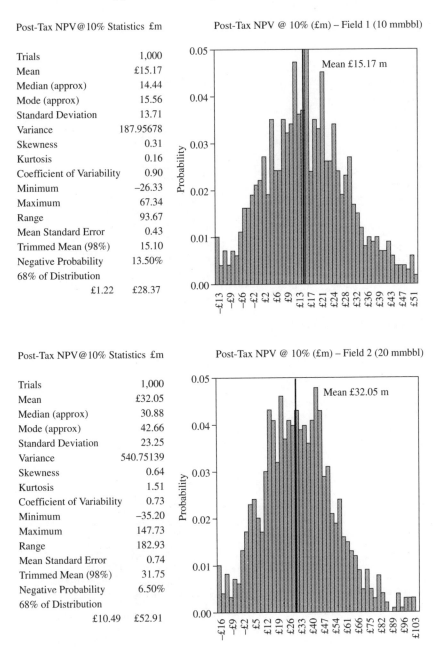

Post-Tax NPV@10% Statistics £m

Post-Tax NPV @ 10% (£m) – Field 1 (10 mmbbl)

Trials	1,000
Mean	£15.17
Median (approx)	14.44
Mode (approx)	15.56
Standard Deviation	13.71
Variance	187.95678
Skewness	0.31
Kurtosis	0.16
Coefficient of Variability	0.90
Minimum	−26.33
Maximum	67.34
Range	93.67
Mean Standard Error	0.43
Trimmed Mean (98%)	15.10
Negative Probability	13.50%
68% of Distribution	
£1.22	£28.37

Post-Tax NPV@10% Statistics £m

Post-Tax NPV @ 10% (£m) – Field 2 (20 mmbbl)

Trials	1,000
Mean	£32.05
Median (approx)	30.88
Mode (approx)	42.66
Standard Deviation	23.25
Variance	540.75139
Skewness	0.64
Kurtosis	1.51
Coefficient of Variability	0.73
Minimum	−35.20
Maximum	147.73
Range	182.93
Mean Standard Error	0.74
Trimmed Mean (98%)	31.75
Negative Probability	6.50%
68% of Distribution	
£10.49	£52.91

Figure 8.18   *Three-field cluster fields at 10 per cent (£m) (mean oil price $18 p/b)*

Post-Tax NPV@10% Statistics £m

Post-Tax NPV @ 10% (£m) – Field 3 (50 mmbbl)

Trials	1,000
Mean	£80.83
Median (approx)	76.02
Mode (approx)	48.04
Standard Deviation	53.33
Variance	2,843.63
Skewness	0.44
Kurtosis	0.02
Coefficient of Variability	0.66
Minimum	−66.11
Maximum	291.39
Range	357.50
Mean Standard Error	1.69
Trimmed Mean (98%)	80.35
Negative Probability	4.50%
68% of Distribution	
£26.67	£134.06

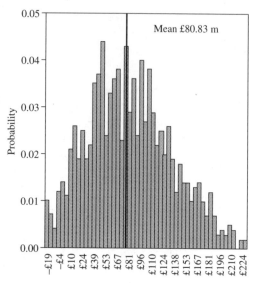

Figure 8.18   (continued)

Post-Tax NPV@15% Statistics £m

Post-Tax NPV @ 15% (£m) – Field 1 (10 mmbbl)

Trials	1,000
Mean	£9.61
Median (approx)	9.35
Mode (approx)	10.95
Standard Deviation	12.08
Variance	145.97677
Skewness	0.24
Kurtosis	0.16
Coefficient of Variability	1.26
Minimum	−31.28
Maximum	53.24
Range	84.52
Mean Standard Error	0.38
Trimmed Mean (98%)	9.57
Negative Probability	22.50%
68% of Distribution	
−£2.50	£21.19

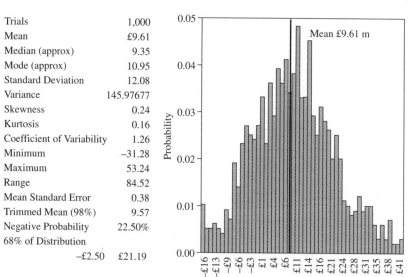

Figure 8.19   *Three-field cluster fields at 15 per cent (£m) (mean oil price $18 p/b)*

Post-Tax NPV@15% Statistics £m

Trials	1,000
Mean	£19.67
Median (approx)	18.62
Mode (approx)	26.60
Standard Deviation	20.10
Variance	404.11522
Skewness	0.55
Kurtosis	1.47
Coefficient of Variability	1.02
Minimum	−41.60
Maximum	119.50
Range	161.10
Mean Standard Error	0.64
Trimmed Mean (98%)	19.44
Negative Probability	14.50%
68% of Distribution	
£0.87	£37.32

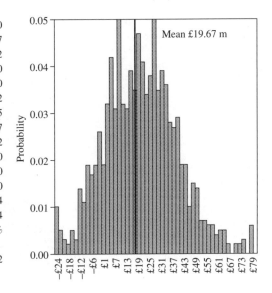

Post-Tax NPV @ 15% (£m) – Field 2 (20 mmbbl)

Post-Tax NPV@15% Statistics £m

Trials	1,000
Mean	£50.51
Median (approx)	46.37
Mode (approx)	61.57
Standard Deviation	45.00
Variance	2,025.34
Skewness	0.39
Kurtosis	0.05
Coefficient of Variability	0.89
Minimum	−84.97
Maximum	217.13
Range	302.11
Mean Standard Error	1.42
Trimmed Mean (98%)	50.21
Negative Probability	12.50%
68% of Distribution	
£5.40	£95.75

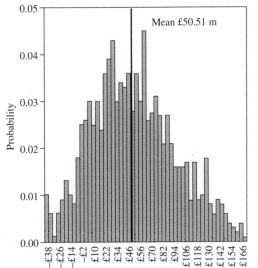

Post-Tax NPV @ 15% (£m) – Field 3 (50 mmbbl)

Figure 8.19 (continued)

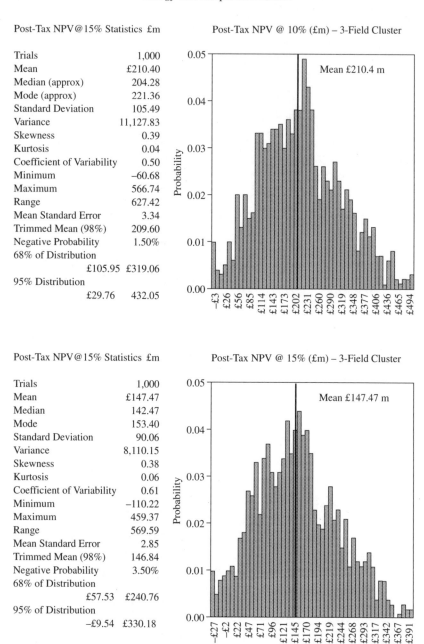

Post-Tax NPV@15% Statistics £m

Trials	1,000
Mean	£210.40
Median (approx)	204.28
Mode (approx)	221.36
Standard Deviation	105.49
Variance	11,127.83
Skewness	0.39
Kurtosis	0.04
Coefficient of Variability	0.50
Minimum	−60.68
Maximum	566.74
Range	627.42
Mean Standard Error	3.34
Trimmed Mean (98%)	209.60
Negative Probability	1.50%
68% of Distribution	
£105.95	£319.06
95% Distribution	
£29.76	432.05

Post-Tax NPV @ 10% (£m) – 3-Field Cluster

Mean £210.4 m

Post-Tax NPV@15% Statistics £m

Trials	1,000
Mean	£147.47
Median	142.47
Mode	153.40
Standard Deviation	90.06
Variance	8,110.15
Skewness	0.38
Kurtosis	0.06
Coefficient of Variability	0.61
Minimum	−110.22
Maximum	459.37
Range	569.59
Mean Standard Error	2.85
Trimmed Mean (98%)	146.84
Negative Probability	3.50%
68% of Distribution	
£57.53	£240.76
95% of Distribution	
−£9.54	£330.18

Post-Tax NPV @ 15% (£m) – 3-Field Cluster

Mean £147.47 m

Figure 8.20   Three-field cluster development (mean oil price $18 p/b)

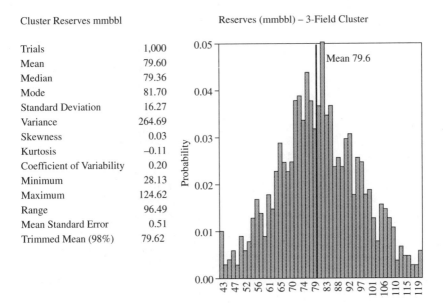

Cluster Reserves mmbbl	
Trials	1,000
Mean	79.60
Median	79.36
Mode	81.70
Standard Deviation	16.27
Variance	264.69
Skewness	0.03
Kurtosis	–0.11
Coefficient of Variability	0.20
Minimum	28.13
Maximum	124.62
Range	96.49
Mean Standard Error	0.51
Trimmed Mean (98%)	79.62

Figure 8.20   (continued)

for the cluster is 57 per cent. (A summary of the coefficient of variations is given in Table 8.5.) The results confirm the major reduction in risk as indicated by this measure.

The probabilities of the NPVs being negative were then examined (Table 8.6). At 10 per cent discount rate the chances of the 10, 20, 50, 35 and 5 mmbbl fields having negative NPVs are, respectively, 11.5, 4.5, 2.5, 4.5, and 31.5 per cent. The probability of the cluster having a negative return is 0.5 per cent. At 15 per cent discount rate the chances of the five fields having negative returns are, respectively, 19.5, 12.5, 8.5, 13.5, and 39.5 per cent. The probability of the cluster having a negative return is 2.5 per cent. There is clearly a large reduction in the downside risk from the cluster developments as a combined investment.

With respect to the upside potential, the chances of the IRR exceeding threshold levels of 20, 25, 40, and 50 per cent were again calculated. The results (Table 8.7) indicate that the chances of the 10 mmbbl field exceeding these hurdles are, respectively, 70.7, 59.2, 26.5 and 13.8 per cent. For the 20 mmbbl field the corresponding chances are 74.6, 61.3, 21.6 and 9.5 per cent. For the 50 mmbbl field they are 79.7, 64.4, 23.8 and 10.4 per cent. For the 35 mmbbl field they are 72.5, 57.5, 20 and 8.7 per cent. For the 5 mmbbl field they are 51.2, 41.9, 21.8 and 14.8 per cent. For the five-field cluster the

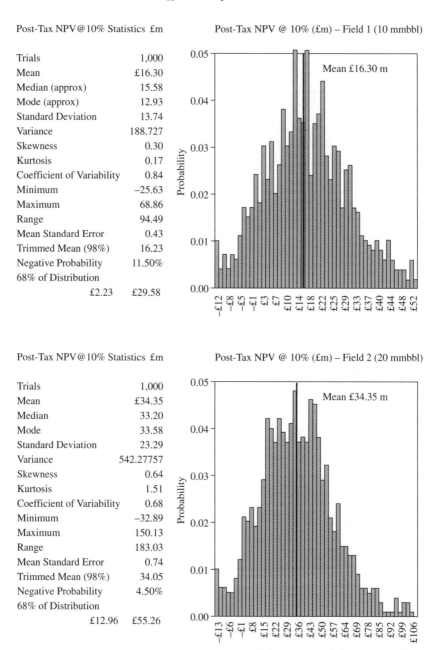

Post-Tax NPV @ 10% Statistics £m

Trials	1,000
Mean	£16.30
Median (approx)	15.58
Mode (approx)	12.93
Standard Deviation	13.74
Variance	188.727
Skewness	0.30
Kurtosis	0.17
Coefficient of Variability	0.84
Minimum	−25.63
Maximum	68.86
Range	94.49
Mean Standard Error	0.43
Trimmed Mean (98%)	16.23
Negative Probability	11.50%
68% of Distribution	
£2.23	£29.58

Post-Tax NPV @ 10% (£m) – Field 1 (10 mmbbl)

Post-Tax NPV @ 10% Statistics £m

Trials	1,000
Mean	£34.35
Median	33.20
Mode	33.58
Standard Deviation	23.29
Variance	542.27757
Skewness	0.64
Kurtosis	1.51
Coefficient of Variability	0.68
Minimum	−32.89
Maximum	150.13
Range	183.03
Mean Standard Error	0.74
Trimmed Mean (98%)	34.05
Negative Probability	4.50%
68% of Distribution	
£12.96	£55.26

Post-Tax NPV @ 10% (£m) – Field 2 (20 mmbbl)

Figure 8.21   Five-field cluster fields at 10 per cent (mean oil price $18 p/b)

Post-Tax NPV@10% Statistics £m

Trials	1,000
Mean	£86.42
Median	81.97
Mode	50.00
Standard Deviation	53.15
Variance	2,824.463
Skewness	0.43
Kurtosis	0.01
Coefficient of Variability	0.61
Minimum	−61.47
Maximum	295.65
Range	357.13
Mean Standard Error	1.68
Trimmed Mean (98%)	85.93
Negative Probability	2.50%
68% of Distribution	
£32.69	£140.61

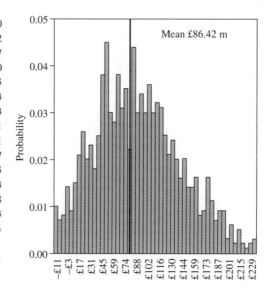

Post-Tax NPV @ 10% (£m) – Field 3 (50 mmbbl)

Post-Tax NPV@10% Statistics £m

Trials	1,000
Mean	£58.90
Median	52.55
Mode	60.16
Standard Deviation	44.18
Variance	1,951.90
Skewness	0.80
Kurtosis	0.71
Coefficient of Variability	0.75
Minimum	−31.30
Maximum	245.74
Range	277.04
Mean Standard Error	1.40
Trimmed Mean (98%)	58.21
Negative Probability	4.50%
68% of Distribution	
£15.94	£101.74

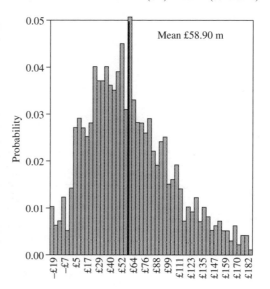

Post-Tax NPV @ 10% (£m) – Field 4 (35 mmbbl)

Figure 8.21   (continued)

Post-Tax NPV@10% Statistics £m

Trials	1,000
Mean	£4.52
Median	3.68
Mode	1.98
Standard Deviation	9.09
Variance	82.71
Skewness	0.64
Kurtosis	0.88
Coefficient of Variability	2.01
Minimum	−22.31
Maximum	40.27
Range	62.57
Mean Standard Error	0.29
Trimmed Mean (98%)	4.43
Negative Probability	31.50%
68% of Distribution	
−£3.76	£12.86

Post-Tax NPV @ 10% (£m) – Field 5 (5 mmbbl)

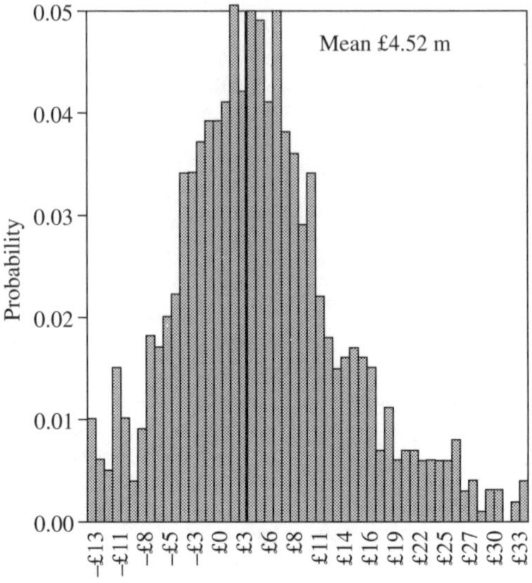

Figure 8.21   (continued)

Post-Tax NPV@15% Statistics £m

Trials	1,000
Mean	£10.68
Median (approx)	10.45
Mode (approx)	11.94
Standard Deviation	12.10
Variance	146.42204
Skewness	0.24
Kurtosis	0.16
Coefficient of Variability	1.13
Minimum	−30.49
Maximum	54.62
Range	85.12
Mean Standard Error	0.38
Trimmed Mean (98%)	10.64
Negative Probability	19.50%
68% of Distribution	
−£1.48	£22.32

Post-Tax NPV @ 15% (£m) – Field 1 (10 mmbbl)

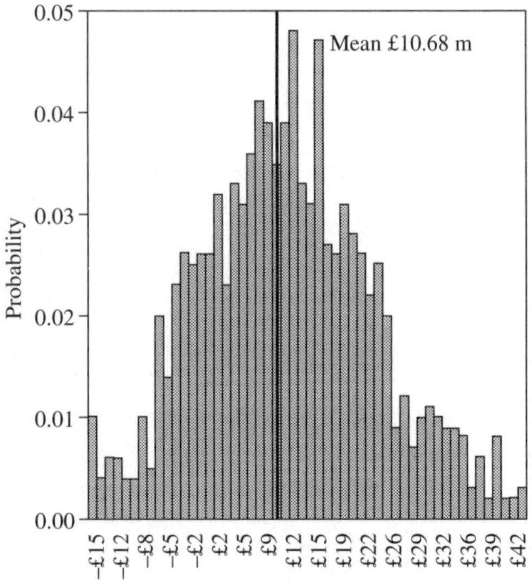

Figure 8.22   Five-field cluster fields at 15 per cent (mean oil price $18 p/b)

Post-Tax NPV@15% Statistics £m

Trials	1,000
Mean	£21.82
Median)	21.09
Mode	28.86
Standard Deviation	20.12
Variance	404.75064
Skewness	0.55
Kurtosis	1.47
Coefficient of Variability	0.92
Minimum	−39.40
Maximum	121.72
Range	161.12
Mean Standard Error	0.64
Trimmed Mean (98%)	21.60
Negative Probability	12.50%
68% of Distribution	
£2.90	£39.47

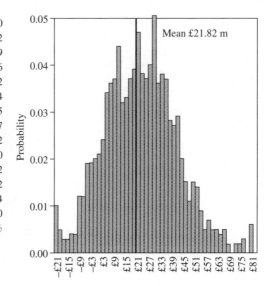

Post-Tax NPV@15% Statistics £m

Trials	1,000
Mean	£55.72
Median (approx)	52.27
Mode (approx)	59.46
Standard Deviation	44.87
Variance	2,013.58
Skewness	0.39
Kurtosis	0.04
Coefficient of Variability	0.81
Minimum	−82.18
Maximum	221.07
Range	303.25
Mean Standard Error	1.42
Trimmed Mean (98%)	55.42
Negative Probability	8.50%
68% of Distribution	
£10.54	£101.91

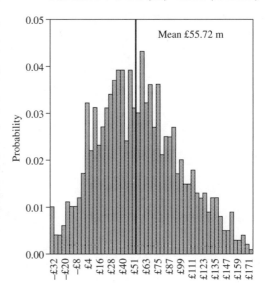

Figure 8.22   (continued)

Post-Tax NPV@15% Statistics £m

Trials	1,000
Mean	£37.49
Median	32.11
Mode	17.96
Standard Deviation	37.64
Variance	1,416.54
Skewness	0.81
Kurtosis	0.91
Coefficient of Variability	1.00
Minimum	−51.91
Maximum	202.74
Range	454.65
Mean Standard Error	1.19
Trimmed Mean (98%)	36.93
Negative Probability	13.50%
68% of Distribution	
£2.31	£73.41

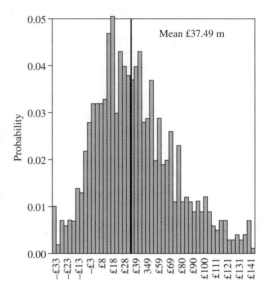

Post-Tax NPV @ 15% (£m) – Field 4 (35 mmbbl)

Mean £37.49 m

Post-Tax NPV@15% Statistics £m

Trials	1,000
Mean	£2.43
Median (approx)	1.76
Mode (approx)	2.18
Standard Deviation	8.44
Variance	71.24
Skewness	0.51
Kurtosis	0.74
Coefficient of Variability	3.48
Minimum	−23.21
Maximum	33.94
Range	57.15
Mean Standard Error	0.27
Trimmed Mean (98%)	2.36
Negative Probability	39.50%
68% of Distribution	
−£5.18	£10.25

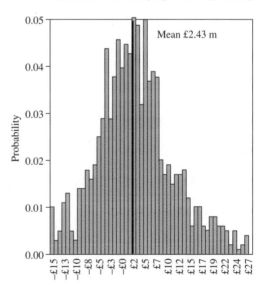

Post-Tax NPV @ 15% (£m) – Field 5 (5 mmbbl)

Mean £2.43 m

Figure 8.22   (continued)

Post-Tax NPV@10% Statistics £m

Trials	1,000
Mean	£327.06
Median (approx)	314.02
Mode (approx)	346.17
Standard Deviation	154.73
Variance	23,939.96
Skewness	0.47
Kurtosis	0.23
Coefficient of Variability	0.47
Minimum	−86.50
Maximum	929.46
Range	1,015.96
Mean Standard Error	4.89
Trimmed Mean (98%)	325.68
Negative Probability	0.50%
68% of Distribution	
	£170.29 £486.71
95% of Distribution	
	£64.77 £656.96

Post-Tax NPV @ 10% (£m) – 5-Field Cluster

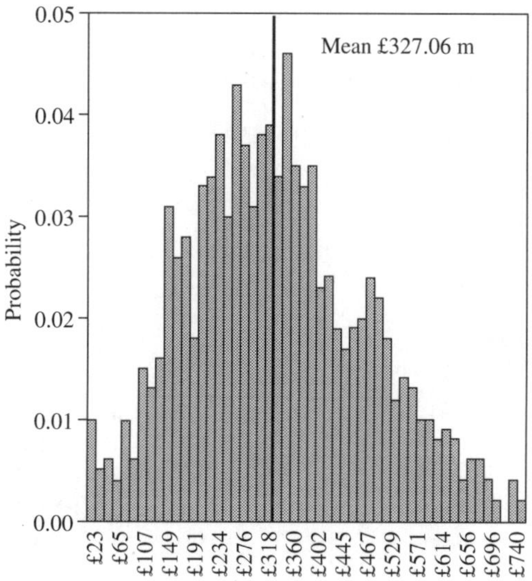

Mean £327.06 m

Post-Tax NPV@15% Statistics £m

Trials	1,000
Mean	£232.80
Median	220.74
Mode	223.44
Standard Deviation	133.59
Variance	17,846.89
Skewness	0.46
Kurtosis	0.26
Coefficient of Variability	0.57
Minimum	−123.45
Maximum	744.71
Range	868.15
Mean Standard Error	4.22
Trimmed Mean (98%)	231.60
Negative Probability	2.50%
68% of Distribution	
	£98.66 £368.61
95% of Distribution	
	£0.77 £520.23

Post-Tax NPV @ 15% (£m) – 5-Field Cluster

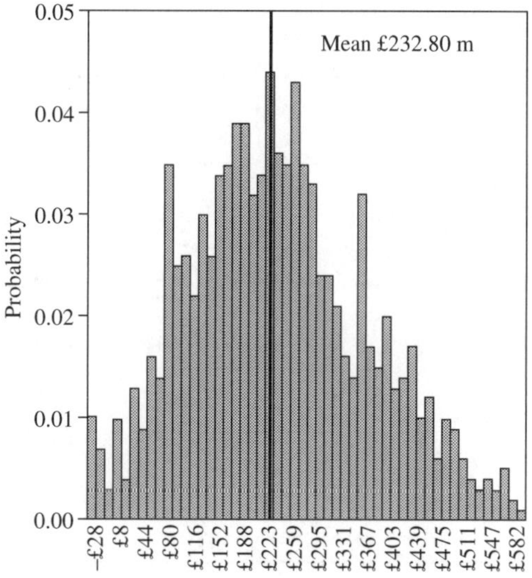

Mean £232.80 m

Figure 8.23   Five-field cluster development (mean oil price $18 p/b)

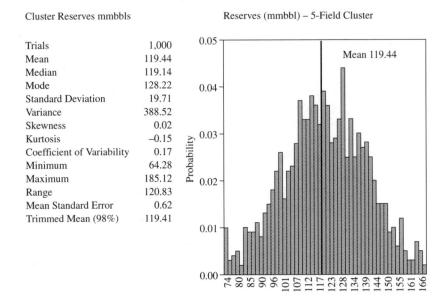

Cluster Reserves mmbbls

Trials	1,000
Mean	119.44
Median	119.14
Mode	128.22
Standard Deviation	19.71
Variance	388.52
Skewness	0.02
Kurtosis	−0.15
Coefficient of Variability	0.17
Minimum	64.28
Maximum	185.12
Range	120.83
Mean Standard Error	0.62
Trimmed Mean (98%)	119.41

Figure 8.23   (continued)

Table 8.5   Coefficients of variation

	NPV at 10%	NPV at 15%		NPV at 10%	NPV at 15%
3-field cluster	0.5	0.61	5-field cluster	0.47	0.57
Field 1 (10 mmbbl)	0.9	1.26	Field 1 (10 mmbbl)	0.84	1.13
Field 2 (20 mmbbl)	0.73	1.02	Field 2 (20 mmbbl)	0.68	0.92
Field 3 (50 mmbbl)	0.66	0.89	Field 3 (50 mmbbl)	0.61	0.81
			Field 4 (35 mmbbl)	0.75	1
			Field 5 (5 mmbbl)	2.01	3.48

Table 8.6   Probability of negative NPV

	NPV at 10%	NPV at 15%		NPV at 10%	NPV at 15%
3-field cluster	1.5%	3.5%	5-field cluster	0.5%	2.5%
Field 1 (10 mmbbl)	13.5%	22.5%	Field 1 (10 mmbbl)	11.5%	19.5%
Field 2 (20 mmbbl)	6.5%	14.5%	Field 2 (20 mmbbl)	4.5%	12.5%
Field 3 (50 mmbbl)	4.5%	12.5%	Field 3 (50 mmbbl)	2.5%	8.5%
			Field 4 (35 mmbbl)	4.5%	13.5%
			Field 5 (5 mmbbl)	31.5%	39.5%

corresponding probabilities are 80.4, 63.5, 16.5 and 4.9 per cent. The conclusion is that there is a greater chance of obtaining an IRR of 20 per cent and above with the cluster compared to any of the five fields individually. The cluster investment also produces a better chance of achieving an IRR of 25 per cent or more than is likely to be attainable on four of the five fields. The chances of the cluster development producing an IRR in excess of 40 or 50 per cent are less with the cluster than with any of the individual fields.

POSSIBLE SCHEMES FOR SHARING COMMON INFRASTRUCTURE COSTS AND THEIR PROBLEMS

To obtain the benefits of shared infrastructure costs and risk sharing it is necessary to devise a scheme to execute the sharing among the licensees in the various fields. It is most likely that there will be separate licensees in the different fields. Even where the same licensees have interests in the different fields, it is most unlikely that the interests of any one company would be the same in the different fields. These factors create complications in the determination of efficiently functioning contractual arrangements among the various licensees. Some possible schemes are outlined in this section, their problems examined, and some solutions proposed.[2]

The first scheme is where the licensees in each field pay a share of the common infrastructure investment costs equal to their respective share of the capacity. In practice this will equate to the corresponding share of reserves. The common infrastructure operating costs are paid for in relation to each field's share of capacity actually used.

Table 8.7   Probability of IRR greater than percentages shown

	20%	25%	40%	50%
5-field cluster	80.4%	63.5%	16.5%	4.9%
Field 1 (10 mmbbl)	70.7%	59.2%	26.5%	13.8%
Field 2 (20 mmbbl)	74.6%	61.3%	21.6%	9.5%
Field 3 (50 mmbbl)	79.7%	64.4%	23.8%	10.4%
Field 4 (35 mmbbl)	72.5%	57.5%	20.0%	8.7%
Field 5 (5 mmbbl)	51.2%	41.9%	21.8%	14.8%

	20%	25%	40%	50%
3-field cluster	76.6%	59.5%	14.6%	4.0%
Field 1 (10 mmbbl)	67.4%	55.8%	23.6%	11.2%
Field 2 (20 mmbbl)	70.7%	56.6%	17.2%	7.6%
Field 3 (50 mmbbl)	74.6%	58.4%	19.4%	7.9%

This type of scheme has some appeal in terms of equity. In practice there are some problems. The common infrastructure has to be financed before reserves of the respective fields are fully known. Where there are different ownership interests involved, conflicts of interest with respect to initial reserves determination can emerge. Of course, re-determinations of reserves can be made through time, and consequential modifications made to ownership interests in fields and thus in the common infrastructure ownership. But such modifications may be costly, and, where recalculation of the cost contributions made in the past is required, difficult problems of compensation arise for parties who had in the event overpaid their cost share.

With respect to the common infrastructure costs, problems arise regarding their equitable sharing in the (very likely) circumstances when different fields in the cluster cease production at different times.

A second scheme involves a modification to the first one with respect to common operating costs. These are shared on a throughput (per barrel) basis. Some of the problems referred to above clearly apply to this scheme as well.

A third possible scheme is where one company finances all the common infrastructure costs. All the other investors then pay tariffs to the asset owner. These tariffs would cover the development and operating costs. There are problems of appropriate tariff determination. The asset owner may feel that he or she, having incurred the investment costs and risks, should levy tariffs reflecting these risks. He or she might try to levy tariffs which would in effect collect a share of any expected economic rents from the fields. Other licensees may feel that the appropriate tariff should cover the costs with only a utility rate of return. There is plenty of scope for differences of view on this matter, and clearly there is a potential conflict of interest among the parties involved.

Under a fourth scheme all licensees would pay a share of the common infrastructure investment costs based on capacity or reserves. Tariffs based on throughput would then be payable by all parties. The revenues would initially be used to cover the common infrastructure operating costs. The remainder of the tariff revenues would be distributed among the different owners of the common infrastructure. The levels of tariff would be set such that, at a minimum, they covered all the investment and operating costs. The scheme is designed to reflect the comparative contributions which each participant makes to the infrastructure.

A principal problem of this scheme relates to tariff determination, especially in the (likely) case where there are different interest shares in the cluster fields. The issues raised with respect to the first and second schemes also arise.

In practice a cluster development could take place where all the fields are developed simultaneously, but it is more likely that field developments will be sequential. The phasing of the fields could vary by several years. The four schemes with their associated problems discussed above can apply to both simultaneous and sequential developments. With the latter, further issues arise which require resolution. Possible solutions are now discussed.

Under a fifth scheme all investors pay a share of the infrastructure investment and operating costs as in the second scheme discussed above. Additional provisions would then be made such that the 'early' field owners compensate 'late' field owners by sharing production from the 'early' fields with them. The amount of the compensation would be related to the relative timing of the 'early' and 'late' field developments.

The problems requiring solution include all those of the second scheme discussed above. In addition there are others relating to the terms of the compensation for the 'late' field owner. Such compensation could be in oil or cash. The amount would depend on what discount rate is appropriate to reflect equitable compensation. There is plenty of scope for differing views on this matter. A technical tax problem could arise for the 'early' producer. He or she may be faced with a tax burden on the production which is in effect transferred to the 'late' producer.

This suggests a tax modification which would in essence introduce tax changes similar to those which were granted in the 1980s for gas banking schemes. This would become a sixth possible scheme. The other problem areas discussed above remain.

A seventh scheme would be the same as the second one except that the investors in the 'late' fields are given a discount on their contribution to the common infrastructure costs. As well as the problem areas discussed in relation to the second scheme, the determination of the appropriate discount requires solution. The question of the rate of discount which should reflect the difference in timing of the field developments is a key issue.

An eighth scheme would base the common infrastructure costs on the present value of the reserves. Common infrastructure operating costs would be shared in accordance with each investor's share of the capacity employed. The problems here lie in the determination of the respective reserves before they are developed. Additionally, the discount rate to reflect the differences in timing has to be determined.

The problems discussed above can be solved. But their resolution may well be very time consuming and project executions thereby delayed. Solution of the problems is clearly easier if the potential conflicts of interest are eliminated or at least reduced. This can be achieved by asset transactions among the investors in the various fields to bring about unitization of interests in the cluster. This means that any one investor would have the same interest in each of the fields. (An extreme case would be where that share was 100 per cent.) Unitization of interests would produce a much better alignment of incentives and greatly reduce any potential conflicts of interest.

There are several requirements for the achievement of unitized interests. First, investors must be willing to trade assets to the extent necessary. Different investors may well have diverging views about the prospects relating to the different fields. While this creates scope for asset transactions it is not necessarily in the direction of producing interest unitization. Preemption rights of existing licensees may hinder transactions. A further requirement is the ability of the respective parties to trade assets to the extent required. Thus investors who should increase their share will have to fund the required investment and may have capital constraints which restrict their ability to execute the deal. Until recently there was a capital gains tax problem inhibiting asset transactions. The rollover relief enacted in 1999 for capital gains tax has significantly reduced the net cost of asset transactions. Other government/industry initiatives, particularly LIFT and DEAL, also help to facilitate asset transactions.

Unitization of field interests will not only reduce conflicts of interest and thus facilitate infrastructure cost sharing, but ensure that the risk-sharing benefits are also secured. These are separate advantages.

SUMMARY AND CONCLUSIONS

The further pace of development of oil and gas in the UKCS depends upon the extent to which the many small fields already discovered can be developed. When viewed as individual investments, many of these are unlikely to be viable. This prompts the notion that a group of fields might be developed jointly to reduce the unit costs. Joint developments could produce worthwhile economies of scale in circumstances where a common infrastructure incorporating a manifold and other associated equipment was employed.

In current conditions for much of the North Sea the most likely development concepts are with subsea completion production systems tied back to existing major infrastructure for processing and onward transportation. There are constraints on the distances over which such developments can be technically and economically undertaken. A mapping exercise was undertaken on all the known fields (278) which do not yet have announced firm development plans. The exercise consisted in the examination of the possible numbers, sizes and locations of potential cluster developments using a common infrastructure, involving their transportation via a common pipeline to further major infrastructure. The initial screening involved the calculation of the numbers of feasible clusters given the current constraints on the distances over which such developments can take place.

The main finding of the initial screening exercise was that there are substantial numbers of clusters in the SNS, CNS and NNS worthy of more detailed examination. Sometimes an undeveloped field was clearly closer to major infrastructure than to the hub of a possible cluster, and thus it is not clear without detailed examination whether such fields are potential members of the cluster. For this reason no clusters are exhibited in the Irish Sea, but it is interesting to note that the Undeveloped Fields Group of PILOT has indicated that two potential clusters in that area are still worthy of examination.

The analysis of the potential economies from the employment of a common infrastructure was undertaken with respect to field sizes and costs which will be typical of the next generation of fields in the UK North Sea. These are generally smaller than the cluster developments which have already been undertaken. It was found that the economies from using a common infrastructure were typically substantial. Under low oil price conditions or very high cost conditions the returns to the cluster development could remain positive in circumstances where the return to investments developed on an individual field basis became negative.

The analysis of the potential risk-sharing benefits of cluster developments found that the total project risks were significantly reduced when the investment was viewed as a cluster rather than individual, separate investments. Further, the downside risks to investors were substantially less when the developments were viewed on a cluster basis. With respect to upside potential, the cluster developments produced higher probabilities of quite attractive rates of return compared to individual investments. Only at very high threshold rates of return were the probabilities of their achievement greater with individual investments compared to the cluster development. The analysis clearly indicates that the risk-sharing benefits indicated by portfolio theory function on a substantial scale in typical North Sea investment conditions.

Cluster developments with common infrastructure require agreements among the various field owners regarding the sharing of the costs involved. A large variety of arrangements is possible including joint ownership of the infrastructure with different possible schemes of charging for its use, and various forms of tariff arrangements, where one party takes the lead role in infrastructure provision. The infrastructure has to be provided in advance of full knowledge of the reserves in the different fields. Where ownership interests differ, this can create conflicts of interest. All the problems are multiplied when the field developments are on a sequential rather than simultaneous basis. In such circumstances the owners of 'late' fields may feel that their contribution to common infrastructure costs should be reduced in relation to that of the owners of 'early' fields.

There is obvious virtue in devising schemes for infrastructure cost sharing which minimize the potential conflicts of interest among the different field investors. This can be achieved by the unitization of field interests whereby one investor has the same share in each of the member fields. To achieve this involves some requirements of investors, particularly (a) a willingness to trade assets, and (b) an ability to finance such deals. The rollover relief for capital gains tax reduces the net cost of such transactions. The LIFT and DEAL schemes should also contribute positively to the achievement of asset transactions. Pre-emption rights of existing licensees may retard asset trading.

The overall conclusion is that cluster developments can make a worthwhile contribution to furthering the development of the UKCS. The benefits from (a) infrastructure cost sharing and (b) project risk sharing can both be substantial. Unitization of field interests can ensure that these benefits are maximized.

NOTES

1. For a discussion of the principle, see chapter 7 of Brealey and Myers (1991).
2. For a full discussion of the schemes including financial modelling of their operation, see Kemp and Stephen (1995).

REFERENCES

Brealey, R.A. and Myers, S.C. (1991), *Principles of Corporate Finance*, London, UK: McGraw-Hill.
Kemp, A.G. and Stephen, L. (1995), *The Economics of Infrastructure Cost Sharing with Cluster Type Developments in the UKCS*, Aberdeen, UK: University of Aberdeen, Department of Economics, North Sea Study Paper No. 53.

9. Modelling underlying energy demand trends

Lester C. Hunt, Guy Judge and Yasushi Ninomiya

INTRODUCTION

This chapter analyses the problems of modelling the underlying energy demand trend (UEDT) when estimating energy demand models. In particular, it emphasizes the need to ensure that a flexible approach is adopted so that the UEDT captures the important influences on energy demand, in addition to the conventional economic variables such as income and price. As Colin Robinson pointed out when writing in a book on energy demand:

> Most of the other chapters in this volume are concerned with the analysis of the past. That is a fascinating subject, but in practical terms, the main value of historical analysis lies in any guide it gives to what may happen in the future. That guidance is always imperfect and sometimes positively misleading. However, in the absence of direct information about the future, the past is the only indicator we have of possible future events. (Robinson, 1992, p. 215)

Our approach is consistent with his view in that a flexible approach to modelling the UEDT ensures that as much information as possible from the past is employed to fully understand the past and hence enhance future projections. Moreover, it emphasizes the importance of correctly specifying the demand function to ensure that the most accurate estimate of the price elasticity of energy demand is obtained. This is particularly important at a time when energy and environmental policy is focused on reducing emissions. If, as found in this study, the price elasticity of energy demand is relatively small then using market mechanisms such as energy taxes, on their own, may not achieve the desired aim – instead, non-market restrictions and regulations may also be needed.

This chapter therefore demonstrates the importance for energy demand modelling of allowing for UEDTs that are stochastic in form.[1] Inherent underlying trends may be non-linear and reflect not only technical progress, which usually produces greater energy efficiency, but also other factors such as changes in consumer tastes and the economic structure that may be working in the opposite direction to technical progress. To illustrate the models, demand functions are estimated for the UK whole economy (aggregate energy) and the UK transportation sector (oil). In addition, it is shown that unless energy demand models are formulated to allow for stochastic trends and seasonals, estimates of price and income elasticities could be seriously biased.

The next section describes the UEDT in detail, briefly touching upon evolving seasonal patterns, followed by a section explaining the econometric methodology. The penultimate section presents the results for the whole economy and the transportation sector followed by a summary and overall conclusion.

'TECHNICAL PROGRESS' AND THE 'UNDERLYING ENERGY DEMAND TREND'

The concept of 'technical progress', when incorporated into energy demand functions, is an important one. It is vital that it is clearly defined and understood. Energy is a *derived demand*, not demanded for its own sake, but for the services it produces in combination with the capital and appliance stock in place at any particular point in time. Therefore, the amount of energy actually consumed in order to obtain the desired level of services depends on the given level of technology embodied in energy appliances. Moreover, the level of technology embedded will have come about through a combination of endogenous and exogenous factors (which are expanded upon below). However, it is argued here that it is not only 'technical progress' that influences energy demand trends; other (exogenous) factors will also influence energy usage, both positively and negatively. The more general concept of the UEDT is therefore introduced, which is illustrated in Table 9.1 and described in more detail below. Given this concept, it is important that the method employed to capture the UEDT is sufficiently flexible to incorporate all of these effects and ensure that potential biases are not introduced into the price and income elasticity estimates.

Autonomous or exogenous 'technical progress' in energy usage can result from a number of factors such as environmental pressures and regulations,

Table 9.1   Underlying energy demand trend

(Pure) Technical energy efficiency		Consumer tastes	Economic structure
Endogenous	Exogenous	Exogenous	Exogenous

and mandated energy efficiency standards. All of these lead to a shift of the
energy demand curve to the left, thus reducing energy consumption at a
given level of income and price (Kouris, 1983b).[2]

It is often argued that in addition to the exogenous factors, 'technical
progress' or improvement in energy efficiency is induced by sustained price
rises (Walker and Wirl, 1993). Or, as argued previously, induced by price
'shocks' above the 'normal bounds' of price changes (Hunt et al., 2000).
Either way, as Jones (1994) emphasizes, it is important to distinguish
between the normal 'price' effects (as measured by the price elasticity of
demand) and the 'endogenous technical progress' effect. Moreover, it is
important that the irreversible nature of the 'technical progress' effect is
recognized and not allowed to bias the (symmetric) price elasticities. In
summary, therefore, the endogenous technical progress referred to in Table
9.1 will be price induced resulting in a (permanent) shift of the energy
demand curve to the left, but is distinct from the normal price effect represented by the price elasticity of demand.

It is further argued, however, that the induced changes in 'technical
progress' can also come about as a result of increases in income or output
(Hunt et al., 2000).[3] In the short run, this will bring about an increase in
energy demand with the given appliance and capital stock (and could be
quite significant before households and firms have time to adjust their stock
of appliances). Over time, however, new and more efficient appliances will
be installed and existing appliances replaced faster than they would be otherwise. Hence, similar to the price effect, a distinction needs to be made
between the long-run income effect and the technical progress effect. The
increase in income will, in the long run, bring about an increase in the
demand for energy (as new appliances and stock are acquired) which represents the long-run income effect. Furthermore, the increase in income may
also induce the replacement of the existing stock of capital with 'upgraded'
more efficient models and hence an irreversible improvement in energy efficiency (and a shift to the left of the (income) energy demand curve).

In addition to the above, it is argued that it is important to capture the
other exogenous factors identified in Table 9.1. The first is *consumer tastes*.
As mentioned above, change in consumer tastes could, *ceteris paribus*,
result in a reduction in the demand for energy.[4] However, it is equally plausible that it could result in an increase in energy demand and hence work in
the opposite direction to the traditional 'technical progress' effect. For
example, it is well known that the efficiency of cars has improved over the
last couple of decades. This will reduce, *ceteris paribus*, the consumption of
energy in the transportation sector. However, this is outweighed by an
increase in demand brought about by an underlying increase in transportation demand. This has been caused by the growth in car size and engine

power and a worsening of traffic conditions in urban areas. Consequently, car fleet fuel intensity has hardly changed. In addition, there has been a shift from public transport to (more energy intensive) private cars (Schipper et al., 1992, p. 123).[5]

In addition, when estimating aggregate energy demand functions, whether at the whole economy or sectoral level, the UEDT will be affected by a change in the *economic structure*. At the whole economy level, a switch from, say, manufacturing to services will affect the aggregate demand for energy. This change is not induced by changes in aggregate output and/or prices but the switch from a sector with a certain level of energy intensity to another sector with a different level of intensity. If therefore, the UEDT is not included, or is modelled inadequately, these changes will be forced to be picked up by the activity and price variables resulting in biased estimates of the income and price elasticities. This equally applies to a change in structure within sectors, for example, the changes over time of the subsectors of manufacturing.

Given this discussion it is important to consider how the UEDT should be captured. The most common procedure in energy demand studies is to utilize a simple linear time trend as an approximation (to 'technical progress'), including the studies by Barker (1995), and Erdogan and Dahl (1997).

The appropriateness or otherwise of utilizing a simple linear time trend is discussed by Beenstock and Willcocks (1981, 1983) who used a linear time trend as a proxy for technical progress. They openly admit that it is not a satisfactory measure but it is better than just ignoring the matter since in their opinion there is undoubtedly technical progress in energy usage (1981, p. 227). However, Kouris (1983a, 1983b) has argued strongly against using a time trend as an approximation for technical progress. He argues that technical progress is an important factor that has always been very difficult to quantify unless a satisfactory way of measuring this phenomenon can be found. Therefore, a simple linear time trend is hardly able to capture its dynamic impact. Moreover, according to Kouris (1983a), most of technical progress is induced by price changes rather than exogenous autonomous technical progress and, thus, technical progress cannot be separated from the long-run price elasticity. Welsch (1989) however, suggests that Kouris's argument leads to *negative* technical progress if the price of energy falls, which he argues is counterintuitive (p. 286).

There is not, therefore, a general consensus concerning the use of a simple time trend to capture 'technical progress'. Moreover, when considering the wider definition of the UEDT that encompasses 'technical progress' and other factors, it would be imprudent, as Kouris argues, to attempt to model it by a simple linear time trend. It is feasible to expect that the UEDT will be non-linear with periods when it could be upward sloping *and/or* periods when it could be downward sloping.[6] Thankfully, recent advances in econometric techniques allow for a much more flexible and general approach. The structural time-series model developed by Harvey and his associates (see for example, Harvey et al., 1986; Harvey, 1989; Harvey and Scott, 1994; and Harvey, 1997) allows for a non-linear stochastic trend that, when used in estimates of energy demand functions, overcomes most, if not all, of the problems discussed above. Moreover, the use of the simple deterministic time trend becomes a limiting case that is present only if statistically accepted by the data.

Before turning to the estimation it is important to consider the possible biases that might exist if the UEDT is not modelled adequately. The failure to model technical progress adequately will result in an overestimate of the 'true' (absolute) price elasticity of demand. This can be clearly seen in Figure 9.1a.[7] Point A represents the initial equilibrium point given the long-run demand curve D_0, price level of P_0, and energy consumption E_0. When the price increases to P_1, energy demand falls to E_1, represented by point B. It is this reduction in demand that represents the 'true' long-run price effect that would come about by changing consumption patterns given the existing energy appliance stock, for example, reducing travel by private car, switching off lights more frequently, lowering central heating temperature and so on (all of which could be reversed if prices fell again). If the UEDT is negative (possibly induced by an 'abnormal' or 'substantial' price rise but also possibly by any combination of the other exogenous factors discussed above) then the demand curve shifts to the left at D_1. Hence, the new equilibrium is represented at point C with energy demand reducing further to E_2; the 'true' UEDT effect is the fall from E_1 to E_2. However, if the estimation procedure ignores the UEDT, the estimated price effect will be from E_0 to E_2 and hence will *overestimate* the price elasticity of demand.

It is important, however, to recognize that this is only one source of bias and it depends on the assumption that the price is rising and that the UEDT is negative as conventionally assumed, whereas the price elasticity can be both negatively and positively biased depending on whether the price is rising or falling and the UEDT is negative or positive. Figure 9.1 also illustrates the alternative biases that may exist for the price effects. Figure 9.1b shows that if the price rises but the UEDT is positive (upward sloping) then the price elasticity will be underestimated if the UEDT is ignored.[8] Figure 9.1c shows that if the price falls but the UEDT is negative (downward sloping) then the price elasticity will be underestimated if the UEDT is ignored.[9] Finally, Figure 9.1d shows that if the price falls but the UEDT is positive (upward sloping) then the price elasticity will be overestimated if the UEDT is ignored.

It is equally important to recognize that similar biases will occur when estimating the income elasticity of demand. Figure 9.2 illustrates the

(a) Negative UEDT (downward sloping) and price rise

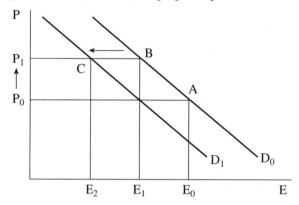

$E_0 - E_1$ = Price effect
$E_1 - E_2$ = UEDT effect
$E_0 - E_2$ = Estimated price effect if UEDT is not modelled
Therefore, price elasticity may be overestimated if UEDT is not incorporated in the model.

(b) Positive UEDT (upward sloping) and price rise

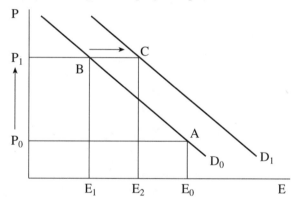

$E_0 - E_1$ = Price effect
$E_1 - E_2$ = UEDT effect
$E_0 - E_2$ = Estimated price effect if UEDT is not modelled
Therefore, price elasticity may be underestimated if UEDT is not incorporated in the model.

Figure 9.1   Possible biases in estimated price elasticities of energy demand

(c) Negative UEDT (downward sloping) and price decline

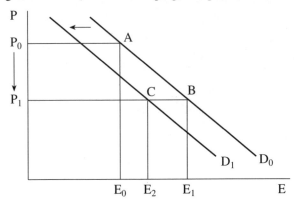

$E_0 - E_1$ = Price effect
$E_1 - E_2$ = UEDT effect
$E_0 - E_2$ = Estimated price effect if UEDT is not modelled
Therefore, price elasticity may be underestimated if UEDT is not incorporated in the model.

(d) Positive UEDT (upward sloping) and price decline

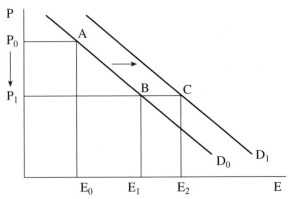

$E_0 - E_1$ = Price effect
$E_1 - E_2$ = UEDT effect
$E_0 - E_2$ = Estimated price effect if UEDT is not modelled
Therefore, price elasticity may be overestimated if UEDT is not incorporated in the model.

Figure 9.1   (continued)

(a) Negative UEDT (downward sloping) and income rise

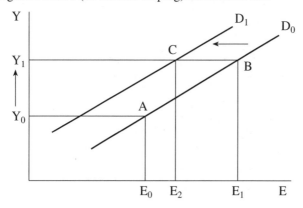

$E_0 - E_1$ = Income effect
$E_1 - E_2$ = UEDT effect
$E_0 - E_2$ = Estimated income effect if UEDT is not modelled
Therefore, income elasticity may be underestimated if UEDT is not incorporated in the model.

(b) Positive UEDT (upward sloping) and income rise

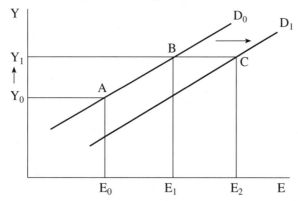

$E_0 - E_1$ = Income effect
$E_1 - E_2$ = UEDT effect
$E_0 - E_2$ = Estimated income effect if UEDT is not modelled
Therefore, income elasticity may be overestimated if UEDT is not incorporated in the model.

Figure 9.2   Possible biases in estimated income elasticities of energy demand

(c) Negative UEDT (downward sloping) and income decline

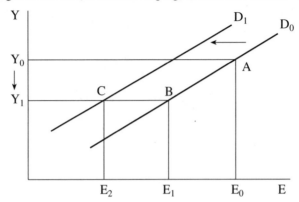

$E_0 - E_1$ = Income effect
$E_1 - E_2$ = UEDT effect
$E_0 - E_2$ = Estimated income effect if UEDT is not modelled
Therefore, income elasticity may be overestimated if UEDT is not incorporated in the model.

(d) Positive UEDT (upward sloping) and income decline

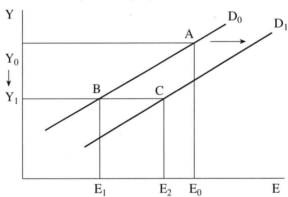

$E_0 - E_1$ = Income effect
$E_1 - E_2$ = UEDT effect
$E_0 - E_2$ = Estimated income effect if UEDT is not modelled
Therefore, income elasticity may be underestimated if UEDT is not incorporated in the model.

Figure 9.2   (continued)

possible biases if the UEDT is not modelled adequately. Figure 9.2a shows that if the income is rising and the UEDT is negative (downward sloping) then the income elasticity will be underestimated if the UEDT is ignored. Figure 9.2b shows that if income is rising and the UEDT is positive (upward sloping) then the income elasticity will be overestimated if the UEDT is ignored. Figure 9.2c shows that if income is falling and the UEDT is negative (downward sloping) then the income elasticity will be overestimated if the UEDT is ignored. Finally, Figure 9.2d shows that if income is falling and the UEDT is positive (upward sloping) then the income elasticity will be underestimated if the UEDT is ignored.

The above discussion illustrates the importance of adequately modelling the UEDT which encompasses the 'technical progress' effect. Given the various influences underpinning the UEDT and hence its expected non-linear (positive and/or negative) nature it should be modelled in the most 'general' or 'flexible' way possible.[10] Moreover, given that in addition prices (and sometimes income) will be falling as well as rising, the resultant biases will vary throughout the estimation period if the UEDT is excluded or modelled inadequately by a simple linear time trend.

METHODOLOGY

Over recent years energy demand modelling has been dominated by the cointegration technique (as discussed in Hendry and Juselius, 2000 and 2001) with 'technical progress' either ignored or approximated by a deterministic time trend.

The over-reliance on the cointegration technique has been questioned (for example, see Maddala and Kim, 1998, pp. 487–8). In particular, Harvey (1997) heavily criticizes the cointegration methodology as unnecessary and/or a misleading procedure due, among other things, to its poor statistical properties.[11] He proposes instead, 'to combine the flexibility of a time series model with the interpretations of regression' and argues that this is 'exactly what is done in the structural time series approach' (p. 200).

Given the discussion in the previous section, a technique is required that allows the UEDT to be modelled in a general and flexible way, and Harvey's structural time-series approach is an ideal tool in these circumstances. Such an approach allows for an unobservable trend that is permitted to vary stochastically over time. Thus the UEDT may be highly non-linear and have periods when it is upward sloping, downward sloping or flat. Moreover, the deterministic linear trend (or no trend at all) is a restricted case of the more general model. Thus, the restricted model is preferred only if it is accepted by the data.

Therefore, the structural time-series model can be combined with an autoregressive distributed lag (ADL) to estimate energy demand functions. This framework allows for both a stochastic trend and stochastic seasonality when estimating the price and income elasticities of aggregate energy demand:

$$A(L)\, e_t = \mu_t + \gamma_t + B(L)\, y_t + C(L)\, p_t + \theta TEMP_t + \varepsilon_t \qquad (9.1)$$

where $A(L)$ is the polynomial lag operator $1 - \phi_1 L - \phi_2 L^2 - \phi_3 L^3 - \phi_4 L^4$, $B(L)$ the polynomial lag operator $\pi_0 + \pi_1 L + \pi_2 L^2 + \pi_3 L^3 + \pi_4 L^4$, and $C(L)$ the polynomial lag operator $\varphi_0 + \varphi_1 L + \varphi_2 L^2 + \varphi_3 L^3 + \varphi_4 L^4$. e_t is the natural logarithm of energy for the appropriate sector, y_t the natural logarithm of the activity variable of the appropriate sector, p_t the natural logarithm of the real price of energy for the appropriate sector, and $TEMP_t$ the average temperature. $B(L)/A(L)$ and $C(L)/A(L)$ represent the long-run activity and price elasticities, respectively, and θ represents the effect of a change in temperature on aggregate energy demand. μ_t is the stochastic trend, γ_t is the stochastic seasonal variation and ε_t is a random white noise disturbance term.[12]

The trend component μ_t is assumed to have the following stochastic process:

$$\mu_t = \mu_{t-1} + \beta_{t-1} + \eta_t \qquad (9.2)$$

$$\beta_t = \beta_{t-1} + \xi_t \qquad (9.3)$$

where $\eta_t \sim NID(0, \sigma_\eta^2)$ and $\xi_t \sim NID(0, \sigma_\xi^2)$. Equations (9.2) and (9.3) represent the *level* and the *slope* of the trend, respectively, and depend upon the variances σ_η^2 and σ_ξ^2, known as the *hyperparameters*. These hyperparameters have an important role in that they govern the shape of the estimated trend model. Table 9.2 illustrates the various trends that can be estimated from this process. Cell (ix) of Table 9.2 represents the most general model when $\sigma_\eta^2 \neq 0$ and $\sigma_\xi^2 \neq 0$ so that both the *level* and *slope* of the trend change stochastically over the sample period. The remaining cells of Table 9.2 represent possible restricted alternatives, depending upon the estimates of the *level* and *slope* of the trend and the hyperparameters, σ_ξ^2 and σ_η^2.[13]

Cells (i), (ii) and (v) illustrate the conventional regression models (ignoring evolving seasonals) that are special cases of the general stochastic trend models. When both variances are zero, namely $\sigma_\eta^2 = 0$ and $\sigma_\xi^2 = 0$, the model reverts to a conventional deterministic linear trend model, cell (v), as follows:[14]

Table 9.2 *Classification of possible stochastic trend models*

Slope	Level		
	No level $lvl = 0, \sigma_\eta^2 = 0$	Fixed level $lvl \neq 0, \sigma_\eta^2 = 0$	Stochastic level $lvl \neq 0, \sigma_\eta^2 \neq 0$
No slope $slp = 0, \sigma_\xi^2 = 0$	(i) Conventional regression but with no constant and no time trend	(ii) Conventional regression with a constant but no time trend	(iii) Local level model (random walk plus noise)
Fixed slope $slp \neq 0, \sigma_\xi^2 = 0$	(iv)	(v) Conventional regression with a constant and a time trend	(vi) Local level model with drift
Stochastic slope $slp \neq 0, \sigma_\xi^2 \neq 0$	(vii)	(viii) Smooth trend model	(ix) Local trend model

Note: The seasonal component is omitted at this stage for simplicity.

$$e_t = \alpha + \beta t + \mathbf{Z}'_t \delta + \varepsilon_t \qquad (9.4)$$

Cells (iii), (vi) and (viii) are restricted versions of the general stochastic trend model but still involve some form of stochastic trend in the level or slope. If $\sigma_\eta^2 \neq 0$ but $\sigma_\xi^2 = 0$, the trend is the local level model with drift provided the slope is non-zero (slp$\neq$0), cell (vi) or the local level model (random walk plus noise) if there is no slope (slp$=$0), cell (iii). If, however, $\sigma_\eta^2 = 0$ but $\sigma_\xi^2 \neq 0$ it is the smooth trend model, cell (viii).

The seasonal component γ_t in equation (9.1) has the following stochastic process:

$$S(L)\gamma_t = \omega_t \qquad (9.5)$$

where $\omega_t \sim NID(0, \sigma_\omega^2)$ and $S(L) = 1 + L + L^2 + L^3$. The conventional case (ignoring the stochastic trend) is again a restricted version of this when the hyperparameter $\sigma_\omega^2 = 0$, with γ_t reducing to the familiar deterministic seasonal dummy variable model. If not, however, seasonal components are moving stochastically over time.

The equations to be estimated therefore consist of equation (9.1) with (9.2) (9.3) and (9.5). All the disturbance terms are assumed to be independent and mutually uncorrelated with each other. As seen above, the hyperparameters σ_η^2, σ_ξ^2, σ_ω^2 and σ_ε^2 have an important role to play and govern the basic properties of the model. The hyperparameters, along with the other parameters of the model, are estimated by maximum likelihood and from these the optimal estimates of β_T, μ_T and γ_T are estimated by the Kalman filter which represent the latest estimates of the *level* and *slope* of the trend and the seasonal components. The optimal estimates of the trend and seasonal components over the whole sample period are further calculated by the smoothing algorithm of the Kalman filter. For model evaluation, equation residuals are estimated (which are estimates of the equation disturbance term, similar to those from ordinary regression) plus a set of auxiliary residuals. The auxiliary residuals include smoothed estimates of the equation disturbance (known as the irregular residuals), the smoothed estimates of the level disturbances (known as the level residuals) and smoothed estimates of the slope disturbances (known as the slope residuals).[15] The software package STAMP 5.0 (Koopman et al., 1995) is used to estimate the energy demand models.

In practice therefore, the general model, equation (9.1), is estimated initially, and a suitable restricted model selected by testing down from the overparameterized model of equation (9.1) which satisfies parameter restrictions without violating a battery of diagnostic tests. In addition, following Harvey and Koopman (1992), normality, kurtosis and skewness statistics for the auxiliary residuals are examined in order to identify outliers and structural breaks and, if necessary, appropriate dummies are included in the models.

A number of checks are undertaken to ensure the acceptability and robustness of the stochastic formulations. First, the stochastic elements are restricted to their deterministic form and/or omitted. This generates six 'general specifications' being initially estimated as follows:

Specification I: Stochastic trend and stochastic seasonals (as discussed above)
Specification II: Stochastic trend and deterministic seasonals
Specification III: Deterministic trend and stochastic seasonals
Specification IV: Deterministic trend and deterministic seasonals
Specification V: No trend and stochastic seasonals
Specification VI: No trend and deterministic seasonals

Each specification is estimated using the general to specific approach as outlined above for specification I. The results therefore indicate the appropriateness of the stochastic specifications. Moreover, they illustrate the impact on the estimated price and income elasticities of any misspecification by assuming a deterministic trend or no trend at all.

Second, (where appropriate) the preferred models for each specification are re-estimated and tested, via likelihood ratio (LR) tests, for the following restrictions:

1. deterministic seasonal dummies;
2. a deterministic time trend; and
3. a deterministic time trend with deterministic seasonal dummies.

This acts as a further check of the stochastic specifications to ensure that they are always accepted by the data.

RESULTS

To illustrate the approach, quarterly unadjusted data for 1971q1–1997q4 are used to estimate an aggregate energy demand function for the UK whole economy and an oil demand function for the UK transportation sector. Data for 1972q1–1995q4 are used to estimate the models; the first four observations are lost due to the four-period lag in the general model and eight observations (for 1996 and 1997) are retained for post-sample prediction tests.

Whole Economy Aggregate Energy Demand

The results for specifications I–VI for the whole economy are given in Table 9.3 (details of the definitions and sources of the data are given in the appendix). Note, each specification has been found individually by following the general to specific procedure outlined in the previous section; therefore, Table 9.3 gives the preferred models for each specification.

For all specifications, GDP (y), the real energy price (p), and air temperature (*TEMP*) are significant drivers of whole economy aggregate energy demand. In addition, the auxiliary residuals for the irregular component indicate that there is a significant impulse shock in energy demand in the first quarter of 1974 – reflecting the first oil crisis and the effect of the UK miners' strike. To capture this outlier, an impulse dummy variable for 1974q1 is included in all specifications, which is always significant. No other signs of outliers or structural breaks were found.

The diagnostic statistics presented in Table 9.3 show that specifications I and II are clearly preferred since the residuals are white noise without any signs of mis-specification; furthermore, these specifications predict well, clearly passing the post-sample prediction tests. On the other hand, specifications III–VI, which include one or more deterministic components, not only suffer from severe autocorrelation, but also consistently fail the prediction tests, even at the 1 per cent level of significance. These signs of mis-specification cannot be removed from specifications III–VI regardless of the number of additional lagged variables.[16] In addition, the LR tests (where applicable) indicate that the stochastic form of the trend is always preferred by the data when they are restricted to being deterministic. Overall, therefore, these results suggest that the stochastic formulation of the UEDT is necessary for the appropriate modelling of UK whole economy aggregate energy demand.

The stochastic seasonal component appears to play a relatively small role; however, other than specification III, the LR tests (where applicable) indicate that the stochastic seasonals are preferred by the data. In particular, the LR test (a) for specification I indicates that the deterministic restriction on the stochastic seasonal is invalid. Overall, this clearly suggests that the specification that includes both the stochastic trend and the stochastic seasonals (I) is preferred by the data.

The estimated elasticities for the different specifications in Table 9.3 are quite different. The long-run income elasticities estimated by the models without any trend (specifications V and VI) are zero. The estimated long-run income elasticities from specifications I–VI are much higher, at around 0.6. This is a clear example of the biased estimated elasticities discussed earlier, which may be brought about by ignoring the UEDT when it should

Table 9.3 Estimated results for UK whole economy energy demand, 1972q1–1995q4

	Specifications					
	(I) Stochastic trend and stochastic seasonals	(II) Stochastic trend and deterministic seasonals	(III) Deterministic trend and stochastic seasonals	(IV) Deterministic trend and deterministic seasonals	(V) No trend and stochastic seasonals	(VI) No trend and deterministic seasonals
Estimated coefficients						
y_t	0.6847** (5.934)	0.8096** (7.316)	0.4705** (4.941)	0.5234** (5.437)		
y_{t-3}	−0.2256* (2.095)	−0.2992** (2.822)	−0.3366** (2.480)	−0.4032** (3.367)		
$\Delta_3 y_t$					0.2955** (3.306)	0.4066** (4.446)
y_{t-4}			0.2340 (1.909)	0.2960** (2.658)		
p_{t-3}	−0.1897** (3.880)	−0.2050** (3.979)	−0.1963** (7.549)	−0.2031** (7.456)	−0.2359** (10.196)	−0.2673** (10.877)
e_{t-1}	0.1848** (3.330)	0.1124* (2.202)	0.3269** (5.661)	0.2731** (4.829)	0.4137** (6.966)	0.3111** (5.173)
$TEMP_t$	−0.0239** (12.117)	−0.0242** (12.005)	−0.0231** (10.179)	−0.0235** (10.131)	−0.0221** (9.221)	−0.0229** (8.955)
$Irr 1974q1$	−0.0764** (4.470)	−0.0761** (4.226)	−0.1001** (4.894)	−0.0990** (4.703)	−0.0974** (4.624)	−0.0987** (4.326)
Long-run estimates						
Income (Y)	0.5632	0.5750	0.5465	0.5725	0	0
Price (P)	−0.2327	−0.2309	−0.2917	−0.2794	−0.4024	−0.3879

155

Table 9.3 (continued)

	Specifications					
	(I) Stochastic trend and stochastic seasonals	(II) Stochastic trend and deterministic seasonals	(III) Deterministic trend and stochastic seasonals	(IV) Deterministic trend and deterministic seasonals	(V) No trend and stochastic seasonals	(VI) No trend and deterministic seasonals
Estimated hyperparameters						
$\sigma_\varepsilon^2 \times 10^{-4}$	1.489	1.969	3.214	3.606	3.442	4.411
$\sigma_\eta^2 \times 10^{-4}$	0.341	0.401	0	0	0	0
$\sigma_\xi^2 \times 10^{-4}$	0	0	0	0	0	0
$\sigma_\omega^2 \times 10^{-4}$	0.094	0	0.055	0	0.136	0
Nature of trend						
Corresponding cell of Table 9.2	Local level with drift (Cell vi)	Local level with drift (Cell vi)	A linear trend (Cell v)	A linear trend (Cell v)	No trend (Cell ii)	No trend (Cell ii)
Average annual growth rate of the estimated UEDT						
1972q1–1995q4	−0.76%	−0.85%	−0.73%	−0.82%	0%	0%
1972q1–1974q4	−0.44%	−0.44%	−0.73%	−0.82%	0%	0%
1975q1–1979q4	−0.64%	−0.67%	−0.73%	−0.82%	0%	0%
1980q1–1984q4	−1.26%	−1.44%	−0.73%	−0.82%	0%	0%
1985q1–1989q4	−0.95%	−1.07%	−0.73%	−0.82%	0%	0%
1990q1–1995q4	−0.42%	−0.48%	−0.73%	−0.82%	0%	0%

Diagnostics

Equation residuals						
Standard error	1.68%	1.65%	1.82%	1.78%	1.99%	2.00%
Normality	0.35	0.82	2.39	1.60	0.19	0.03
Kurtosis	0.35	0.41	0.00	0.06	0.00	0.00
Skewness	0.00	0.41	2.39	1.54	0.19	0.02
H(30)/H(31)	0.91	0.99	0.97	1.28	0.75	0.54
r(1)	−0.07	−0.03	0.24*	0.27**	0.24*	0.28**
r(4)	0.04	0.12	0.29**	0.33**	0.28**	0.40**
r(8)	0.02	0.04	0.14	0.17	0.11	0.21*
DW	2.12	2.03	1.47	1.42	1.48	1.37
$Q_{(x,n)}$	$Q_{(8,6)} = 6.21$	$Q_{(8,7)} = 4.62$	$Q_{(8,7)} = 34.34$**	$Q_{(8,8)} = 40.62$**	$Q_{(8,7)} = 35.36$**	$Q_{(8,8)} = 51.62$**
R^2	0.99	0.99	0.99	0.99	0.98	0.98
R^2_s	0.84	0.84	0.81	0.82	0.77	0.77

Auxiliary residuals

Irregular						
Normality	0.67	2.83	0.57	0.37	0.23	0.04
Kurtosis	0.30	0.02	0.37	0.26	0.11	0.02
Skewness	0.38	2.81	0.20	0.10	0.11	0.03
Level						
Normality	0.75	0.11	n/a	n/a	n/a	n/a
Kurtosis	0.00	0.00	n/a	n/a	n/a	n/a
Skewness	0.74	0.11	n/a	n/a	n/a	n/a
Slope						
Normality	n/a	n/a	n/a	n/a	n/a	n/a
Kurtosis	n/a	n/a	n/a	n/a	n/a	n/a
Skewness	n/a	n/a	n/a	n/a	n/a	n/a

Table 9.3 (continued)

		Specifications				
	(I) Stochastic trend and stochastic seasonals	(II) Stochastic trend and deterministic seasonals	(III) Deterministic trend and stochastic seasonals	(IV) Deterministic trend and deterministic seasonals	(V) No trend and stochastic seasonals	(VI) No trend and deterministic seasonals
Predictive tests (1996Q1–1997Q4)						
$\chi^2_{(8)}$	9.62	14.06	23.55**	25.66**	24.15**	25.64**
Cusum t	1.34	1.20	4.34***	4.30***	4.40***	4.34***
LR tests						
Test (a)	4.25*	n/a	2.23	n/a	7.50**	n/a
Test (b)	28.27**	29.67**	n/a	n/a	n/a	n/a
Test (c)	33.92**	n/a	n/a	n/a	n/a	n/a

Notes:

$\Delta_3 y_t$ denotes $y_t - y_{t-3}$.

t-statistics from STAMP 5.0 are given in parentheses.

** Indicates significant at the 1% level and * indicates significance at the 5% level.

Normality is the Bowman–Shenton statistic, approximately distributed as $\chi^2_{(2)}$.

Skewness statistic is approximately distributed as $\chi^2_{(1)}$.

H(30) is the test for heteroscedasticity, approximately distributed as $F_{(30, 30)}$.

r(1), r(4) and r(8) are the serial correlation coefficients at the 1st, 4th and 8th lags, respectively, approximately distributed as N(0,1/T).

DW is the Durbin–Watson test for first-order autocorrelation.

$Q_{(x,n)}$ is the Box–Ljung Q-statistics based on the first xth residuals autocorrelation and distributed as $\chi^2_{(n)}$.

R^2 is the coefficient of determination.

R_s^2 is the coefficient of determination based on the differences around the seasonal mean (see Harvey, 1989, p. 268).

$\chi^2_{(8)}$ is the post-sample predictive failure test.

Cusum t is the test of parameter consistency, approximately distributed as the t-distribution.

The restrictions imposed for the LR test are explained in the text.

be included.[17] Given the shape of the estimated UEDT for specification I (see Figure 9.3 below) it is not surprising that there is no great divergence between the estimated long-run income elasticities for specifications I–IV; the UEDT, in this case, can be reasonably approximated by a deterministic trend. In a similar fashion, the estimated long-run price elasticity does not vary considerably between specifications I and IV. However, the estimates for specifications V and VI, without a trend at all, are larger (in absolute terms). This is another example of biased estimates caused by inappropriate modelling of the UEDT.[18]

It is useful to discuss the shape of the UEDT for the preferred specification (I) in some detail. It is the local level with drift trend (cell (vi) of Table 9.2). It includes a stochastic trend level with a fixed slope. The estimated UEDT has a clear 'downward' shape over the period driven entirely by the stochastic movement of the level as illustrated in the top right-hand chart of Figure 9.3. This implies that the UEDT in the energy demand declined almost continuously, even after controlling for the income and price effects. However, looking more closely at the top left-hand chart of Figure 9.3, it can be seen that there was a substantial decline during the early 1980s towards the mid-1980s, but the decline diminished in the late 1980s and the early 1990s. The different estimated average annual growth rates of the UEDT over various subperiods are summarized in Table 9.3, and this emphasizes the non-linearity of the UEDT. In summary, therefore, the UEDT generally declines, but *not* at a fixed rate as the conventional deterministic model assumes.

Evolution of the stochastic seasonal component is illustrated in the bottom half of Figure 9.3. Although its stochastic movement is relatively moderate in contrast to the estimated UEDT, it is observed that the demand in the first and the second quarters gradually increased and decreased respectively over time, suggesting that conventional seasonal dummies are too restrictive. Not surprisingly, the LR test (a) rejects the restriction of deterministic dummies in favour of the stochastic formulation as seen in Table 9.3.

Table 9.4 summarizes some previous estimates of long-run energy demand elasticities for the UK whole economy. It can be seen that the estimates from our preferred specification, of 0.56 and −0.23 for the income and price elasticity, respectively, fall in the middle of those given in Table 9.4. Of all the studies given in Table 9.4 only Welsch (1989) includes a time trend as a proxy for the UEDT, the other studies all ignoring it completely. The inclusion of a deterministic time trend is considered as an important issue by Welsch. Although the estimated long-run income and price elasticities are 0.71 and −0.11, which are somewhat different from the estimates obtained here,[19] the results are still consistent with those here: that is, when

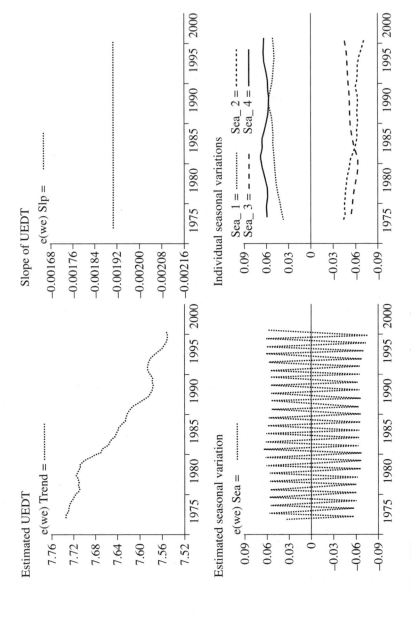

Figure 9.3   UK whole economy aggregate energy demand

Table 9.4 Previous energy demand studies for UK whole economy aggregated energy demand

Study (years)	Technique / model used	Data used	Estimated long-run income and price elasticities
Westoby and Pearce (1984)	Dynamic log-linear (manufacturing output/GDP ratio included)	Annual data 1954–80 (27 obs.)	$\eta_y = 0.760$ $\eta_p = -0.210$ No trend included
Welsch (1989)	Static/dynamic log-linear reduced form by OLS	Annual data 1970–84 (15 obs.)	$\eta_y = 0.71$ $\eta_p = -0.11$ Trend included but no details given
Hunt and Manning (1989)	Log-linear EG 2-step	Annual data 1967–86 (20 obs.)	$\eta_y = 0.38$ to 0.49 $\eta_p = -0.30$ to 0.33 No trend included
Hunt and Witt (1995)	Johansen–VECM	Annual data 1967–94 (28 obs.)	$\eta_y = 0.23$ $\eta_p = -0.29$ No trend included

Note: η_y = the long-run income elasticity, η_p = the long-run price elasticity.

Sources: Hunt and Lynk (1992), Atkinson and Manning (1995), Fouquet (1996) and Clements and Madlener (1999) with some additions and modifications.

the trend (deterministic or stochastic) is completely ignored, a lower income elasticity and a higher price elasticity (in absolute terms) are generated. Welsch argues that the lower price elasticity implies that energy efficiency improvement is mostly induced by autonomous technical progress rather than being price induced, and a higher income elasticity is led by the separation between pure income effect and technical progress effect (p. 290). This is a case where the deterministic time trend acts as a reasonable approximation of the UEDT – as illustrated above.

Transport Oil Demand

Table 9.5 reports the estimated results for all six specifications for UK transportation oil demand. Unlike for the whole economy, there are no autocorrelation problems, with all specifications passing the diagnostic tests presented. However, specifications II, IV and VI, with deterministic seasonals, all fail the post-sample prediction tests, thus indicating that stochastic seasonals are necessary for the oil transportation demand.[20]

The results for specifications I and II (with a stochastic trend) are the most parsimonious with a lag of only one quarter on y required to capture the adjustment to the long run. Specifications III and VI (with a deterministic trend) need the largest number of lagged variables with complex dynamics. Specifications V and VI also have a rather complex lag structure with the temperature variable insignificant and hence excluded – in contrast to the other specifications.

In determining the preferred specification for transportation oil demand, those with deterministic seasonal dummies (II, IV and VI) are rejected given their poor forecasting performance. The choice is therefore between specification I with a stochastic trend, specification III with a deterministic trend and specification VI with no trend (all with stochastic seasonals). There is little to choose between these specifications in terms of the diagnostics. However, specification I with the stochastic trend is preferred given that it is the most parsimonious of the models and more importantly the LR tests (a) and (c) clearly reject the restriction of a deterministic trend.

The shape of the estimated UEDT for specification I is given in the top left-hand chart of Figure 9.4. This shows that the UEDT is generally upward sloping; therefore, after controlling for the normal income and price effect, the use of transportation energy has been increasing. This illustrates that over the past 25 years (other than the last few years of the estimation period) the sector has become more energy intensive. This increase in energy intensity shown by the upward UEDT reflects a shift in the energy demand curve to the right, *ceteris paribus*. This is consistent with Schipper et al. (1992, pp. 145–6). However, the different estimated average annual

Table 9.5 Estimated results for UK transportation oil demand, 1972q1–1995q4

	Specifications					
	(I) Stochastic trend and stochastic seasonals	(II) Stochastic trend and deterministic seasonals	(III) Deterministic trend and stochastic seasonals	(IV) Deterministic trend and deterministic seasonals	(V) No trend and stochastic seasonals	(VI) No trend and deterministic seasonals
Estimated coefficients						
y_t	0.5634** (5.387)	0.5912** (6.031)	0.4381** (5.006)	0.4757** (5.393)	0.4128* (5.937)	0.4657** (6.702)
y_{t-1}	0.2327* (2.266)	0.2746** (2.834)				
y_{t-2}			−0.2389* (2.511)	−0.2605** (2.716)		
p_t	−0.1285** (4.323)	0.1269** (4.120)				
p_{t-2}			−0.1042** (4.369)	−0.1120** (4.595)	−0.0429* (2.596)	−0.0487** (2.746)
Δp_t			−0.1896** (5.576)	−0.1930** (5.575)	−0.1702** (4.717)	0.1713** (4.618)
e_{t-1}			0.5728** (7.947)	0.5391** (7.615)	0.6515** (11.401)	0.6065** (10.636)
$TEMP_t$	0.0045** (2.901)	0.0047** (2.818)	0.0041* (2.266)	0.0044* (2.369)		

Table 9.5 (continued)

	Specifications					
	(I) Stochastic trend and stochastic seasonals	(II) Stochastic trend and deterministic seasonals	(III) Deterministic trend and stochastic seasonals	(IV) Deterministic trend and deterministic seasonals	(V) No trend and stochastic seasonals	(VI) No trend and deterministic seasonals
Long-run estimates						
Income (Y)	0.7961	0.8658	0.4662	0.4667	1.1843	1.1835
Price (P)	−0.1285	−0.1269	−0.2438	−0.2430	−0.1230	−0.1237
Estimated hyperparameters						
$\sigma_\varepsilon^2 \times 10^{-4}$	0.736	1.106	2.083	2.315	2.393	2.828
$\sigma_\eta^2 \times 10^{-4}$	0.798	0.799	0	0	0	0
$\sigma_\xi^2 \times 10^{-4}$	0	0	0	0	0	0
$\sigma_\omega^2 \times 10^{-4}$	0.039	0	0.030	0	0.006	0
Nature of trend						
Corresponding cell of Table 9.2	Local level with drift (Cell vi)	Local level with drift (Cell vi)	A linear trend (Cell v)	A linear trend (Cell v)	No trend (Cell ii)	No trend (Cell ii)
Average annual growth rate of the estimated UEDT						
1972q1–1995q4	0.54%	0.41%	0.60%	0.65%	0%	0%
1972q1–1974q4	−0.06%	−0.28%	0.60%	0.65%	0%	0%
1975q1–1979q4	1.03%	0.92%	0.60%	0.65%	0%	0%

1980q1–1984q4	0.63%	0.57%	0.60%	0.65%	0%	0%
1985q1–1989q4	0.85%	0.61%	0.60%	0.65%	0%	0%
1990q1–1995q4	0.08%	0.00%	0.60%	0.65%	0%	0%
Diagnostics						
Equation residuals						
Standard error	1.51%	1.52%	1.47%	1.44%	1.63%	1.61%
Normality	0.31	0.43	2.97	0.19	1.16	0.49
Kurtosis	0.00	0.26	1.93	0.14	0.15	0.36
Skewness	0.31	0.18	1.04	0.06	1.01	0.13
H(30)/H(31)	0.75	1.03	0.93	1.14	0.79	1.13
r(1)	0.02	0.05	−0.10	−0.05	−0.06	0.02
r(4)	−0.05	0.07	−0.08	−0.04	0.03	0.13
r(8)	−0.02	0.04	0.04	0.04	0.05	0.08
DW	1.95	1.87	2.18	2.07	2.12	1.95
$Q_{(x,n)}$	$Q_{(8,6)}=0.60$	$Q_{(8,7)}=5.50$	$Q_{(8,7)}=4.34$	$Q_{(8,8)}=5.52$	$Q_{(8,7)}=5.87$	$Q_{(8,8)}=11.23$
R^2	0.99	0.99	0.99	0.99	0.99	0.99
R_s^2	0.54	0.54	0.57	0.58	0.47	0.48
Auxiliary residuals						
Irregular						
Normality	2.81	0.73	0.27	0.01	0.70	0.58
Kurtosis	2.70	0.59	0.00	0.01	0.67	0.55
Skewness	0.11	0.14	0.27	0.00	0.03	0.03
Level						
Normality	1.22	0.57	n/a	n/a	n/a	n/a
Kurtosis	0.89	0.43	n/a	n/a	n/a	n/a
Skewness	0.34	0.14	n/a	n/a	n/a	n/a

Table 9.5   (continued)

	Specifications					
	(I) Stochastic trend and stochastic seasonals	(II) Stochastic trend and deterministic seasonals	(III) Deterministic trend and stochastic seasonals	(IV) Deterministic trend and deterministic seasonals	(V) No trend and stochastic seasonals	(VI) No trend and deterministic seasonals
Slope						
Normality	n/a	n/a	n/a	n/a	n/a	n/a
Kurtosis	n/a	n/a	n/a	n/a	n/a	n/a
Skewness	n/a	n/a	n/a	n/a	n/a	n/a
Predictive tests (1996Q1–1997Q4)						
$\chi^2_{(8)}$	11.98	20.27**	11.97	17.01*	12.88	17.97*
Cusum t	−0.45	−0.47	−1.37	−1.37	−2.30	−2.38
LR tests						
Test (a)	7.45**	n/a	2.08	n/a	4.53*	n/a
Test (b)	48.50***	41.53**	n/a	n/a	n/a	n/a
Test (c)	48.97***	n/a	n/a	n/a	n/a	n/a

Note: See notes for Table 9.3.

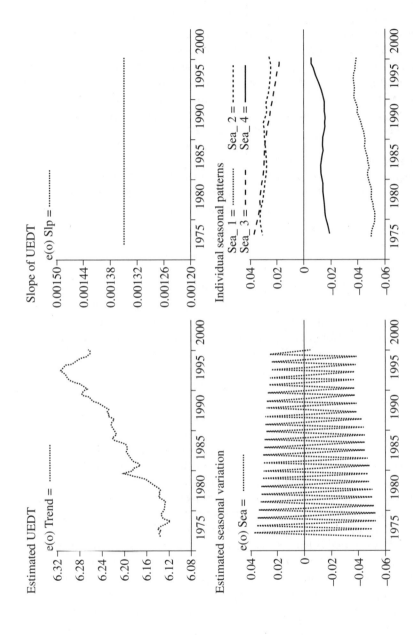

Figure 9.4 UK transportation oil demand

growth rates of the UEDT over various subperiods summarized in Table 9.4, emphasize again the non-linearity of the UEDT. In the oil transportation case, therefore, although the UEDT is generally increasing, it is *not* at a fixed rate as the conventional deterministic model would assume.

The hyperparameter of the seasonal components is relatively small compared to that of the level indicating that the stochastic movement in the seasonal component is not as large as the stochastic fluctuation of the trend. However, the changes in the seasonal pattern are still found to be stochastic and, as already stated, are clearly preferred to conventional deterministic seasonal dummies. The pattern is illustrated in the bottom charts of Figure 9.4. This shows that the magnitude of seasonal fluctuations has diminished since the early 1980s, in particular, the first and fourth quarter increase and, conversely, the second and third quarter demand gradually declines over time. Note that since the model includes the temperature variable, these seasonal movements can be considered as a non-temperature-induced seasonal pattern.

The estimated long-run elasticities for income and price are also different between the models, which are roughly divided into three groups: no-trend models (specifications V and VI), deterministic trend models (specifications III and IV) and stochastic trend models (specifications I and II). The estimated income elasticities by the no-trend models are higher than other models including either the deterministic or the stochastic trend. This is another example of the overestimation of the income elasticity by a model that ignores the UEDT when it is upward sloping and GDP is increasing over the sample period. In contrast, the estimated long-run price elasticities given by the no-trend models are almost identical to those of the stochastic trend models.

The estimated long-run income and price elasticities from the preferred model are 0.80 and −0.13, respectively. Table 9.6 summarizes the estimated elasticities of UK petrol demand from previous studies – none of which considers the UEDT. It can be seen that there are substantial differences between the estimates with most giving a much higher income elasticity than that found here – Dargay's (1992) conventional model being the exception. These higher estimates are consistent with the biases outlined earlier: that is, the income elasticity is overestimated if the 'true' upward-sloping UEDT is omitted during a period when income is increasing. Other than Fouquet et al. (1997), where the long-run price elasticity is constrained to zero, all estimated long-run price elasticities given in Table 9.6 are greater (in absolute terms) than the −0.13 estimated here. Given the volatility in the real energy price variable, it is not possible to 'predict' any bias. However, given our statistical results it suggests that these previous results are overestimates (in absolute terms).

Table 9.6 Previous energy demand studies for UK transport oil demand

Study (years)	Technique / model used	Data used	Estimated LR elasticities
Dargay (1992)	Unrestricted ECM irreversible demand model	Annual data 1960–88 (29 obs.)	$\eta_y = 1.49$ $\eta_p = -0.15$ (only for max. price) $\eta_p = -0.10$ (for price fall and rise, but insignificant at 10% level)
	Unrestricted ECM conventional reversible demand model	Annual data 1960–88 (29 obs.)	$\eta_y = 0.70$ (insignificant at 10% level) $\eta_p = -0.40$ (insignificant at 10% level)
Dargay (1993)	Log-linear EG 2-step (structural form model)	Annual data 1950–91 (42 obs.)	$\eta_y = 1.5$ $\eta_p = -0.7$ to -1.4
Hodgson and Miller (1995)	DTI energy model	Annual data 1954–88 (35 obs.)	$\eta_y = 0.81$ $\eta_p = -0.3$
Franzén and Sterner (1995)	Dynamic log-linear model	Annual data 1960–88 (29 obs.)	$\eta_y = 1.6$ $\eta_p = -0.4$
Fouquet et al. (1997)	Log-linear EG 2-step	Annual data 1960–94 (35 obs.)	$\eta_y = 1.95$ to 2.05 $\eta_p = 0$
Ninomiya (1997)	Log-linear EG 2-step (structural form model)	Annual data 1955–94 (40 obs.)	$\eta_y = 1.0$ to 1.1 $\eta_p = -0.18$

Note: None of the studies includes any trend. η_y = the long-run income elasticity, η_p = the long-run price elasticity.

SUMMARY AND CONCLUSION

This chapter has highlighted the important concept of the underlying energy demand trend, which encompasses technical progress, consumer tastes and changing economic structure. It has also shown that it is important to include the UEDT in the general form when estimating energy demand elasticities and that the appropriate econometric technique employed is flexible enough to allow the UEDT to take a non-linear form – as dictated by the data.

The structural time-series model has therefore been used to estimate the UEDT (and evolving seasonals) for the UK whole economy and transportation sector. A non-linear downward-sloping UEDT is found for whole economy aggregate energy demand, whereas a non-linear upward-sloping UEDT is found for transportation oil demand. Moreover, it is clearly demonstrated that the stochastic form of the UEDT and the seasonals are preferred to the deterministic alternatives.

An important policy implication is the low estimated price elasticity of demand for the transportation sector coupled with an upward-sloping UEDT. This illustrates that any improvement in the technical energy efficiency in the energy appliances (cars, lorries and so on) has been more than cancelled out by (a) an increase in more-energy-using luxury/comfortable appliances and/or (b) greater utilization of the appliances. Given this, and the relative price insensitivity, energy policy should focus more on changes in people's lifestyle, via advertising campaigns, stricter regulations and so on in order to reduce oil demand and hence emissions – rather than an over-reliance on market mechanisms such as energy taxes.

DATA APPENDIX

The data set is quarterly seasonally unadjusted for the period from 1971q1 to 1997q4.

Energy Consumption

The energy consumption data for the whole economy refers to UK final consumption of aggregate energy in million tonnes of oil equivalent (mtoe), E(we). For the transportation sector the energy consumption data refers to UK final consumption of 'petroleum' in million tonnes of oil equivalent (mtoe), E(o). These were taken from various issues of *UK Energy Trends* up to June 1999. Data before 1992 have been converted to mtoe from millions of therms. *e(we)* and *e(o)* represent the natural logarithms of E(we) and E(o), respectively.

Activity

The nominal and constant prices expenditure estimates of UK gross domestic product GDP(E) at market prices were kindly supplied by the Office of National Statistics (ONS) since the seasonally unadjusted data are not published. Therefore the activity variable for both the whole economy and the transportation sector, (Y), is the constant GDP(E) series re-based and indexed to 1990 = 100. The implicit GDP(E) price deflator at 1990 = 100 was calculated from the nominal and constant price series. y represents the natural logarithm of Y.

Energy Prices

The real price index for the whole economy, P(we), is a weighted average of the real price indexes form the manufacturing sector, the transportation sector, P(o), and the residential sector. The nominal aggregate price series for the residential sector is a weighted average of different fuels from the GB domestic fuel price index (taken from various issues of *UK Energy Trends* up to June 1999). The nominal aggregate price series for the industrial sector is a weighted average of different fuels from the GB industrial fuel price index (taken from various issues of *UK Energy Trends* up to June 1999). The nominal price series for transportation oil is the oil and petrol index from the GB domestic fuel price index (taken from various issues of *UK Energy Trends* up to June 1999). For all three subsectors the nominal indexes were deflated by the GDP(E) deflator and re-based to 1990 = 100 to give the real energy price indexes for the three subsectors. $p(we)$ and $p(o)$ represent the natural logarithms of P(we) and P(o), respectively.

Temperature

$TEMP_t$ refers to the average GB quarterly temperature in degrees celsius taken from various issues of *UK Digest of Energy Statistics* (*DUKES*).

NOTES

1. In addition, underlying seasonal influences are also modelled in a stochastic way.
2. Kouris (1983b) actually identifies consumer tastes as another exogenous factor that leads to less energy consumed (for a given level of income and prices). The preference here, however, is to separate this out from 'technical progress' given the ambiguous expected sign, as discussed later.
3. There is also some debate in the literature as to whether income has a distinct role in energy demand functions (see Kouris, 1983b; Beenstock and Willcocks, 1983; Welsch, 1989). The view taken here, in agreement with Beenstock and Willcocks and Welsch, is

that income should be included in the general specification and only omitted if accepted by the data, see Hunt et al. (2000) for more discussion.

4. For example, if it is a result of a government advertising campaign to encourage energy conservation.

5. Another example, at the disaggregated level, is the significant switch in energy for space heating from coal to gas that occurred during the 1960s and 1970s in many industrial countries. The reason why consumers switched from coal is not fully explained by economic factors, but by the desire to use the cleaner and more convenient alternative energy source. Clearly, in this case the effect on the UEDT for gas was operating in the opposite direction to any legitimate technical improvements also taking place.

6. Note, if the UEDT is *negative* the underlying trend is *downward sloping* whereas if the UEDT is *positive* the underlying trend is *upward sloping*. This was noted by Hogan and Jorgenson (1991) who found that 'technical progress' is not always energy saving but could also be energy using.

7. Figure 9.1a is similar to the figure in Walker and Wirl (1993, p. 188).

8. If the rise in the UEDT is sufficiently large, but ignored, then the resultant estimated price elasticity could be positive.

9. If the fall in the UEDT is sufficiently large, but ignored, then the resultant estimated price elasticity could be positive.

10. Harvey et al. (1986), when analysing the employment–output relationship also argued that 'a stochastic trend offers an intuitively more appealing way of modelling variables like productivity and technical progress, and offers a way out of the problems caused by constraining them to be deterministic' (p. 975).

11. Harvey actually concludes the paper by stating that the 'recent emphasis on unit roots, vector autoregressions and co-integration has focussed too much attention on tackling uninteresting problems by flawed methods' (p. 200).

12. That is, $\varepsilon_t \sim NID(0, \sigma_\varepsilon^2)$.

13. Cells (iv) and (vii) are ignored since it is not possible to estimate models of this type.

14. Ignoring the seasonality for simplicity.

15. In practice the level and slope residuals are only estimated if the level and slope components are present in the model, that is, η_t and/or ξ_t are non-zero.

16. Therefore, the results shown in Table 9.3 are estimated by the models after deleting the insignificant variables at the 5 per cent level. Again, the deletion has no discernible effect on the diagnostics – which are consistently poor.

17. That is, the exclusion of the UEDT may lead to an underestimation of the long-run income elasticity when the UEDT is generally downward sloping.

18. In contrast, the differences between modelling seasonality appear to have little effect on the estimated income and price elasticities. This is to be expected, since the estimated hyperparameters for the seasonals are much smaller (0.009) than those of the trend (0.341) as seen in Table 9.3.

19. These differences may be caused by the significantly different estimation period used in the studies. Haas et al. (1998) show that the estimation using the data covering only the period before the plummeting in oil prices, around 1985, tends to produce much higher values for both income and price elasticities compared to the estimation using the data that include the period after the fall (p. 125).

20. This is despite the LR test (a) for specification III suggesting that the restriction of deterministic seasonals is acceptable by the data.

REFERENCES

Atkinson, J. and Manning, N. (1995), 'A survey of international energy elasticities', in Barker, T., Ekins, P. and Johnstone, N. (eds), *Global Warming and Energy Demand*, London, UK: Routledge, pp. 3–105.

Barker, T. (1995), 'UK energy price elasticities and their implication for long-term

CO$_2$ abatement', in Barker, T., Ekins, P. and Johnstone, N. (eds), *Global Warming and Energy Demand*, London, UK: Routledge, pp. 227–53.

Beenstock, M. and Willcocks, P. (1981), 'Energy consumption and economic activity in industrialised countries', *Energy Economics*, **3** (4), 225–32.

Beenstock, M. and Willcocks, P. (1983), 'Energy and economic activity: a reply to Kouris', *Energy Economics*, **5** (3), 212.

Clements, M.P. and Madlener, R. (1999), 'Seasonality, cointegration, and forecasting UK residential energy demand', *Scottish Journal of Political Economy*, **46** (2), 185–206.

Dargay, J.M. (1992), 'The irreversible effects of high oil prices: empirical evidence for the demand for motor fuels in France, Germany and the UK', in Hawdon, D. (ed.), *Energy Demand: Evidence and Expectations*, Guildford, Surrey, UK: Surrey University Press, pp. 165–82.

Dargay, J.M. (1993), 'The demand for fuels for private transport in the UK', in Hawdon, D. (ed.), *Recent Studies of the Demand for Energy in the UK*, Guildford, Surrey, UK: Surrey Energy Economics Discussion Paper No. 72, Department of Economics, University of Surrey.

Erdogan, M. and Dahl, C. (1997), 'Energy demand in Turkey', *Journal of Energy and Development*, **21** (2), 173–88.

Fouquet, R. (1996), 'The growth of the cointegration technique in UK energy demand modelling and its relationship to dynamic econometrics', in Mackerron, G. and Pearson, P. (eds), *The UK Energy Experience: Model or Warning?*, London, UK: Imperial College Press, pp. 295–308.

Fouquet, R., Pearson, P., Hawdon, D. and Robinson, C. (1997), 'The future of UK final user energy demand', *Energy Policy*, **25** (2), 231–40.

Franzén, M. and Sterner, T. (1995), 'Long-run demand elasticities for gasoline', in Barker, T., Ekins, P. and Johnstone, N. (eds), *Global Warming and Energy Demand*, London, UK: Routledge, pp. 106–20.

Haas, R., Zochling, J. and Schipper, L. (1998), 'The relevance of asymmetry issues for residential oil and natural gas demand: evidence from selected OECD countries, 1970–95', *OPEC Review*, **22** (2), 113–46.

Harvey, A.C. (1989), *Forecasting, Structural Time Series Models and the Kalman Filter*, Cambridge, UK: Cambridge University Press.

Harvey, A.C. (1997), 'Trends, cycles and autoregressions', *Economic Journal*, **107** (440), 192–201.

Harvey, A.C., Henry, S.G.B., Peters, S. and Wren-Lewis, S. (1986), 'Stochastic trends in dynamic regression models: an application to the employment–output equation', *Economic Journal*, **96** (384), 975–85.

Harvey, A.C. and Koopman, S.J. (1992), 'Diagnostic checking of unobserved-components time series models', *Journal of Business and Economic Statistics*, **10** (4), 377–89.

Harvey, A.C. and Scott, A. (1994), 'Seasonality in dynamic regression models', *Economic Journal*, **104** (427), 1324–45.

Hendry, D. and Juselius, K. (2000), 'Explaining cointegration analysis: Part I', *Energy Journal*, **21** (1), 1–42.

Hendry, D. and Juselius, K. (2001), 'Explaining cointegration analysis: Part II', *Energy Journal*, **22** (1), 75–120.

Hodgson, D. and Miller, K. (1995), 'Modelling UK energy demand', in Barker, T., Ekins, P. and Johnstone, N. (eds), *Global Warming and Energy Demand*, London, UK: Routledge, pp. 172–87.

Hogan, W.W. and Jorgenson, D.W. (1991), 'Productivity trends and the cost of reducing CO_2 emissions', *Energy Journal*, **12** (1), 67–86.

Hunt, L.C., Judge, G. and Ninomiya, Y. (2000), *Modelling Technical Progress: An Application of the Stochastic Trend Model to UK Energy Demand*, Guildford, Surrey, UK: Surrey Energy Economics Discussion Paper, No. 99, Department of Economics, University of Surrey.

Hunt, L.C. and Lynk, E.L. (1992), 'Industrial energy demand in the UK: a cointegration approach', in Hawdon, D. (ed.), *Energy Demand: Evidence and Expectations*, Guildford, Surrey, UK: Surrey University Press, pp. 143–62.

Hunt, L.C. and Manning, N. (1989) 'Energy price- and income-elasticities of demand: some estimates for the UK using the co-integration procedure', *Scottish Journal of Political Economy*, **36** (2), 183–93.

Hunt, L.C. and Witt, R. (1995), *An Analysis of UK Energy Demand Using Multivariate Cointegration*, Guildford, Surrey, UK: Surrey Energy Economics Discussion Paper No. 86, Department of Economics, University of Surrey.

Jones, C.T. (1994), 'Accounting for technical progress in aggregate energy demand', *Energy Economics*, **16** (4), 245–52.

Koopman, S.J., Harvey, A.C., Doornik, J.A. and Shephard, N. (1995), *STAMP 5.0*, London, UK: International Thompson Business Press.

Kouris, G. (1983a), 'Fuel consumption for road transport in the USA', *Energy Economics*, **5** (2), 89–99.

Kouris, G. (1983b), 'Energy consumption and economic activity in industrialised economies: a note', *Energy Economics*, **5** (3), 207–12.

Maddala, G.S. and Kim, I. (1998), *Unit Roots, Cointegration and Structural Change*, Cambridge, UK: Cambridge University Press.

Ninomiya, Y. (1997), 'An empirical analysis of petrol demand in the UK using the reduced form model and the structural form model', unpublished MSc thesis, Guildford, Surrey, UK: Surrey Energy Economics Centre (SEEC), Department of Economics, University of Surrey.

Robinson, C. (1992), 'The demand for electricity: a critical analysis of producer forecasts', in Hawdon, D. (ed.), *Energy Demand: Evidence and Expectations*, Guildford, Surrey, UK: Surrey University Press, pp. 215–34.

Schipper, L., Meyes, S., Howarth, R.B. and Steiner, R. (1992), *Energy Efficiency and Human Activity: Past Trends, Future Prospects*, Cambridge, UK: Cambridge University Press.

Walker, I.O. and Wirl, F. (1993), 'Irreversible price-induced efficiency improvements: theory and empirical application to road transportation', *Energy Journal*, **14** (4), 183–205.

Welsch, H. (1989), 'The reliability of aggregate energy demand functions: an application of statistical specification error tests', *Energy Economics*, **11** (4), 285–92.

Westoby, R. and Pearce, D. (1984) 'Single equation models for the projection of energy demand in the UK 1954–80', *Scottish Journal of Political Economy*, **31** (3), 229–84.

10. Long-run carbon dioxide emissions and environmental Kuznets curves: different pathways to development?

Peter J.G. Pearson and Roger Fouquet

INTRODUCTION: COLIN ROBINSON AND THE EVOLUTION OF ENERGY MARKETS

Colin Robinson's studies of energy economics and the lucidity with which he has conveyed his findings have inspired many: we are glad to join in acknowledging his achievements and example. For us, his grasp of the evolution of the UK energy system and of world petroleum markets, and his imaginative blending of economic, econometric and political economic analysis, showed the value of an historical understanding of the long-run development of energy markets.

A long interest in transitions in developing countries between traditional biomass fuels and modern fuels and their environmental consequences, which developed at the University of Surrey in collaboration with Paul Stevens (Pearson and Stevens, 1987; Pearson, 1988a, 1992), has grown at Imperial College into an interest in very long-run transitions in the UK. Our recent studies of energy use and of energy prices (Fouquet and Pearson, 1998, 2003) highlight the influences over hundreds of years of economic, as well as political and historical factors: thus energy demands and supplies have interacted with prices, profits and economic activity, with the evolving attributes of fuels, technologies and services, and with the lives and legacies of energy and environmental policies. The exploration of how long-term energy markets, prices and technological innovations interact with economic development and environment illuminates the past, helps understand how we got where we are today, and may yield insights into possible energy/environmental futures in the developing world.

This mainly descriptive chapter extends the long-run analysis to a preliminary investigation of the relationship between economic development and energy-related environmental quality, in the form of carbon dioxide emissions. This chapter focuses on the per capita emissions of four industrialized countries at different stages in their development, over periods of more than one hundred years, in order to raise questions about these experiences and to consider their relevance for currently developing countries. This is done through a discussion of the potential pathways that three of the largest developing countries might follow, as their economies and energy systems mature. The usefulness of examining long time series in this area is being increasingly recognized – for example, it is pleasing to see the paper by Panayotou et al. (2000), which explores long-run relationships between carbon dioxide emissions, income, structural change and trade, in a set of industrialized countries, including the UK.[1]

The next section outlines the data sources that underpin the work in this chapter with the following section discussing the environmental Kuznets curve. The subsequent section examines the carbon emission paths followed by four post-industrialized economies (the UK, the United States, Germany and Japan). Decomposition analysis is used in the next section to begin to explore the changing relationship between economic development and carbon dioxide emissions. This is followed by a section examining the relationships between emissions and income for China, India and Indonesia, with the subsequent section looking at their decomposition. This is followed by a section that tries to systematize the experiences of the four industrialized countries, followed by the penultimate section that uses this approach to examine the evolution of developing-country emissions. The final section draws together the findings and suggestions from the work.

DATA

The analysis in this chapter stems from a recently assembled data series on carbon dioxide emissions, energy use and economic activity. Annual data for the UK, relating to primary energy consumption and gross domestic product from the eighteenth century to the present day, had already been collected from the works of many pioneers in economic historical series, including William Beveridge (Fouquet and Pearson, 1998). Carbon dioxide emissions (measured in tonnes of carbon) were estimated for specific fuels and economic sectors, using the methods proposed by Salway (1996). For the other countries, historical carbon dioxide emissions are available from the US CO_2 Information and Analysis Center (CDIAC, 2001). Primary energy use and real gross domestic product data are principally from Mitchell's *International Historical Statistics*, which draws on UN data (Mitchell, 1994). Issues clearly arise about the accuracy and reliability of the data, in relation to both the longer-run historical experience of the industrialized countries and the experience of the developing countries.

Hence, the analysis undertaken should be interpreted with appropriate caution.

EMISSIONS, INCOME AND ENVIRONMENTAL KUZNETS CURVES

The central relationship between per capita carbon dioxide emissions and per capita real income over time is examined. However, because the underlying processes and influences are complex and controversial, recent research on the emissions–income relationship is briefly reviewed.

In the past ten years, there has been much interest in associations between measures of environmental quality (ranging from pollutant emissions or concentrations to deforestation and municipal waste) and real per capita income. Initially, empirical studies used only cross-section or panel data sets and simple reduced forms. Inferring time-series results, these studies tended to focus on those empirical relationships that suggested an inverted U- or bell-shape, the *environmental Kuznets curve* (EKC), for several measures of declining environmental quality (for example, World Bank, 1992; Selden and Song, 1994; Arrow et al., 1995). The EKC graph represents environmental quality initially worsening as income grows, until countries cross an income threshold and pass over a turning point; environmental quality then improves as they go down the right-hand-side segment of the curve. For carbon dioxide, a postulated EKC underlies some forecasts of rapidly rising emissions from developing economies, where incomes are well below potential turning points, and of stabilizing or declining emission levels in industrialized countries thought to be approaching or beyond such a turning point.

A key issue has been whether the EKC represents a 'natural' growth process that should not be disturbed, and/or whether other factors, especially policy, have the power to influence the slope and position of the curve (Panayotou, 1993). In terms of the underlying processes, Pearson (1994) emphasized the importance of resource endowments, and of dynamic adjustments in the demand for, and supply and regulation of environmental quality, in influencing the pollution–income relationship. Relevant factors include: energy resources, markets and prices; demographic changes; shifts in the shares of different sectors with different pollution intensities (for example, from agriculture to heavy and then light industry, and to commerce and services); technological change and increasing returns associated with the development of 'cleaner' technologies (that is, costs that fall with learning, scale and time); fuel substitution to higher-quality fuels (for example, to electricity); the possible export of polluting

industries to poorer countries (the 'pollution haven' hypothesis); and
increasing willingness to pay for environmental quality as income and
knowledge grow, along with developing political willingness/capacity to
reduce distortions and internalize externalities via regulation.[2]

As with other two-dimensional reduced-form econometric relationships,
initial sightings of the EKC led to a flurry of activity: to criticize or re-
model the empirical approaches and debate their findings, and to backfill
the neglected theoretical foundations (see, for example, Stern, 1996;
Andreoni and Levinson, 1998; Cole, 1999; Lopez and Mitra, 2000; Stagl,
1999; Bosquet and Favard, 2000; Harbaugh et al., 2000; Panayotou, 2000;
Anderson, 2001). On the empirical side, relationships between environmental quality and income have been shown to be sensitive to both sample and
empirical specification. Empirical approaches have explored: alternative
data types (cross-section, panel and, too rarely, time-series data) from
different sources (including, for income, usually UN, World Bank or World
Resources Institute, and for carbon dioxide, mainly CDIAC or the
International Energy Agency [IEA]); various functional forms (linear or
log-linear in the variables, with quadratic and sometimes cubic income
terms, flexible spline functions, switching regimes, Gamma and Weibull distributions), estimation methods (ranging from least squares to Bayesian
Markov chain Monte Carlo methods) and specifications (time and country
fixed effects, random effects, and use of additional economic, demographic
or political variables). Theoretical developments have led to the articula-
tion of processes at both the macroeconomic level (for example, demographic, structural, technological, trade-related and political/institutional
factors) and the microeconomic level (the demand for environmental
quality, pricing, fuel substitution and energy efficiency). For example, in
their dynamic simulation model, Anderson and Cavendish (2001) demonstrate clearly how

> [T]he effect of income growth on pollution varies with income elasticities and
> price elasticities; with the rate at which low polluting practices can feasibly be
> incorporated into the capital stock through new investment and retrofitting;
> with the rate of retirement of old practices; and above all with the timing of pol-
> icies and their effect on technology development. (p. 742)

For carbon emission pathways, in particular, there is still much room for
further research. While some initial studies suggested that carbon dioxide
emissions might continually increase with income, several recent papers
have suggested the plausibility of inverse U-shapes, at least for some sets of
countries and time periods (for example, Schmalensee et al., 1998; Galeotti
and Lanza, 1999; Panayotou et al., 1999, 2000; Anderson, 2001; Anderson
and Cavendish, 2001; Halkos and Tsionas, 2001). However, there remain

issues of theoretical, statistical and empirical robustness and concerns about a lack of overlap in income/emissions observations in panel data for high-income industrialized and low-income developing countries. Because income is such a key influence, the relations between emissions and income are a useful starting point for understanding emission pathways, although taken on its own the EKC postulate offers an oversimplified reduced form. In what follows, the inverse U-shape is treated as an insufficiently tested hypothesis – or set of hypotheses. In addition, it is not assumed that any single curve could adequately represent the diversity of resources, geographies, markets and institutions across the countries examined in this chapter.

The EKC literature rarely asks what happened to the original Kuznets curve, after which the environmental version was named. In 1954, Simon Kuznets postulated an inverse U-shaped relation between a measure of income inequality and income, initially based on a limited data set of five economies at a single time-point (Kuznets, 1955). Fields (1999) reviews recent studies that have re-examined the relationship, in particular by looking at data on experience within countries and over time. Of 48 countries drawn from the Deininger and Squire (1998) data set, the Gini coefficient of inequality of income shares followed an inverted U-shape in only five countries, a U-shape in four, while in the remaining 39 countries (81 per cent of the sample) there was no statistically significant quadratic that coupled the Gini with national income. Fields concludes that, 'The Kuznets curve is neither a law nor even a central tendency. The pattern is that there is no pattern' (p. 24). And he asks,

> What is it about the countries in which inequality has been growing that differentiates them from ones in which inequality has been declining? The way to learn the answer is by doing a number of case studies and then look for similarities and differences in the patterns. It is there that the research frontier lies. (p. 10)

The approach here accords with the spirit of this comment, although the brief 'case studies' that are examined here do not pretend to have explored the issues in sufficient depth.

CARBON EMISSIONS AND INCOME IN FOUR INDUSTRIALIZED COUNTRIES

With the aid of graphs the relationships between per capita carbon dioxide emissions and per capita real income (GDP) in four industrialized countries are examined. Experience in the UK suggests a non-linear relationship, with considerable variability. Figure 10.1a graphs estimates of per

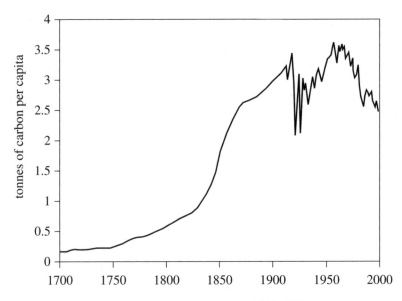

Figure 10.1a   UK: CO_2 emissions per capita, 1700–1998

capita emissions since the eighteenth century, while Figure 10.1b graphs the emissions–income relationship for 1870–1998. As per capita incomes rose from about $1,500 (in 1990 US dollars) in about 1750 to about $2,250 by the 1840s, there was a gradual increase from about 0.5 to 1 tonne of carbon (hereafter, tC) per capita. This was followed by a rapid rise to 2.75tC as incomes doubled to about $4,600 between the 1840s and 1900. There was then a slower rise to a peak of about 3.2tC per capita at about $5,000 in the 1920s. For income levels between $5,000 and $10,000, and over the period between the 1920s and the 1970s (apart from exceptional events, like the 1926 General Strike), emissions fluctuated between about 3.2tC and 2.5tC, climbing back to a peak of 3.2tC by the early 1970s. Emissions fell from 3tC at an income level of around $12,000 in the late 1970s to 2.5tC at an income level of $18,000 by the late 1990s. This gives some suggestion of an inverted U-shape, that is, an environmental Kuznets curve, for the UK. Total UK emissions in 1999 were 149mtC.

Patterns of energy use and their interaction with the UK's economic development underlie this emissions pathway (Fouquet and Pearson, 1998), as do the fossil fuel carbon emission factors (the emission factor of oil is about three-quarters that of coal, while that of gas is just over half that of coal). Figure 10.1c shows what happened to primary energy use in the UK over the 1700–1998 period. The rapid growth in the use of

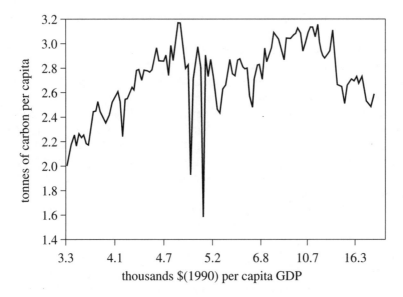

Figure 10.1b   UK: CO$_2$ emissions and income, 1870–1998

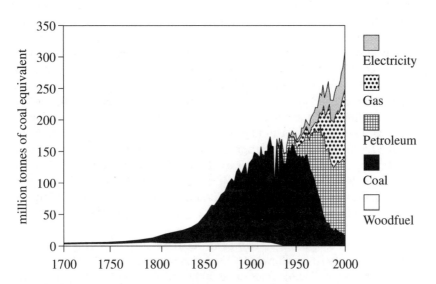

Figure 10.1c   UK: primary energy use, 1700–1998

domestically produced coal during the second half of the nineteenth century, associated with rapid industrial and urban growth, is of course particularly striking; so is coal's subsequent relative and absolute decline in importance. Coal displaced wood in the eighteenth century. It was then displaced, initially by imported petroleum, particularly after the Second World War. This was accompanied by growth in primary electricity (hydro and nuclear) and then by increasing penetration of gas, following the discovery and exploitation of North Sea oil and gas reserves in the last decades of the twentieth century. In particular, the 1990s saw the liberalization of the electricity sector, with the 'dash for gas', the uptake of combined cycle gas turbines and an increased nuclear share in electricity generated (Pearson, 2000).

Figure 10.2a shows the relationship between carbon dioxide emissions per capita and real GDP per capita in the USA. There was an initial rapid growth from 0.6tC at per capita incomes of about $2,500 in 1870, to 4tC at $6,000 by about 1920, followed by a gradual growth from 4 to 5.5tC from the 1930s to the late 1970s, at income levels between $6,000 and $18,000 per capita. Finally, there was a small decline from 5.7 to 5.2 between income levels of about $18,000 in the late 1970s, to about $23,000 by the 1990s (total US emissions in 1998 were 1,494mtC). There is less suggestion of an inverted U-shape than for the UK's graph. Figure 10.2b, which shows primary energy use in the USA for 1870–1998, reveals different patterns from those of the UK, particularly in association with the rapid growth in energy use, especially petroleum, from the 1930s to the oil price shocks of 1973–74 and 1979–80, and with the growing use of coal in the last decades of the twentieth century.

Germany (Figure 10.3a) also exhibited rapid emissions growth: from 1tC per capita at income levels of about $1,900 in 1870, to 3.5tC at incomes of about $3,300 by 1900. Between these income levels at the turn of that century and the income levels of $5,000, which were reached in the 1940s, emissions fluctuated around the 3tC mark. After the Second World War and until 1970, there was rapid growth from 3 to 4.5tC, as incomes grew to about $12,000. From the 1980s, as incomes went from $16,000 per capita to $20,000, carbon emissions fell to about 3.5tC. Germany's emissions in 1998 were 242mtC. Figure 10.3b shows primary energy use in Germany from 1870 to 1998. Coal use dominated and continued to grow until the 1960s, with increasing penetration of petroleum, then gas and primary electricity.

Per capita carbon emissions in the Japanese economy (Figure 10.4a) grew very slowly from below 0.1tC at per capita incomes of about $200 in 1870 to about 0.5tC at incomes of $3,500 by the end of the 1950s. This was followed by explosive growth to 2.2tC at incomes of $13,000 by the late

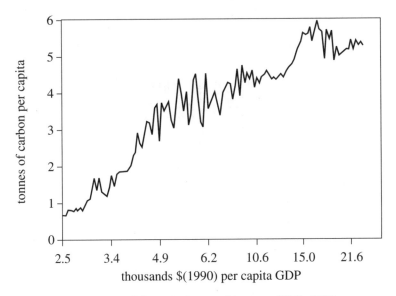

Figure 10.2a   USA: CO₂ emissions and income, 1870–1998

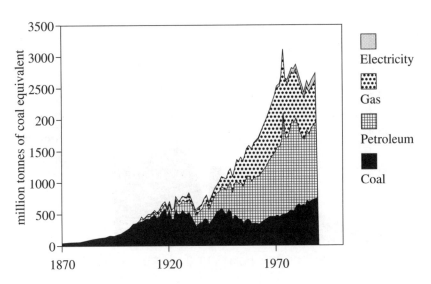

Figure 10.2b   USA: primary energy use, 1870–1998

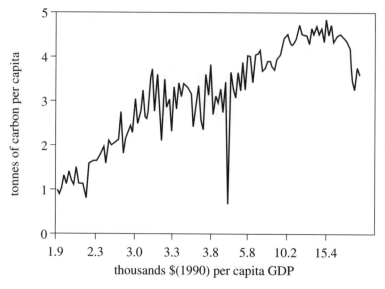

Figure 10.3a   Germany: CO$_2$ emissions and income, 1870–1998

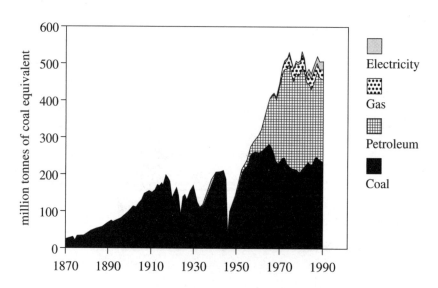

Figure 10.3b   Germany: primary energy use, 1870–1998

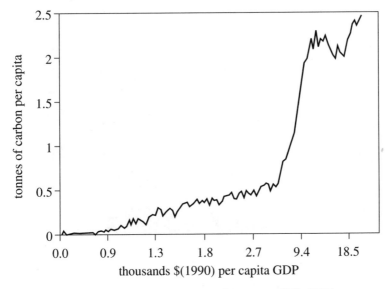

Figure 10.4a   Japan: CO_2 emissions and income, 1870–1998

1970s. There was then stagnation and a rise to 2.1–2.3tC, at incomes between \$13,000 and \$20,000, without a clear sustained pattern emerging. Japan's total emissions in 1997 were 336mtC. Figure 10.4b shows the patterns of primary energy use in Japan for 1870–1998. The increase in coal use after the Second World War is evident, as is the decline in imported coal and the penetration of nuclear electricity after the two oil price shocks of the 1970s.

DECOMPOSITION FOR FOUR INDUSTRIALIZED COUNTRIES

To explore further the factors that underlie emissions growth, it is helpful to break down energy-related CO_2 emissions into the elements of the 'Kaya identity' (Jepma et al., 1996; IEA/OECD, 1991; Ogawa, 1991). This identity decomposes gross[3] carbon dioxide emissions (C) into four components: carbon intensity (C/E), energy intensity (E/GDP), per capita income (GDP/Pop) and population (Pop). That is,

$$C = C/E * E/GDP * GDP/Pop * Pop. \qquad (10.1)$$

Energy in a competitive market

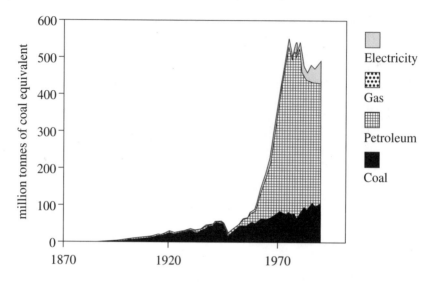

Figure 10.4b   Japan: primary energy use, 1870–1998

Alternatively, by dividing both sides of the equation by population, per capita carbon emissions can be represented as:

$$C/Pop = C/E * E/GDP * GDP/Pop. \qquad (10.2)$$

Figures 10.5–8 display the decomposed elements for the four countries discussed above. Before considering them, however, it is worth warning that while the decomposition offers valuable initial insights, it also abstracts from the underlying complexities (Pearson and Fouquet, 1996, 1997). For example: (a) the identity's right-hand-side terms are themselves aggregates subject to several influences (for example, the energy-intensity term, E/GDP, is affected by changes in the energy efficiency of individual processes and by structural change in the composition of sectoral output[4]); (b) the terms are not independent and are interrelated in complex, often non-linear ways (for example, there is an extensive literature on the relationship between energy intensity and GDP, while GDP and population tend to be inversely related[5]).

Figure 10.5 graphs the carbon intensity of primary energy use for the four countries from 1870 to 1998. These intensities reflect the evolving fuel mixes depicted in Figures 10.1b–4b, and in particular reflect the changing shares of fossil fuels. The UK is the only country showing a clearly rising trend at the end of the nineteenth century. The second half of the twenti-

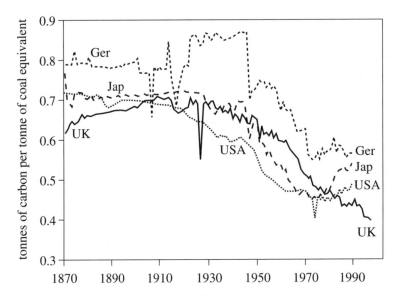

Figure 10.5   Carbon intensities of four countries, 1870–1998

eth century is characterized by broadly declining trends in carbon intensity and a range of values lying between 0.75 (for Germany in the 1950s) and 0.4 (UK in the 1990s). The USA and Japan show some evidence of rising trends after 1970, partly associated with developments in coal use. Nevertheless, the carbon intensities of all four countries at the end of the twentieth century lie significantly below their values at its start.

Figure 10.6 shows increasing primary energy intensities for three of the four countries over the 50 years from 1870 to 1920. The UK's falling trend, which continued through to the end of the twentieth century, reflects its earlier industrialization. Japan's post-Second World War increase in intensity continued as its economy matured, until the oil price shocks of the 1970s exposed its vulnerability to the rising costs of imported fuels. Energy intensity in the USA also declined rapidly after the oil shocks. By the end of the twentieth century, the primary energy intensities of three of the countries had fallen significantly below their levels at the start of the twentieth century, while Japan's intensity had begun to fall below its 1910 value.

Levels of real GDP per capita are shown in Figure 10.7. After relatively slow growth up to about 1930, the enhanced performance of the USA, Germany and, to a lesser extent, the UK, over the second half of the twentieth century is striking, with Japan's very rapid rise occurring somewhat later. Even in the UK, incomes tripled between 1930 and the end of the

Energy in a competitive market

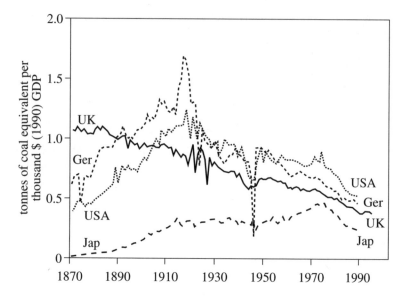

Figure 10.6   Primary energy intensities of four countries, 1870–1998

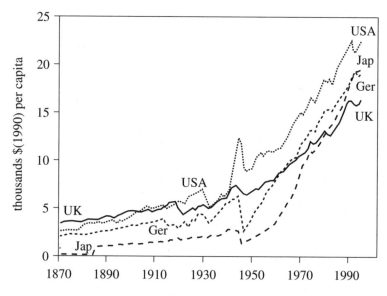

Figure 10.7   GDP per capita of four countries, 1870–1998

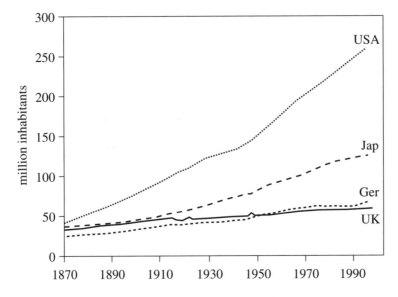

Figure 10.8   Population of four countries, 1870–1998

century. The growth in incomes has exerted a strong positive influence on energy consumption and emissions in all four countries.

Figure 10.8 shows significant differences in population sizes and growth rates in the four countries. The growth in the USA throughout the period, and to a lesser extent in Japan from the beginning of the twentieth century, suggests how much population growth has contributed to the growth in total carbon emissions for these two countries in particular.

RELATIONSHIPS BETWEEN CARBON EMISSIONS AND INCOME FOR THREE DEVELOPING COUNTRIES

The relationships between per capita emissions and real income for a set of three very large developing countries, China, India and Indonesia, over the 1870–1998 period are now considered – see Figures 10.9–11. In each country, as long as per capita income levels remain significantly below about $900–$1,000, carbon emissions are both small (fractions of a tonne), and show little tendency for rapid growth. The picture changes significantly once GDP per capita moves above these levels but even here, the emission and income levels show some striking diversity. For China (Figure 10.9a),

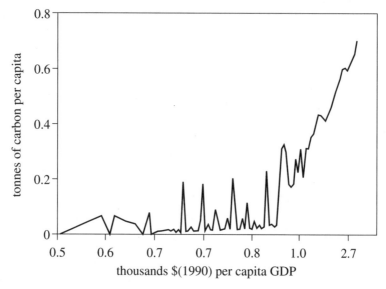

Figure 10.9a   China: CO₂ emissions and income, 1870–1998

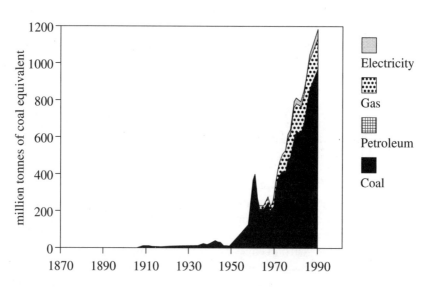

Figure 10.9b   China: primary energy use, 1870–1998

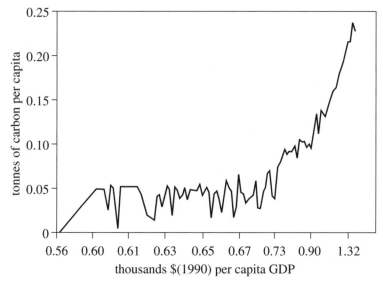

Figure 10.10a   India: CO₂ emissions and income, 1870–1998

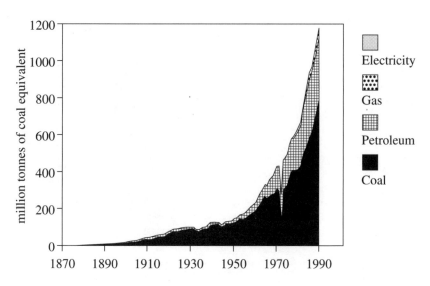

Figure 10.10b   India: primary energy use, 1870–1998

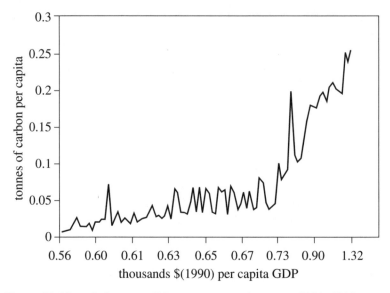

Figure 10.11a   Indonesia: CO_2 emissions and income, 1870–1998

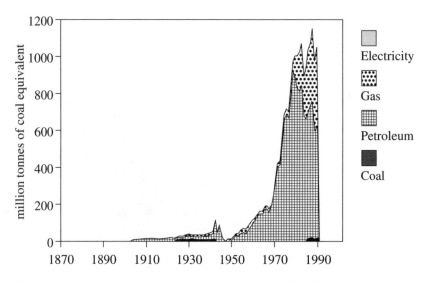

Figure 10.11b   Indonesia: primary energy use, 1870–1998

the growth in emissions was from about 0.2 to 0.7tC per capita as incomes grew from $900 to $2,700. For India (Figure 10.10a), there was an increase from about 0.1 to 0.25 for incomes between $900 and $1,300. In Indonesia (Figure 10.11a), by contrast, the rise was from an even lower base, 0.05tC, and a higher per capita income level, $1,300, leading to emissions of 0.25tC at income levels of $2,500. Total emissions for China were 918mtC in 1994, for India were 272mtC in 1996 and for Indonesia were 69mtC in 1996.

As Figures 10.9b–11b indicate, all three countries are drawing on their significant fossil fuel reserves, with coal use dominant in China and India, and petroleum dominant in Indonesia. In the figures, each country shows significant increases in primary energy use after the Second World War, with particularly fast growth rates over the three most recent decades. Because of the very small shares of imported petroleum in India and China, there is no obvious impact of the oil price shocks of the 1970s on total primary energy use (although the economic impact was significant for countries with limited foreign exchange reserves: Pearson, 1988b). For Indonesia, however, not surprisingly this period shows significant increases in gas and declines in petroleum use, and a small increase in coal use from the 1980s. One major caveat arises in relation to these graphs and the decomposition graphs below, however, since their data do not go beyond the early 1990s. More recent data from the *BP Statistical Review* (BP, 2001) seem to confirm earlier suggestions of a significant recent fall in primary energy use in China: having risen through the first half of the 1990s, it fell from 887 million tonnes of oil equivalent (mtoe) in 1996 to 752.7 mtoe in 2000. This was because of annual reductions in coal use from 1996 (676.9 mtoe) to 2000 (480.1 mtoe) – a figure that represents a 28 per cent fall and that lies 10 per cent below the 1990 level. Neither India nor Indonesia experienced similar declines between 1996 and 2000. China appears to have undertaken striking reforms in coal and other industry structures and prices, which could have significant impacts on its future carbon and energy intensities.

DECOMPOSITION FOR THREE DEVELOPING COUNTRIES

The carbon emissions for China, India and Indonesia can be decomposed into the four elements of the Kaya identity. Figures 10.12–15 show the results up to the early 1990s. The carbon intensities, particularly up to the post-Second World War period, and especially for China, are not easy to interpret and there are serious questions about the reliability and comprehensiveness of the data. For most of the post-war period, however, there is

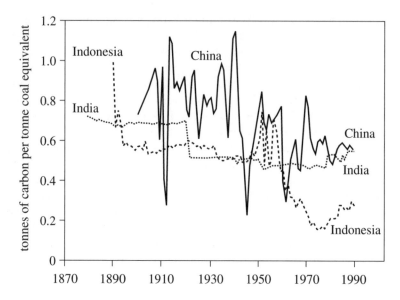

Figure 10.12   Carbon intensities of three developing countries, 1870–1998

little obvious sign in the graphs of any systematic fall in carbon intensities, with some suggestion of a rising intensity in Indonesia after earlier declines. However, as noted above, the 1996–2000 BP data on primary energy use alter the post-1996 picture for China.

Figure 10.13 shows the paths of primary energy intensity for the three countries. As well as the presence of much variability, the most dominant trends indicate significant increases in energy intensity over the period, especially in the second half of the twentieth century. On the other hand, there are some indications of falling intensities in China and Indonesia in recent years (but none for India), again associated with energy liberalization and the removal of price subsidies; however, it would be premature to conclude that they necessarily herald major longer-term declines in energy intensity, given the relatively early stages of mechanization, industrialization and urbanization in these two countries.

Figure 10.14 shows real GDP per capita, and again indicates the relatively rapid growth rates in all three countries in the second half of the twentieth century, particularly over the two most recent decades, with Indian growth rates appearing somewhat slower than those of China and Indonesia. These income levels are, of course, only a fraction of those enjoyed in the four industrialized countries (Figure 10.7).

Figure 10.15 shows population in the three countries. Both the absolute numbers (now over 2 billion people, more than twice the population of the

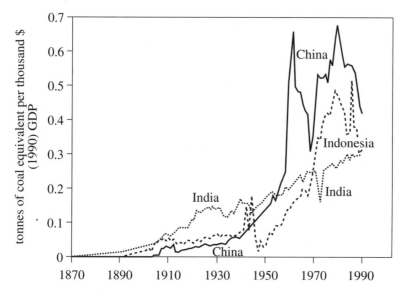

Figure 10.13   Primary energy intensities of three developing countries,
1870–1998

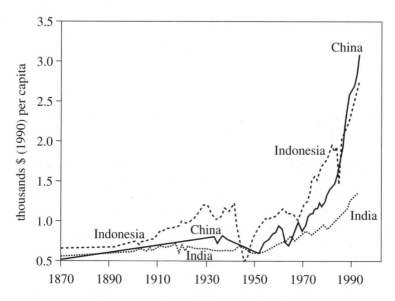

Figure 10.14   GDP per capita of three developing countries, 1870–1998

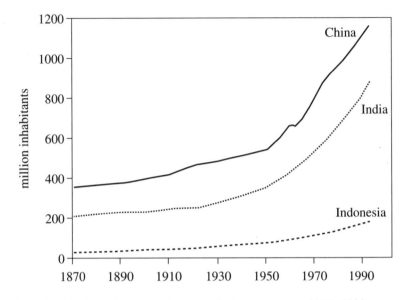

Figure 10.15   Population of three developing countries, 1870–1998

OECD countries)'and the growth rates are particularly striking, especially over the most recent four decades. The combination of rising population and real income levels will exert substantial upward pressure on energy demand which, if not countered by falling carbon and energy intensities, is likely to translate into striking increases in the total emissions of these developing countries (Pearson and Fouquet, 1996, 1997).

PATTERNS OF CARBON DIOXIDE GROWTH IN INDUSTRIALIZED COUNTRIES

Reviewing the experiences of the four post-industrialized economies (Figures 10.1–4), some patterns in per capita emissions may be tentatively suggested, although there are also significant variations in emissions, income levels and timing. The patterns, and their variations, have been conditioned by differences and similarities across a range of influences: in political, economic, energy and environmental institutions and policies, in levels and patterns of economic activity, urbanization and industrialization, and in the availability, costs and prices of indigenous and imported resources and technologies.[6] These influences deserve more investigation and analysis than they have received, both here and elsewhere.

The first pattern exhibits relatively dormant, low levels of per capita carbon emissions, which are associated with low shares of fossil fuels and significant use of traditional biomass fuels. This is followed by growth from this low-carbon base, during which all the elements of the Kaya identity tend to rise. For the UK, for example, this began at about $1,500 (in 1750) at 0.3–0.4tC, whereas in Japan, a century and a half later (about 1890), it started at about $1,000 and at 0.05tC. This pattern tended to coincide with medium economic growth rates and the beginnings of substitution towards fossil fuels.

The third pattern reflects rapid growth from a medium per capita carbon base. The main features are a large absolute increase in per capita emissions, fast economic growth, industrialization, and major fuel substitution – generally towards relatively high carbon fuels. The beginning of the pattern ranges between Germany's $1,900 in about 1870, and Japan's $3,500 in about 1960 – with the UK starting at $2,250 in about 1840, and the USA at $2,500 in about 1870. Japan had limited indigenous energy resources, relied increasingly on imported fuels, especially petroleum in the second half of the twentieth century, and had lower energy intensity than the other three countries, resulting in a somewhat lower-carbon pathway. Germany's emissions were influenced by its burning of lower-quality coal and lignite with less efficient combustion and relatively high carbon content. For these kinds of reasons, per capita carbon emissions at the beginning of this rapid growth pattern ranged between 0.5 and 1tC. The range of emissions during this pattern also varies: for the UK, it was between 1 and 3tC; for the USA, 0.6 and 6tC; for Germany, 1 and 4.5tC; and for Japan 0.5 and 2.3tC.

A fourth pattern is a slowing down or even stagnation of per capita carbon dioxide emissions. This may even be followed by a fifth pattern of declining emissions – and these two patterns may fuse, in the sense that there is a flattening and then a decline. Where per capita carbon emissions stabilize, they can do so at different combinations of carbon and per capita income levels, as in the UK and Germany: the turning point was at about $12,000 in the UK and $14,000 in Germany. In the USA, if per capita emissions prove to show a persisting decline, the turning point would be at about $18,000. It is not clear that Japan has experienced a decline from an obvious peak. Thus, these fourth and fifth patterns show differing behaviour between countries, as they follow different pathways, and not all of the four industrialized countries can be said to have entered or sustained a fifth, declining pattern.

Although five useful patterns have been identified, it is also important to acknowledge the differences between the four industrialized countries' experiences. Consider for example, the variations in: the take-off of the rapid growth third pattern (ranging between incomes of $1,900 and $3,500

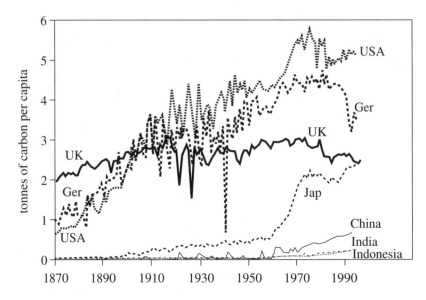

Figure 10.16 CO_2 emissions per capita of seven countries, 1870–1998

and emissions of 0.5tC and 1.0tC per capita); in the highest level of carbon emissions reached (ranging between 2.3tC and 6tC); and – where experienced – in the turning points (starting, in the lowest case, at incomes of $12,000 per capita).

POSSIBLE CARBON DIOXIDE GROWTH TRENDS IN THREE DEVELOPING COUNTRIES

It has been argued that the patterns experienced in the industrialized countries can be suggestive of the different pathways that currently developing nations might follow. Figure 10.16 shows the graphs of emissions against time for all seven countries. Earlier, it was seen that the observed second pattern – of growth in per capita carbon emissions from a low base – started at a range of between $1,000 per inhabitant in Japan and $1,500 in the UK, while carbon emissions ranged from 0.05 to 0.4tC. The three developing countries examined have all reached or passed something like this second pattern, experiencing emissions of 0.05–0.3tC at per capita incomes in the range of $900–$1,300. At present, India emits 0.25tC at an income level of about $1,300; Indonesia emits 0.25tC at $2,500; and China emits 0.70tC at $2,700.

The third pattern, showing rapid growth in emissions from a medium base, occurred in the industrialized countries at per capita income levels of about \$1,900–\$3,500, and with take-off emission levels ranging from 0.5 to 1.0tC. Comparing these figures, China could be close to the third pattern experience, based on its per capita income and emission levels. Indonesia also seems close to the rapid growth pattern, with an income level of \$2,500 per capita – although it has a relatively low level of carbon emissions, partly because of the relatively high share of petroleum in its primary energy mix. India may still be some distance away from rapid growth, with a relatively low level of per capita income and emissions, \$1,300 and 0.25tC, respectively.

The entry of China and Indonesia into the third pattern, followed later by India, would lead to major increases in world emissions. It would be valuable, therefore, to know more about whether, and if so when, these developing countries might follow the industrialized economies through the third, fourth and even fifth patterns – and what policy or other influences might shift their experience to be closer to that of either Japan (reaching 2.5tC) or the USA (reaching 6tC per capita). It has been suggested that the Kaya identity, equations (10.1) and (10.2), with its elements of carbon intensity, energy intensity, per capita income and population, can provide a useful starting point for a deeper analysis and understanding. The following are a few preliminary suggestions about possible influences on carbon and energy intensities, drawing on industrialized-country experience.

First, it seems likely that successfully growing developing countries will continue to switch towards mechanized industry as their economies mature, first towards heavier industry, then towards lighter industry and eventually the service and commercial sectors. Urbanization and the growth of modern transport also tend to raise energy and fossil fuel consumption, while pressures grow for enhanced provision of modern fuels in rural areas. Second, in these three countries, there is also still substantial availability of high-carbon fuels, especially coal, which for several reasons could be cheaper than it was in the past in some of the industrialized countries. In addition, industrialized countries may try harder to export their coal to economies where the external cost of carbon is not yet being internalized. Third, although globalization may increase opportunities to 'export' some of their pollution to even poorer countries, following industrialized-country experience, these economies have not yet developed to a point where this is economically attractive.[7] If anything, they may 'import' emissions from post-industrialized economies through the development of more polluting industries previously concentrated there. In the near and medium terms, therefore, structural shifts seem likely to generate upward pressure on both energy and carbon intensity.

Fourth, there have been upward pressures on energy prices, especially for the removal of subsidies, as developing countries move towards energy market liberalization and as they seek to encourage inward flows of investments from revenue-hungry independent energy companies. Any such upward step-changes in prices could, however, be countered in the future by efficiency improvements associated with restructuring and competition.

Fifth, in some countries more efficient technologies are gradually being introduced that use lower-carbon and often better-quality (high-value/attribute) fuels, like gas – and at much earlier phases of development than in the industrialized countries (Anderson, 2001). And, although several forms of lower-carbon and carbon abatement technologies (for example, some renewable energy technologies) are currently not economically attractive, if they continue to develop in the industrialized countries, their costs will fall as they move along learning curves. This could be reinforced by the post-Kyoto flexible mechanisms (for example, Clean Development Mechanism (CDM) projects). Sixth, increasing knowledge and willingness to pay for environmental quality may mean the demand for reductions in greenhouse gases (and in other fossil-fuel-related emissions) will be greater in developing countries than it was at the same stages of development in industrialized countries (from which it has until recently been absent). Seventh, international processes for the internalization of global externalities will be more advanced for developing countries than they were for the industrialized countries when they were at similar levels of economic development, through mechanisms such as the Kyoto Protocol and its successors (especially given US pressure for the involvement of developing countries in emissions restraint). Each of these last three influences implies some downward pressure on carbon intensity, although it is hard to gauge their timing and extent.

In current conditions, it seems unlikely that the downward influences on carbon intensities in particular, will prevail over the medium term. When added to continuing relatively rapid growth in GDP per capita and population, it seems very likely that China, India and Indonesia will move towards a third pattern of rapid carbon emissions growth from a medium base, implying very large rises in total global carbon emissions. On the other hand, pressures associated with the last three factors have the potential to imply that (in terms of tonnes of carbon per capita) the emissions path could lie much closer to Japan's experience than that of the USA.

Given their indigenous fossil fuel resources and their current low levels of per capita income, it is also likely to be a long time before these countries could reach the fourth pattern of stabilized per capita emissions experienced by some of the industrialized countries. It is also much too early to say whether and when they might reach a fifth pattern of declining per capita emissions (although it is clear that it would require the possibility of major reductions in carbon intensities). Prospects for these two patterns are heavily dependent on the development and dissemination of lower or zero carbon energy technologies.

CONCLUSION

The aim of this chapter was to examine the pathways of carbon emissions followed by a group of post-industrialized countries and by a group of large developing countries and so to raise some questions about what the experiences of the former might indicate for the pathways and choices of the latter. As well as many common elements, including four or five apparent 'patterns' in the relationships between emissions, income and time, there are also considerable variations in the pathways within and between the two country groups. Although the underlying economic, technological and policy processes and parameters have not been explored in detail in this chapter, arguably deeper analyses would yield richer insights and lessons from these historical experiences. There is a need to compare past with present and then to look forward, asking what might in the future change, in areas ranging from more efficient and lower-carbon technologies to national and international markets, institutions and policies.

Drawing on the Kaya identity, this chapter has suggested some influences on developing-country carbon and energy intensities. This is important because it is clear that if developing-country per capita incomes and population continue to grow rapidly,[8] the growth in total carbon emissions could only be contained through substantial falls in carbon and energy intensities. It has been argued elsewhere (Pearson and Fouquet, 1996, 1997), that there are likely to be limits to what can be achieved economically in reducing energy intensity in the developing world over the next few decades. This then puts considerable pressure on lowering carbon intensity, through the uptake of lower- or zero-carbon fuels (and carbon sequestration), although Figure 10.12 suggests little sign of any systematic decline in carbon intensities in the three countries in the period from the Second World War to the early 1990s. This raises key issues about adverse trade-offs between carbon constraints and income growth, which might in turn only be resolved through technology development and transfer (especially in renewables) and through successful negotiation and cooperation between the industrialized and developing nations.[9]

In terms of the emissions–income relationship, the variability in the experience of four industrialized countries shows that countries can follow significantly different paths at different times. The message to take from this analysis and from the recent EKC literature is that a country's trajectory can be influenced by a range of exogenous and endogenous factors. Many of these influences change over time and are amenable to national or international policy intervention: income growth is not a substitute for active policy making, the pursuit of technological innovation or the building of capacity and institutions. And if industrialized countries wish the developing countries to pursue trajectories different from their own historical experience – and from those that the developing countries themselves might choose – they will have to help make the emissions–income relationship different from what it would otherwise be.

NOTES

1. We found this paper after the presentation of an earlier version of this chapter at the SEEC (Surrey Energy Economics Centre) conference in 2000.
2. However, as Panayotou (2000) notes, this did not apply in the past to carbon dioxide, a global pollutant for which the potential for environmental damage is only now being appreciated.
3. Net CO_2 emissions = gross emissions – re-absorption, where re-absorption includes sequestration, recirculation or fixing of CO_2.
4. As the decomposition literature shows (Boyd et al., 1987). See also: Ang and Lee (1996), Linn and Chang (1996) and Sinton and Levine (1994).
5. Particularly where rising (women's) income levels tend to depress fertility rates (Galor and Weil, 1996). And, as Anderson (1994) and others have observed, a carbon control scenario that significantly restrained per capita income growth could make the population grow faster than it would otherwise have done.
6. For an exposition of these influences, see Pearson (1994).
7. And, in terms of total carbon emissions, this simply shifts the emissions location of a global pollutant whose impacts are independent of that location.
8. For example, in the World Energy Council/International Institute for Applied Systems Analysis (WEC/IIASA) scenarios for 1990–2050, developing-country real GDP per capita grows at rates between 1.75 and 3.6 per cent per year and population grows at 1.52 per cent per year (WEC/IIASA, 1995).
9. For a similar suggestion, see Panayotou et al. (2000).

REFERENCES

Anderson, D. (1994), 'Energy, environment and economy', Tennessee, USA: Paper presented in celebration of the Bicentennial of the University of Tennessee.
Anderson, D. (2001), 'Technical progress and pollution abatement: an economic view of selected technologies and practices', *Environment and Development Economics*, **6** (3), 283–311.
Anderson, D.A. and Cavendish, W. (2001), 'Dynamic simulation and environmental policy analysis: beyond comparative statics and the environmental Kuznets curve', *Oxford Economic Papers*, **53** (4), 721–46.

Andreoni, J. and Levinson, A. (1998), *The Simple Analytics of the Environmental Kuznets Curve*, Cambridge, MA, USA: NBER Working Paper No. 6739, National Bureau of Economic Research.

Ang, B.W. and Lee, P.W. (1996), 'Decomposition of industrial energy consumption: the energy coefficient approach', *Energy Economics*, **18** (1–2), 129–43.

Arrow, K., Bolin, B., Costanza, R., Dasgupta, P., Folke, C., Holling, C.S., Jansson, B.-O., Levin, S., Mäler, K.-G., Perrings, C. and Pimentel, D. (1995), 'Economic growth, carrying capacity, and the environment', *Science*, **268** (5210), 520–21.

Bosquet, A. and Favard, P. (2000), *Does S. Kuznets' Belief Question the Environmental Kuznets Curves?*, Milan, Italy: Working Paper 106, Fondazione Eni Enrico Mattei.

Boyd, G.A., McDonald, J.F., Ross, M. and Hanson, D.A. (1987), 'Separating the changing composition of U.S. manufacturing production from energy efficiency improvements: a divisia index approach', *Energy Journal*, **8** (2), 77–96.

BP (2001), *BP Statistical Review of World Energy 2001*, London, UK: BP plc.

CDIAC (2001), *Trends – a Compendium of Data on Global Change*, Tennessee, USA: Carbon Dioxide Information Administration Center, Oak Ridge National Laboratory (http://cdiac.esd.ornl.gov).

Cole, M.A. (1999), 'Limits to growth, sustainable development and environmental Kuznets curves: an examination of the environmental impact of economic development', *Sustainable Development*, **7** (2), 87–97.

Deininger, K. and Squire, L. (1998), 'New ways of looking at old issues: inequality and growth', *Journal of Development Economics*, **57** (2), 259–87.

Fields, G.S. (1999), *Distribution and Development: A Summary of the Evidence for the Developing World*, Cornell, USA: A background paper for the World Development Report 2000.

Fouquet, R. and Pearson, P.J.G. (1998), 'A thousand years of energy use in the United Kingdom', *Energy Journal*, **19** (4), 1–41.

Fouquet, R. and Pearson, P.J.G. (2003), 'Long run energy prices (1500–1996)', in Mackerron, G., Pearson, P.J.G. and Horsnell, P. (eds), *A New Era for Energy? Price Signals, Industry Structure and Environment*, Oxford, UK: Oxford University Press, forthcoming.

Galeotti, M. and Lanza, A. (1999), *Desperately Seeking (Environmental) Kuznets*, Milan, Italy: Nota di Lavoro 2.99, Fondazione Eni Enrico Mattei.

Galor, O. and Weil, D.N. (1996), 'The gender gap, fertility and growth', *American Economic Review*, **86** (3), 374–87.

Halkos, G.E. and Tsionas, E.G. (2001), 'Environmental Kuznets curves: Bayesian evidence from switching regime models', *Energy Economics*, **23** (2), 191–210.

Harbaugh, W., Levinson, A. and Wilson, D. (2000), *Re-examining the Empirical Evidence for an Environmental Kuznets Curve*, Cambridge, MA, USA: NBER Working Paper 7711, National Bureau of Economic Research.

IEA/OECD (1991), *Greenhouse Gas Emissions: The Energy Dimension*, Paris, France: Organization for Economic Cooperation and Development.

Jepma, C.J., Asaduzzaman, M., Mintzer, I., Maya, R.S. and Al-Moneef, M. (1996), 'A generic assessment of response options', in Bruce, J.P., Lee, H. and Haites, E.F. (eds), *Climate Change 1995: Economic and Social Dimensions of Climate Change*, Cambridge, UK: Cambridge University Press, pp. 227–62.

Kuznets, S. (1955) 'Economic growth and income inequality', *American Economic Review*, **45** (1), 1–28.

Linn, S.J. and Chang, T.C. (1996), 'Decomposition of SO_2, NO_x and CO_2 emissions from energy use of major economic sectors in Taiwan', *Energy Journal*, **17** (1), 1–17.

Lopez, R. and Mitra, S. (2000), 'Corruption, pollution and the Kuznets environment curve', *Journal of Environmental Economics and Management*, **40** (2), 137–50.

Mitchell, B.R. (1994), *International Historical Statistics*, Cambridge, UK: Cambridge University Press.

Ogawa, Y. (1991), 'Economic activity and the greenhouse effect', *Energy Journal*, **12** (1), 23–35.

Panayotou, T. (1993), *Empirical tests and policy analysis of environmental degradation at different stages of economic development*, Geneva, Switzerland: World Employment Programme Research, Working Paper 238, International Labour Office.

Panayotou, T. (2000), *Economic Growth and the Environment*, Cambridge, MA, USA: Centre for International Development (CID) Working Paper No. 56, Harvard.

Panayotou, T., Peterson Zwane, A. and Sachs, J. (2000), *Is the Environmental Kuznets Curve Driven by Structural Change? What Extended Time Series May Imply for Developing Countries*, Cambridge, MA, USA: Consulting Assistance on Economic Reform Project (CAER) II Discussion Paper No. 80, Harvard Institute for International Development.

Panayotou, T., Sachs, J. and Peterson, A. (1999) *Developing Countries and the Control of Climate Change: Empirical Evidence*, Cambridge, MA, USA: CAER II Discussion Paper No. 45, Harvard Institute for International Development.

Pearson, P.J.G. (1988a), *Energy Transitions in Less-developed Countries: Analytical Frameworks for Practical Understanding*, Cambridge, UK: Energy Discussion Paper No. 40, Cambridge Energy Research Group.

Pearson, P.J.G. (1988b), 'Economic linkages of the petroleum sector with the rest of the economy', in Khan, K. (ed.), *Petroleum Development in Developing Countries: Legal, Economic and Policy Issues*, London, UK and New York, USA: Belhaven Press, pp. 207–20.

Pearson, P.J.G. (1992), 'Greenhouse gas scenarios and global warming: the role of third world countries', in Bird, G. (ed.), *International Aspects of Economic Development*, London, UK: Academic Press, pp. 125–67.

Pearson, P.J.G. (1994), 'Energy, externalities and environmental quality: will development cure the ills it creates?', *Energy Studies Review*, **6** (3), 199–216.

Pearson, P.J.G. (2000), 'Electricity liberalisation, air pollution and environmental policy in the UK', in MacKerron, G. and Pearson, P.J.G. (eds), *The International Energy Experience: Markets, Regulation and the Environment*, London, UK: Imperial College Press, pp. 289–302.

Pearson, P.J.G. and Fouquet, R. (1996), 'Energy efficiency, economic efficiency and future carbon dioxide emissions from the developing world' *Energy Journal*, **17** (4), 135–60.

Pearson, P.J.G. and Fouquet, R. (1997), 'Energy efficiency, carbon intensity and future carbon dioxide emissions from the developing world', in *Proceedings of the International Energy Agency Workshop on Biomass Energy: Key Issues and Priority Needs*, Paris, France: IEA/OECD, pp. 313–34.

Pearson, P.J.G. and Stevens, P.J. (1987), 'Integrated energy forecasting and Policy in LDCs: problems and prospects', *Pacific and Asian Journal of Energy*, **1** (1), 33–43 (reprinted in Stevens, P. (ed.) (2000), *The Economics of Energy*, Cheltenham, UK: Edward Elgar, pp. 479–89).

Salway, A.G. (1996), *UK Greenhouse Gas Emission Inventory, 1990 to 1994*, UK: AEA Technology for the Department of the Environment.

Schmalensee, R.A., Stoker, T.M. and Judson, R.A. (1998), 'World carbon dioxide emissions: 1950–2050', *Review of Economics and Statistics*, **80** (1), 15–27.

Selden, T.M. and Song, D. (1994), 'Environmental quality and development: is there a Kuznets curve for air pollution emissions?', *Journal of Environmental Economics and Management*, **27** (2), 147–62.

Sinton, J.E. and Levine, M.D. (1994), 'Changing energy intensity in Chinese industry: the relative importance of structural shift and intensity change', *Energy Policy*, **22** (3), 239–55.

Stagl, S. (1999), *Delinking Economic Growth from Environmental Degradation? A Literature Survey on the Environmental Kuznets Curve Hypothesis*, Vienna, Austria: Working Paper No. 6, Series on Growth and Employment in Europe, Wirtschaftsuniversität Wien.

Stern, D.I. (1996), 'Economic growth and environmental degradation: the environmental Kuznets curve and sustainable development', *World Development*, **24** (7), 1151–60.

WEC/IIASA (1995), *Global Energy Perspectives to 2050 and beyond*, London, UK: World Energy Council.

World Bank (1992), *World Development Report*, Oxford, UK: Oxford University Press.

11. UK emissions targets: modelling incentive mechanisms

Bridget Rosewell and Laurence Smith

INTRODUCTION

As a method for achieving the UK's Kyoto Protocol target reduction in greenhouse gas emissions levels of 12.5 per cent on 1990 levels, and the government's own 20 per cent reduction in carbon dioxide emissions, the government is in the process of introducing a domestic emissions trading scheme. This chapter describes part of the contribution of 'the Environment Business' to the design of the UK Emissions Trading Scheme (ETS).[1]

The development of the ETS has proceeded largely through the actions of a group of businesses which came together to form the Emissions Trading Group (ETG). This group of companies has worked with the Department for the Environment, Transport and the Regions (DETR), the Department of Trade and Industry (DTI) and HM Treasury (HMT) to put forward an emissions trading scheme which would be acceptable to business and the government. The Environment Business is part of the ETG.

The main part of the UK ETS will be a cap-and-trade scheme, where companies will accept absolute emissions targets in each year of the scheme. They will be given enough emissions permits to cover their target and will have to have enough permits at the end of each year to cover their emissions for that year. Companies will be able to trade in these permits, selling permits if they produce fewer emissions than their target, or buying permits if they produce more emissions than their target. At the time of writing the plan is that the UK ETS will be voluntary.

As part of their discussions, the ETG concluded that companies would not be willing to sign up to a voluntary ETS unless they were provided with a financial incentive to do so. The Environment Business developed a computer model of UK firms to allow different options for the design of the UK ETS and the incentive to be compared. More specifically, this chapter assesses:

- the level of incentive required to secure an acceptable level of participation in the emissions trading scheme;

- the expected cost to government over the lifetime of the incentive; and
- the carbon savings expected to be secured by the incentive.

It does this for a number of different scenarios concerning:

- the type of financial incentive;
- emissions abatement cost curves; and
- participation of the power sector.

THE MODEL

Cost–Benefit Calculation

The model has been based on the financial cost–benefit calculation made by individual firms facing different cost structures. Firms examine the costs/benefits of accepting a fixed target and compare them to the costs/benefits of continuing as present. The decision of a firm to accept a target for emissions is a voluntary one and will depend on:

- the cost of reducing emissions to the firm concerned;
- the risk of being unable to meet targets;
- the expected price of trading permits in the market once it starts; and
- other benefits, such as IPPC[2] flexibility, credit for early action and access to international mechanisms.

The model looks at the first two of these. It does not attempt to value any of the other benefits for individual firms. To the extent that these are important, they will increase the effectiveness of any of the incentives which are modelled here, since they will raise the likelihood of at least some firms signing up for any given incentive.

The model principles also start from the conclusions drawn from the work of the Incentives Working Group. This has shown that trading by itself is insufficient to provide an incentive for firms to sign up to the targets that would make it possible. In the context of the model, therefore, the existence of a possible trading system is not included in the calculation that a firm makes in deciding whether to accept a target or not.

Such inclusion is not possible, since inclusion of the benefit of being able to sell permits would only be one-sided – firms could sign up to sell but no one would sign up to buy and hence the market would be empty. However, this does not mean that a market that could develop once targets were accepted is irrelevant. It is here a risk management tool, since the existence of a market can lower the risk premium attached to a failure to meet targets, as it provides the option to buy permits if targets are breached and the potential to sell if they are unexpectedly easy.

The Firms

All firms with over 500 employees were included in the model, 3,425 of them, with the parameters for each firm in the model set by the following method.

Data on carbon emissions were taken from Volterra (2000).[3] The number of firms in each sector was obtained from DTI (1998). This document also contains figures for the number of firms with over 500 employees and the proportion of total turnover accounted for by firms with over 500 employees. These figures are shown in Table 11.1.

The number of firms with more than 500 employees in each sector were split up into firms under negotiated agreements (NAs), firms that pay the full rate of the Climate Change Levy (CCL) and firms that do not pay CCL. The splits were calculated in proportion to the emissions in each of these categories. The emissions attributed to these firms were calculated by multiplying the total emissions in the category by the proportion of turnover accounted for by firms with more than 500 employees. Table 11.2 shows the number of firms and their emissions by sector on this basis. These estimates have been used in the model in all but the groups of industries covered by NAs.

Abatement Costs

The model requires that firms set any benefit of reducing their emissions (such as lower CCL payments or a specific payment) against the costs of achieving this reduction. This means that the costs of abatement are a key input into the model. Given the apparent lack of any very certain information about this, a number of scenarios are included in this chapter, which are dealt with below.

Incentive Duration

It became clear in discussion of the ETG Steering Group that targets under any scheme could not become operational until 2002. It was also agreed that any scheme would need to end at the start of the commitment period. Thus the model has been run over the period from 2002 to 2007, inclusive. It was not possible to adjust the model to allow for different speeds of take-up of

Table 11.1 Firm data

Sector	Carbon emissions mt	Covered by CCL NA	CCL not NA	No. of firms	No. of firms >500 employees	Proportion of turnover
Metals	11.0	8.6	2.4	2,450	35	0.581
Non-metallic mineral products	2.9	2.7	0.2	5,065	55	0.489
Chemicals	5.9	5.0	0.9	3,915	100	0.653
Mechanical engineering	1.8	0.3	1.5	38,975	165	0.293
Electrical engineering	0.9	0	0.9	7,955	110	0.600
Vehicles	1.8	0.3	1.5	3,140	80	0.813
Food, drink & tobacco	3.5	0.8	2.7	7,345	175	0.691
Textiles, leather and clothing	1.2	0.6	0.6	13,735	85	0.300*
Paper	3.8	2.4	1.4	2,585	35	0.350*
Plastics & rubber	1.6	0.1	1.5	6,800	65	0.318
Other manufacturing	1.8	0	1.8	56,280	245	0.526
Water	0.8	0	0.8	75	15	0.600*
Construction	1.0	0	1.0	124,680	130	0.192
Mining	0.6	0	0.6	1,270	10	0.200*
Oil/gas/coke	9.1	0	0	255	5	0.800*
Power	13.5	0	0	215	25	0.950*
Agriculture	3.0	0	3.0	64,535	5	0.010*
Public sector	8.1	0	8.1	153,350	590	0.479
Commerce	13.9	0	13.9	822,715	1,495	0.437
Totals	86.2	20.8	42.8	1,315,340	3,425	

Note: * = estimated values.

Source: DTI (1998).

Table 11.2   Number of firms and their emissions by sector

Sector	Number of firms	Tax type	Tax level	Average emissions	Total emissions
Metals	8	CCL	30	0.174	1.394
Non-metallic mineral products	4	CCL	30	0.024	0.098
Chemicals	15	CCL	30	0.039	0.588
Mechanical engineering	138	CCL	30	0.003	0.440
Electrical engineering	110	CCL	30	0.005	0.540
Vehicles	67	CCL	30	0.018	1.220
Food, drink & tobacco	135	CCL	30	0.014	1.886
Textiles, leather and clothing	43	CCL	30	0.004	0.180
Paper	13	CCL	30	0.038	0.490
Plastics & rubber	61	CCL	30	0.008	0.477
Other manufacturing	245	CCL	30	0.004	0.947
Water	15	CCL	30	0.032	0.480
Construction	130	CCL	30	0.001	0.192
Mining	10	CCL	30	0.012	0.120
Oil/gas/coke	5	none	0	1.456	7.280
Power	25	none	0	0.513	12.825
Agriculture	5	CCL	30	0.006	0.030
Public sector	590	CCL	30	0.007	3.880
Commerce	1,495	CCL	30	0.004	6.074

the incentive. Thus as far as the modelling work is concerned, all firms decide as soon as the incentive becomes available.[4]

Impact of CCL Negotiated Agreements

Certain industry sectors have entered into negotiations with the DETR to reduce the amount of CCL that companies in these sectors will have to pay, if they meet emissions reduction targets. The negotiated agreements cover a specified number of firms and their associated emissions. These figures have been used in place of the estimates of numbers of larger firms. Information on baselines and expected emissions reductions were provided in confidence by the DETR.

The baseline from which a CCL firm must operate in order to be eligible for incentives to sign up to absolute targets is based on the NA for its sector. This has been achieved by adjusting the abatement cost functions to add in the cost of reaching the required baseline.

The new baselines, by effectively raising the costs of emissions reduction, substantially reduce the ability of such firms to sign up to any incentive scheme. However, they are still able to sign up if payments are sufficiently high or there exist abatements which can be made at relatively low (though positive) costs.

The Workings of the Model

The targets to which firms sign up are set in advance by the government and are a fixed percentage reduction by 2008 on their current emissions levels, achieved by a straight line reduction from 2001. Costs and benefits are calculated for each year and the benefit/credit is made in the year in question. For modelling purposes, this is the most straightforward way to do the calculations. It does not prevent an approach that in practice uses a series of milestones and makes credits in particular years during the period.

For simplicity a percentage reduction from the beginning of the period is taken. In practice, there could be a bigger reduction taken from a grandfathered baseline. Such a target would give credit for early action. The issues surrounding the choice of baseline have been discussed elsewhere in the ETG. The period over which grandfathering could be possible depends on data availability, industrial restructuring and corporate changes; but the analysis here abstracts from these issues.

There are a number of additional assumptions which are made to make the model operational. They are as follows:

- If firms are not subject to CCL or any targets it is assumed that they would continue to produce the same amount of emissions in every year.
- All firms are assumed to be profit maximizers and to decide on whether to agree to absolute permits by considering only changes in costs and revenues.
- The only costs that change under the schemes are costs directly related to changes in emissions levels.

The firms that face CCL charges have an incentive to reduce their pollution levels up to the amount where the reduction in these charges equals the pollution abatement costs. This gives a level of pollution produced and an associated amount of government revenue. For each firm the reduction in carbon emissions due to CCL is worked out by finding the minimum of its cost function including abatement and CCL costs. Since we are assuming that without these costs a firm will continue to produce the same amount of pollution in all future years, then they will be the same each year and so the reduction in emissions due to CCL costs will be the same in every year (that is, will not be cumulative).

These estimates are those produced for the firms which are covered by the model because they are assumed to be likely to be interested in an incentive scheme. They are therefore only a subset of all firms, and thus the results should not be confused with the overall effects of CCL, which affects a large amount of emissions not taken into account in this model.

The incentive to accept a binding target operates in addition to this. The model takes into account the effect of any additional reductions in carbon emissions on the cost to the firm and on government revenues. For each firm signing up to the scheme, its costs can be calculated using the combination of the new CCL costs and the firm's abatement costs.

Firm Behaviour

Each firm minimizes its cost function and produces the associated level of pollution emissions, unless the firm's target requires it to produce fewer emissions in which case the firm produces at the target level. Figure 11.1 shows that if the firm signs up to this scheme then the emissions it produces will be equal to the lowest line in Figure 11.1, which will be below its target in earlier years and on target thereafter.

If a firm's costs under the incentive scheme are lower than its costs outside the scheme, it signs up for the scheme. If this is not the case, it remains outside and so behaves as it would under the normal CCL regime.

Government revenue from this firm is the revenue from CCL at the new rates. The total cost to the government and extra carbon reduction (in addition to the original effects of CCL) is then worked out according to which firms sign up to the scheme.

SCENARIOS

Treatment of the Power Generation Sector

There has been an intensive debate over the extent to which carbon associated with electricity use and production should be allocated to the power sector. Various models have been suggested.

After discussion with the DETR, three scenarios have been produced. One allocates the emissions associated with production of electricity for the domestic sector to the power industry. This is because domestic consumers are unlikely to 'own' carbon directly. This amounts to 13.5 million tonnes of carbon (mtC). The second allocates the carbon associated with electricity use for all firms outside negotiated agreements and employing fewer than 500 people (23.8mtC) to the sector. The third allocates both of these.

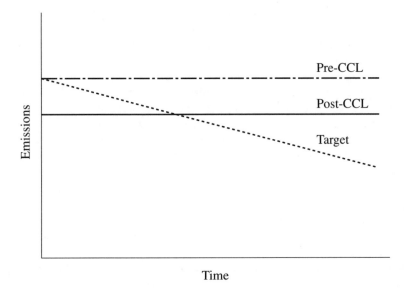

Notes:
Pre-CCL emissions are those that the firm would produce in the absence of any incentives or CCL.
Post-CCL emissions are those that the firm would produce after the effects of CCL (at the new lower rate).
Target emissions are those that the firm has to meet.

Figure 11.1   Emissions production and targets

Results for all of these possibilities are included as no decision has yet been made on the rules of allocation. A scenario in which the power sector is unable to join the scheme is also included.

The Estimation of Abatement Costs

In many ways this is the most difficult issue as the margin of uncertainty is large. Moreover, one reason for having an incentive scheme is to kick-start trading so that market information about abatement costs can be generated. Until this happens, we are largely ignorant of many of the most important aspects of abatement costs.

Clearly, the success of any incentive to accept a cap on emissions will depend on what the costs really are in practice. (Prior to this it will in fact depend on what companies think their costs might be, even before they actually begin to estimate in earnest.) Improving the estimates of abatement costs has been a priority.

Previous models used a central estimate that gives a reduction of 10 per cent of emissions for any firm in any sector for £50 per tonne of carbon. This was based on BP Amoco estimates and early experience with their trading scheme.

Alternative sources of abatement costs essentially rest on estimates made by ETSU (1999) and incorporated into the ERM (2000) model of trading developed for the DTI. These are based upon the discounted costs of introducing new technology and the energy/carbon saving that is associated with such pieces of kit. Process changes are not included. There are difficulties in using and interpreting the cost curves that have been developed. Some comments on these estimates are made below.

ETSU, *Savings Supply Curves*

This report (ETSU, 1999) provides estimates of all cost effective (ACE) and all technically possible (ATP) savings for 13 sectors: the most energy intensive. These estimates are made for both 1995 and 2010, where the difference is mostly a matter of the likely uptake on a 'business as usual' (BAU) basis between those years, combined with new investments becoming possible. The results are summarized in Table 11.3.

Table 11.3   Summary of carbon savings (mtc)

	1995	2010
Cost-effective carbon saving	9.4	7.8
Technical potential carbon saving	13.9	9.7

Uptake on a BAU basis means that all potential savings fall over time, and it is also noticeable that much of the saving can be achieved on a cost-effective basis. This means that the cost per tonne of achieving such savings is negative. In the context of a model based on a cost–benefit model of firm decisions, where projects with negative costs would be undertaken anyway, such investments would essentially come under the BAU category. It is therefore difficult to interpret these negative costs in any sensible light.

It would be possible to take only that portion of the cost curve which is positive. However, a detailed examination of these data shows that this curve has two features that appear to be common to almost all industries. One is that only a small number of possible investments have positive costs. The other, related, feature is that the curve becomes vertical extremely quickly. In many industries an apparently vertical curve is reached at costs of £0.5 per tonne of CO_2 (£0.14 per tonne of carbon). It seems extremely unlikely that no carbon savings are possible past this point, but should this be true then no economic incentive of any kind is likely to be effective in bringing down emissions.

The other possibility is that the definition of cost effective is unhelpful for the purposes here (and hence how these negative costs were arrived at), but there is no firm information as to how it is arrived at.

ERM, *Assessing the Impacts of an Emissions Trading System on UK Industry*

This model (ERM, 2000), developed for the DTI, enables the user to gauge the amount of trading that is likely to take place when a particular target reduction is chosen. Depending on the target, sectors will trade if they can get below the target at a cost which is less than the price that other sectors are willing to pay. The model produces a price at which demand equals supply and which is the marginal cost of abatement for the sectors in the model. Thus it requires estimates of abatement costs, though the model only covers manufacturing industry.

The abatement costs in the ERM model are based on the ETSU data but operate on a year-by-year basis. The model adds on to the ETSU system a view on the rate of take-up for any particular technology based upon 'S' curves. Each year only a portion of any given technology, with its associated cost, is expected to be taken up. In other respects, the cost curves are similar as they are based on a ranking of technologies by cost by sector – the cheapest technology is introduced first, followed by the next cheapest and so on. These cost relationships recur year by year in each sector.

While the data used are based on the same sources, the cost functions look rather different, with several industries showing reductions being possible at higher costs. Table 11.4 shows the results from the ERM model, when six years of potential reductions in carbon are taken together. Six years was used as being the time period between the introduction of a scheme and the beginning of the commitment period, and hence that used in the model. The reductions included here are those associated with negative costs (cost effective) as well as those which are possible at costs up to the relevant limit. Thus at a cost of £50 per tonne, the sectors in the model can provide reductions in emissions of one million tonnes. This represents a reduction in emissions of 4 per cent.

At a cost of £100 per tonne, the increase is little higher than at £50, at 1.23 million tonnes or 4.6 per cent. As in the ETSU estimates, the costs escalate at fairly low level of reductions. Also as in the ETSU estimates, most of the technologies which are costed show negative costs – they are in the cost-effective bracket.

Energy in a competitive market

Table 11.4   Reduction in emissions (mtC) 2002–2007

Sector	Cost per tonne of carbon, £				Total emissions mtC
	30	50	70	100	
Iron & steel	0.471	0.529	0.537	0.562	8.26
Ferrous metals	0.019	0.019	0.020	0.024	0.27
Ceramics	0.010	0.011	0.011	0.011	0.30
Glass	0.037	0.040	0.045	0.061	0.61
Primary aluminium	0.040	0.041	0.042	0.056	0.47
Secondary aluminium	0.004	0.004	0.005	0.006	0.06
Brick	0.009	0.014	0.014	0.014	0.34
Cement	0.013	0.016	0.029	0.031	1.55
Chemicals	0.161	0.166	0.172	0.172	5.74
Food	0.024	0.052	0.061	0.073	3.05
Non-ferrous foundries	0.014	0.014	0.023	0.023	0.30
Non-metallic minerals	0.001	0.001	0.003	0.003	0.53
Other non-ferrous	0.010	0.012	0.020	0.021	0.19
Paper	0.039	0.041	0.055	0.055	2.29
Plastic	0.005	0.009	0.010	0.010	1.52
Textiles	0.058	0.074	0.081	0.104	0.74
Totals	0.914	1.041	1.128	1.226	26.22

Implications for Modelling

There are two serious problems raised by these abatement cost estimates. The first is the obvious lack of coverage of major sectors. There are no cost curves for the utilities sectors or commerce, for example. Even within manufacturing, there are some gaps. The ERM estimates for engineering, for example, are based on very little evidence, even though there are some estimates in ETSU. There is no way of providing estimates of such sectors except to use cost curves which are based on the average cost curves of the sectors as a whole. The other difficulty is with the estimates themselves:

- they are based only on technological investments;
- they produce a surprisingly large number of negative costs; and
- they suggest that only limited investments with positive costs are even possible.

This is not to suggest that such cost curves are not possible, but does perhaps imply that these are at one end of the range of likelihood. There may well be a variety of investments which could produce savings which are not covered here. Equally, it seems reasonable to think that cost curves may not rise as strongly once costs become positive as has been suggested in these curves. It is as if the technologies that have been included are those which are most practical and well known – these then have negative costs. On the other hand, there may well be technologies which are less well developed and whose costs are at the moment positive or unknown, but which could produce effective reductions in emissions at relatively low costs in due course. Two additional scenarios have therefore been developed:

- ERM cost curves added over six years, with non-estimated sectors showing abatement costs at the average for all the estimated sectors – that is, 4 per cent reduction at £50 per tonne; and
- as above but with the reduction on average being 8 per cent at £50 per tonne.

The second of these is based on a rule of thumb used by the US government that firms only tell it half of their possible emissions reductions. The original scenario is still used and in all cases, a random distribution of plus or minus 10 per cent is taken around the average for individual firms.

Three scenarios have been produced that cover a range of possibilities. In our opinion, the technically based costs are likely to be at the top end of the cost range, since they take no account of savings which can be made on other bases, or of developments which are not currently well costed. On the other hand, the initial trades in the BP Amoco scheme may be too low (though trades have apparently taken place at well below this price).

Incentive Type

After discussions with the ETG and the DETR, the number of possible incentive types was reduced to two:

1. *Performance credit* Firms which sign up to a performance credit receive the credit level for each tonne of reduction to which they sign up. They sign up to the scheme if the credit they receive is higher than the combined effect of their abatement costs and the reduction in CCL they pay from lowering their emissions.
2. *Reduction in CCL rate* Firms which sign up to absolute targets receive a reduction in the rate of CCL that they pay on each tonne of carbon produced. Therefore they have lower CCL costs both because they produce fewer emissions and because they pay a lower rate of CCL on their emissions.

The results depend on the scale of the reduction in CCL and the percentage reduction of emissions which is built in to the target. Care needs to be taken over the firms in NAs as they will already receive an 80 per cent reduction in CCL rate, thus any further reduction cannot be greater than 20 per cent. To make the incentives fair, these firms must have the same absolute reduction in CCL paid per tonne of CO_2 as firms not in NAs.

RESULTS

Tables 11.5–11.8 summarize the results of the model based around achieving a saving of 2mtC in 2007. They include firms from all sectors with the emissions given to the power sector specified. There is no discounting. For each abatement cost scenario, two tables are given:

Table (a)   shows the results for the cheapest way of achieving a reduction of 2mtC; and

Table (b)   shows the cheapest results for achieving this reduction with the extra condition that firms have to sign up for an emissions reduction of at least 10 per cent.

The average yearly cost of the incentive is the average of the payments over the six years. However, since the incentive is given on a pounds per tonne of carbon reduction basis and reduction targets are straight line increasing, the payments in the first year are much smaller than the average and will rise linearly to become much bigger than the average in the final year.

Performance Credit

The ERM scenario is the scenario with the highest abatement costs and this can be seen to lead to the highest average yearly cost and the highest credit level to achieve the desired reduction (Tables 11.5a and b). Travelling down the tables, the amount of emissions allocated to the power sector increases and as a result the cost of achieving an emissions reduction of 2mtC becomes less. This is because the power sector has abatement costs fixed at £50 per tonne for a 4 per cent reduction (see section on implications for modelling, above). Thus as the power sector's emissions are increased, the 4 per cent increases in absolute terms but the price remains at £50 per tonne, that is emissions reductions are higher for the same cost. The number of firms signing up decreases travelling down the tables since greater reductions from the power sector mean that fewer firms need to be motivated to achieve the desired total reductions.

Table 11.5a   ERM scenario

Emissions allocated to power sector	Average yearly cost £m	Emissions reduction mtC	Credit level £/tC	Number of firms signing up	Percentage emissions reduction
None	135	1.97	110	2,857	10
Domestic	85	1.88	80	1,677	7
Small firms	70	1.99	70	74	7
Domestic & small firms	55	2.19	50	30	5

Table 11.5b   ERM scenario > 10 per cent emissions reduction

Emissions allocated to power sector	Average yearly cost £m	Emissions reduction mtC	Credit level £/tC	Number of firms signing up	Percentage emissions reduction
None	135	1.97	110	2,857	10
Domestic	132	2.01	110	1,956	12
Small firms	120.7	2.11	100	1,536	11
Domestic & small firms	125	2.60	90	947	10

This effect is particularly obvious where there is no lower limit on the reduction. In this case a limited number of firms are able to 'scoop the pool' – 30 firms sign up for a 5 per cent reduction. In none of these scenarios do any CCLA firms sign up.

In this scenario, costs are approximately half those in the first one, and the pattern is fairly similar. However, where reductions are set to at least 10 per cent per firm, the number of firms signing up falls to 77 for 'Domestic' but then jumps back up to 1,391 for 'Small firms' (Tables 11.6a and b). This is due to the link between percentage emissions reduction and the payments to firms. When the percentage emissions reduction is decreased, the total incentive paid to each firm decreases linearly. Abatement cost curves are non-linear so in some cases these will cross with abatement costs being higher than the incentive at lower levels of reduction. No CCLA firms sign up under this scenario.

The 'Domestic & small firms' average yearly cost in Tables 11.6a and b is larger than the 'Small firms' average yearly cost due to the fact that emissions reductions are higher. Due to the discrete nature of the modelling, 2.42mtC was the closest figure to 2mtC (Tables 11.7a and b). Some CCLA firms sign up in this scenario, but only where the power sector does not participate.

Energy in a competitive market

Table 11.6a   ERM scenario with reductions doubled

Emissions allocated to power sector	Average yearly cost £m	Emissions reduction mtC	Credit level £/tC	Number of firms signing up	Percentage emissions reduction
None	67.8	2.09	40	2,857	13
Domestic	30.6	2.01	30	77	10
Small firms	21.7	2.17	20	30	7
Domestic & small firms	21.9	2.19	20	30	5

Table 11.6b   ERM scenario with reductions doubled > 10 per cent emissions reduction

Emissions allocated to power sector	Average yearly cost £m	Emissions reduction mtC	Credit level £/tC	Number of firms signing up	Percentage emissions reduction
None	67.8	2.09	40	2,857	13
Domestic	30.6	2.01	30	77	10
Small firms	45.7	2.33	30	1,391	13
Domestic & small firms	58.7	3.19	30	1,391	13

Reduction in CCL Rate

In both ERM scenarios, 2 million tonnes of carbon reduction cannot be achieved so Table 11.8 shows the cost of achieving a 1mtC reduction. The power sector does not pay CCL so it is not motivated to sign up to targets, therefore the power sector scenarios are redundant in this case.

CONCLUSIONS

There are a large number of unknowns around firms' abatement costs and willingness to sign up to targets. Any modelling work thus has to include many assumptions. Therefore it is reassuring that the results for the different scenarios give figures that are comparable.

Reducing the CCL rate as an incentive for signing up to emission targets is shown to be much less effective than the performance credit, and reducing the CCL rate does not allow the target of 2 million tonnes of carbon reduction to be achieved in two out of the three cost curve scenarios. Thus

Table 11.7a £50 per tonne for 10 per cent reduction in carbon

Emissions allocated to power sector	Average yearly cost £m	Emissions reduction mtC	Credit level £/tC	Number of firms signing up	Percentage emissions reduction
None	82.7	2.06	50	3,154	9
Domestic	46.9	2.15	40	510	10
Small firms	32.6	2.17	30	30	7
Domestic & small firms	21.2	2.15	20	29	5

Table 11.7b £50 per tonne for 10 per cent reduction in carbon > 10 per cent emissions reduction

Emissions allocated to power sector	Average yearly cost £m	Emissions reduction mtC	Credit level £/tC	Number of firms signing up	Percentage emissions reduction
None	83.8	2.16	50	3,104	10
Domestic	46.9	2.15	40	510	10
Small firms	43.7	2.02	40	419	11
Domestic & small firms	51.7	2.42	40	418	11

Table 11.8 Summary

Scenario	Average yearly cost £m	Emissions reduction mtC	% reduction in CCL rate	Number of firms signing up	Percentage emissions reduction
ERM	75.4	1.10	15	2,848	9
ERM with reductions doubled	37.2	1.00	7	2,852	12
£50 a tonne for 10% reduction in carbon	43.8	1.01*	7	2,678	9

Note: *For comparison purposes the cost here of reducing by 2mtC is £98 million.

a performance credit is the recommended incentive mechanism. For the performance credit, the average annual cost varies between £20 million and £135 million depending on the scenario.

EPILOGUE

After this research was completed, much has happened, some of it as a result of the research.

The work detailed in this chapter formed the basis for the successful bid in the government's Comprehensive Spending Review, Spring 2000. This led to the government announcing funding of £30 million available in 2002 (with the expectation of similar amounts in future years) for incentives for companies to sign up to the emissions trading scheme. The incentive outlined was very similar to the performance credit described in this document.

The DETR published their consultation document on the UK Emissions Trading Scheme towards the end of 2000 (DETR, 2000). This set out the proposed rules for a trading scheme and invited interested parties to comment. The government decided that there should be an auction scheme to allocate the incentive money. The Environment Business updated its models according to these rules and provided updated results to the DETR. The auction to allocate the incentive money took place over 11–12 March 2002. Thirty-four organizations were successful and pledged over four million tonnes of carbon dioxide reduction. The UK Emissions Trading Scheme officially started on 2 April 2002.

NOTES

1. Except where indicated, this chapter describes work carried out up to June 2000. Significant extra work and updates to the computer modelling have been carried out since this date. These are detailed in the Epilogue. When the work was carried out The Environment Business was part of Volterra Consulting Ltd.
2. Integrated Pollution Prevention and Control. A European Directive. For more information see http://europa.eu.int/comm/environment/ippc/.
3. From the table showing 'Estimated 1998 UK GHG emissions by final use (MTC equivalent)' in Appendix 1.
4. Since this work was carried out it has been decided that the duration of the initial ETS and incentive payments will be from 2002 until 2006, inclusive.

REFERENCES

DETR (2000), *A Greenhouse Gas Emissions Trading Scheme for the United Kingdom*, London, UK: Department for the Environment, Transport and the Regions.
DTI (1998), *Small and Medium Enterprise Statistics for the United Kingdom*, London, UK: Department of Trade and Industry Statistical Bulletin.
ERM (2000), *Assessing the Impacts of an Emissions Trading System on UK Industry*, London: UK: Environmental Resources Management Report, May.
ETSU (1999), *Savings Supply Curves*, London, UK: Energy Technology Support Unit Report, November.
Volterra (2000), *Emissions Targets – Modelling Incentives*, London, UK (Volterra Consulting Report).

Index